Praise for

The Politically Incorrect Guide® to The Supreme Court

"Is the judiciary the federal government's 'least dangerous' branch, as Alexander Hamilton predicted it would be? It depends on which of two antithetical approaches to the law we adopt—the progressive vision of politicized judging, or the constitutionalist view that courts must faithfully say what the law is. In *The Politically Incorrect Guide® to the Supreme Court*, John Yoo and Robert Delahunty brilliantly and engagingly lay out the stakes for our nation in making the right choice."

—**Andrew C. McCarthy**, bestselling author of *Ball of Collusion*, former federal prosecutor, and *National Review* contributing editor

"Discover the real but previously untold story of the Supreme Court by reading this book! Authors Delahunty and Yoo unveil the unvarnished history of the Court and its justices and then dissect the Court's decisions on abortion, the right to bear arms, religion and free speech, and the welfare state. They explain how the new conservative majority on the Court can honor the Founders' vision for America against today's rising progressive tide."

—**Senator Mike Lee**

The Politically Incorrect Guide® to

The Supreme Court

The Politically Incorrect Guides® to...

American History
Thomas E. Woods Jr.
9780895260475

The American Revolution
Larry Schweikart
Dave Dougherty
9781621576259

The Bible
Robert J. Hutchinson
9781596985209

The British Empire
H. W. Crocker III
9781596986299

Capitalism
Robert P. Murphy
9781596985049

Catholicism
John Zmirak
9781621575863

Christianity
Michael P. Foley
9781621575207

The Civil War
H. W. Crocker III
9781596985490

Communism
Paul Kengor
9781621575870

The Constitution
Kevin R. C. Gutzman
9781596985056

Darwinism and Intelligent Design
Jonathan Wells
9781596980136

English and American Literature
Elizabeth Kantor
9781596980112

The Founding Fathers
Brion McClanahan
9781596980921

Global Warming and Environmentalism
Christopher C. Horner
9781596985018

The Great Depression and the New Deal
Robert P. Murphy
9781596980969

Hunting
Frank Miniter
9781596985216

Immigration
John Zmirak and Al Perrotta
9781621576730

Islam (And the Crusades)
Robert Spencer
9780895260130

Jihad
William Kilpatrick
9781621575771

The Middle East
Martin Sieff
9781596980518

The Presidents, Part 1
Larry Schweikart
9781621575245

The Presidents, Part 2
Steven F. Hayward
9781621575795

Real American Heroes
Brion McClanahan
9781596983205

Science
Tom Bethell
9780895260314

The Sixties
Jonathan Leaf
9781596985728

Socialism
Kevin D. Williamson
9781596986497

The South (And Why It Will Rise Again)
Clint Johnson
9781596985001

The Vietnam War
Phillip Jennings
9781596985674

Western Civilization
Anthony Esolen
9781596980594

Women, Sex, and Feminism
Carrie L. Lukas
9781596980037

The Politically Incorrect Guide® to The Supreme Court

John Yoo and Robert J. Delahunty

Regnery Publishing
WASHINGTON, D.C.

Cataloging-in-Publication data on file with the Library of Congress

ISBN: 978-1-68451-355-0
eISBN: 978-1-68451-432-8

Library of Congress Control Number: 2023932931

Published in the United States by
Regnery Publishing
A Division of Salem Media Group
Washington, D.C.
www.Regnery.com

Manufactured in the United States of America

10 9 8 7 6 5 4 3 2 1

To Dr. Irena Delahunty and Sook Hee Yoo, M.D.

Contents

PART I

Judicial Review

CHAPTER 1

Least Dangerous?

The Supreme Court, Alexander Hamilton predicted, "will always be the least dangerous" branch.[1] Hamilton got it wrong. The 2021–2022 term displayed the Supreme Court's power as never before. On June 24, 2022, in *Dobbs v. Jackson Women's Health Organization*, the justices reversed *Roe v. Wade*, the 1973 case that had recognized a constitutional right to abortion. *Dobbs* sent the question back to the states to decide.[2] In May 2022 someone had leaked a draft of the *Dobbs* opinion, which provoked a legion of pro-abortion protesters to descend on the justices' homes—one of whom planned to assassinate Justice Brett Kavanaugh—and triggered overwhelming criticism from progressive lawyers, professors, and politicians. Senate Majority Leader Chuck Schumer and House Speaker Nancy Pelosi issued a joint statement on the day of the leak to warn, "If the report is accurate, the Supreme Court is poised to inflict the greatest restriction of rights in the past fifty years—not just on women but on all Americans."[3] This great tragedy was the Supreme Court's refusal to decide abortion disputes any longer—a ruling that sent the question back to the states to decide through democratic means.

It's Not Just *Dobbs*

Dobbs was no anomaly. The Court issued other groundbreaking decisions in the last final two weeks of the 2021–2022 term. In *New York State Rifle & Pistol Association v. Bruen*, the justices limited gun control by expanding the Second Amendment right to bear arms.[4] In *West Virginia v. EPA*, handed down on the last day of the term, the Court pushed back against the expanding reach of the Administrative State.[5] In other major cases from that term, the Court demonstrated its firm control over the question of religion in public life, allowing a high school football coach to lead players in prayer at the end of games.[6] It even intervened in the COVID emergency by striking down presidential orders suspending evictions and requiring vaccines at work.[7]

And 2022 was no anomaly either. In the past few years, the Court has decided that Presidents Obama and Biden could defer the removal of illegal aliens who were brought to the United States as children.[8] It held that President Donald Trump could impose a "Muslim ban" restricting immigration from several Islamic countries.[9] It explained that states could not exclude churches from participating in state grant programs on an equal footing with secular groups.[10] It read the First Amendment to bar the government from limiting independent campaign contributions and spending.[11] The Court has even intervened in politics—it turned away challenges to the results of the 2020 election[12] and rejected cases inviting it to overturn partisan redistricting maps,[13] but also allowed Democratic state courts to replace congressional redistricting maps enacted by Republican legislators.[14]

And the Court shows no signs of slowing down. In a case against Harvard and North Carolina Universities argued in the fall of 2022, the justices will decide whether schools can continue to consider race when admitting students.[15] Also in the 2022–2023 term, the Court will review whether the government can use environmental laws to limit the right of property owners to develop their land.[16] It will further address whether individual rights to privacy extend to new technologies such as smartphones and self-driving cars, and whether social media companies must recognize free speech rights for their users. Not only has the Court expanded its powers to decide many of our society's fundamental questions, now most Americans seem content to have judges, rather than elected politicians, make the calls—at least until a Supreme Court decision doesn't go their way.

I'll See You in Court!

"There is hardly any political question in the United States that sooner or later does not turn into a judicial question." —a keen observation of French thinker Alexis de Tocqueville in 1835, after he traveled throughout the United States investigating what made the New World so different from the Old[17]

These cases, and others spanning sex, race, religion, and speech, underscore the Court's unmatched influence over American society. Its authority to "say what the law is," as Chief Justice John Marshall put it in the foundational 1803 decision *Marbury v. Madison*,[18] has placed it at the center of our nation's most controversial and sensitive issues. But this great power comes at a price, because our Founders created a Supreme Court deliberately insulated from political influence. Once nominated by the president and confirmed by the Senate, Supreme Court justices serve for life at a salary that cannot be reduced. Unlike presidents and members of Congress, federal judges need never return to the people for approval of their actions.

If the justices get the wrong answer—or, even worse, substitute their own ideas for those of the Founders—the American people can reverse the error only by amending the Constitution, something that requires the approval of two-thirds of the House and Senate and three-quarters of the state legislatures. (The states have never used the alternative procedure, which requires them to call a convention.)

Rather than mount a challenge to the Court, our presidents and Congress defer to the justices to settle our most divisive national controversies. Whereas a hundred years ago there would have been a lively debate over the Court's power to reverse the decisions of elected legislatures, today

Nice Work, If You Can Get It

Supreme Court justices have job protections that would make a tenured professor or unionized schoolteacher blush.

debate concentrates instead on *which* laws the Court should strike down. Nevertheless, the anti-democratic or "counter-majoritarian" feature of striking down acts of Congress, the president, and the states remains the central challenge posed by the nature of the Supreme Court. Americans must constantly reconsider whether the power to block the will of the majority should rest in the hands of nine judges who, after the president has nominated and the Senate confirmed them, enjoy their jobs for life.

My, How Things Have Changed

The Court's supremacy in our lives is recent—and runs counter to American history. Abraham Lincoln, for one, did not believe that the Supreme Court should have the vast power that it wields today. Lincoln rose to prominence because of his opposition to Chief Justice Roger Taney's opinion in *Dred Scott v. Sandford* that blacks could never become citizens of the United States and that the federal government had no power to limit the spread of slavery in the territories.[19] In his first inaugural address, delivered even as the South descended into secession, Lincoln made clear his opposition to the Court. "I do not . . . deny that such decisions must be binding in any case, upon the parties to a suit, as to the object of that suit," he said. Decisions of the Court should receive "very high respect and consideration, in all parallel cases, by all other departments of the government."[20] At times it might even be worth following erroneous decisions because the costs of reversing them could be high. But, Lincoln argued, "if the policy of the government, upon vital questions, affecting the whole people, is to be irrevocably fixed by decisions of the Supreme Court . . . the people will have ceased, to be their own rulers, having to that extent, practically resigned their government, into the hands of that eminent tribunal."[21]

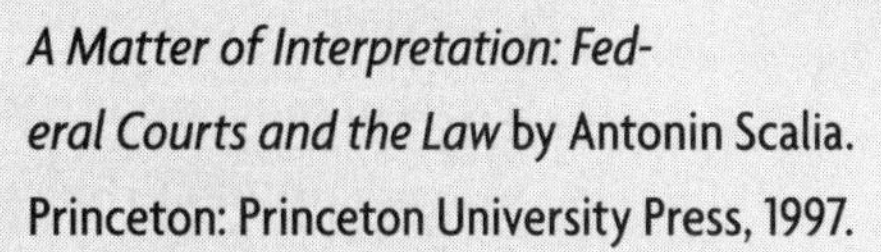

A Matter of Interpretation: Federal Courts and the Law by Antonin Scalia. Princeton: Princeton University Press, 1997.

On this question, as on many others, Lincoln understood the deeper structures of American politics and society. He was also harking back to an older understanding of constitutional interpretation, one closer to the Founding. In our nation's early years, the president and Congress decided the great constitutional questions first, and the Supreme Court followed years later. On, for example, the great question of whether the United States could operate a national bank—the precursor to the Federal Reserve—President George Washington fully aired the constitutional arguments when deciding whether to veto the bill to establish the bank. Secretary of State Thomas Jefferson argued in the cabinet that the bank exceeded the limited powers of the federal government, and Congressman James Madison opposed it on the floor of the House. Secretary of the Treasury Alexander Hamilton, however, persuaded President Washington that the bank was "necessary and proper"—in the words of Article I, Section 8, Clause 18—to the execution of explicit constitutional powers granted to the government. That was all in 1789, the first year of our Republic under the new Constitution. The Supreme Court would not address the national bank for thirty years, until *McCulloch v. Maryland*.[22] We can tell the same story of the nation's struggles over the powers of the presidency, federal versus state power over the economy, military conscription, states' rights, freedom of speech, and the spread of slavery. Before the Civil War, the great debates over these and other constitutional issues arose between figures like Madison, Hamilton, Jefferson, James Monroe, John Quincy Adams, Andrew Jackson, Daniel Webster, John Calhoun, Abraham Lincoln, Stephen Douglas, William Lloyd Garrison, and Frederick Douglass in the halls of Congress, the state legislatures, public meetings, election campaigns, pamphlets, and the press. Rarely did the Supreme Court get there first.

Today, the Court has expanded its power to decide society's important questions while the president and Congress watch from the sidelines. Gay marriage is a case in point. Until the twenty-first century, both the federal government and virtually all states had refused to recognize same-sex marriages. In 2008 that deeply blue state, California, had voted by popular initiative to ban gay marriage, and Democratic Party nominee and President Barack Obama had campaigned in 2008 and 2012 against it as well. Over time, however, several states had legalized such unions, and attitudes began to change, particularly among the young. Then in 2015, in *Obergefell v. Hodges*, the Supreme Court held that the Constitution itself, through the Due Process Clause of the Fourteenth Amendment, required all states to recognize gay marriage. In order to reach that result—while refusing to find that gays, like racial minorities, constituted a class entitled to heightened judicial protection—the Court had to declare that any restriction singling out gays could only arise out of malicious hatred rather than rational public policy.[23] While this made for a clear rule of law, it effectively ended prospects for political compromise. After all, the Supreme Court found that restrictions on gays could arise only from bigotry. Rather than allowing societal change to come about through debate, give-and-take, and compromise in the states, the Supreme Court decided to short-circuit the political process and seize control over the issue.

This development makes Lincoln's challenge even more acute: How do we reconcile the Court's authority to interpret the Constitution with the people's right to govern themselves? How do we define the line between constitutional law, on the one hand, and politics, on the other? Progressives answer by denying that any such dividing line exists and demanding that we treat law as just another form of politics. We saw this attitude on display during the 2019 Senate confirmation hearings on Brett Kavanaugh's appointment to the Supreme Court. Progressive senators, supported by their expert witnesses, advanced a view of judges as simply enablers of a political party's policies. They cross-examined Kavanaugh on his decisions based on whether the outcomes favored certain interest groups: minorities, women, environmental organizations, and the like. In their view, it would seem that the only difference between a judge and a member of Congress is that the former wears a robe.

Unequal Justice?

President Obama said he was looking to appoint judges with "empathy"[24]—though no one thought he meant empathy for corporations or the police.

Two Ways of Judging

If judges simply advance political goals, then progressives are at least honest in their desire for a judge who favors their causes and supporters. Under this view Democrats should only pick judges who rule in favor of unions, racial minorities, and criminal suspects. Republicans should only want judges who always rule in favor of business or landowners. The courts only provide a different kind of arena—one populated by lawyers, judges, and legal arguments instead of candidates, campaign platforms, and elections—for the fundamental political struggle for control over society.

Our constitutional order rejects this politicized approach. Judges must be blind to the race or gender, wealth or beliefs of the parties who appear before them. In Chief Justice John Roberts's metaphor, judges are umpires who

Judging, or Legislating?

In 2005, at a panel discussion at Duke University, the future Justice Sotomayor stated, "All of the legal defense funds out there, they're looking for people with Court of Appeals experience. Because it is—Court of Appeals is where policy is made. And I know, and I know, that this is on tape, and I should never say that. Because we don't 'make law.'" Sotomayor's mocking tone made clear that she was deriding the idea that judges "don't 'make law.'"[25]

Accepting His Limitations

"Judges are like umpires. Umpires don't make the rules, they apply them. The role of an umpire and a judge is critical. They make sure everybody plays by the rules, but it is a limited role. Nobody ever went to a ball game to see the umpire." —John Roberts, testifying in his confirmation hearings for the position of chief justice of the Supreme Court[28]

call balls and strikes but do not play in the game itself.[26] In other words, as even the progressive Justice Elena Kagan put it in her confirmation hearings, "The question is not, 'Do you like this party or do you like that party? Do you favor this cause or do you favor that cause?' . . . The question is what the law requires."[27] Justice Sotomayor, who accepts that the judicial function subsumes policy-making, is an outlier.

Who wins and who loses should not be the point of a court case. It's the method that judges use to interpret the law and apply it to the parties that matters. Thomas Jefferson viewed judging as a mechanical exercise. He hoped that judges would take the law written by the legislature and apply it to the facts presented by the parties with as little discretion as possible. Of course, judging is not easy, and judges are human. But the ideal is that everyone is equal in the court of law—that there are no favorites before blind justice—is as old as the Republic itself. Properly applied, it would vindicate Hamilton's prediction that the courts would be the "least dangerous [branch] to the political rights of the Constitution."[29]

A Book You're Not Supposed to Read

The Least Dangerous Branch: The Supreme Court at the Bar of Politics by Alexander M. Bickel. 2nd ed. New Haven, Connecticut: Yale University Press, 1986.

These two opposing visions of the courts have given birth to distinct approaches to judging. The first approach has a lot in common with the way state judges decide the cases that Americans are most likely to encounter in their personal lives: criminal trials, contract and property disputes, and civil lawsuits over accidents. Judges in these cases apply what is known to lawyers as the "common law," which we inherited from Great Britain and which is still the foundation of the law of the states. Common law judges are free, within constitutional bounds, to create the rules as they see fit, when they apply established precedents to novel situations. They often exercise the equivalent of legislative power—when they, rather than the elected legislature, make rules on property, contract, and torts—though most states check this power by subjecting judges to regular elections. Importing the common law model into the federal judiciary, however, will create judges who do not feel themselves bound by the written Constitution or by the laws enacted by Congress. Supreme Court justices will find themselves tempted to lead the people to where they "should be," rather than to apply the legislation that reflects where the people are. There will be nothing to limit a justice but his imagination and his fellow justices.

Might Makes Right?

The great liberal justice William J. Brennan reportedly said that the most important rule in the Supreme Court is the "Rule of Five": the number of justices needed to produce a majority, and hence the power to change the law.[30]

The alternative, conservative view, as expounded by Chief Justice Roberts at his confirmation hearing, is that the judge is an umpire—as bound as a philosopher-king is free. An umpire judge relies on a few basic principles: The people, through their elected representatives, make the law. The law is composed of words, those words have meaning, and that meaning is fixed at the time of the law's passage. The judge must determine the words' meaning as understood by those who enacted the law. This method of judging is called "originalism" when applied to the Constitution and "textualism" when applied to statutes or regulations.

A Book You're Not Supposed to Read

A Debt against the Living: An Introduction to Originalism by Ilan Wurman. New York: Cambridge University Press, 2017.

Common Good Constitutionalism by Adrian Vermeule. Cambridge, United Kingdom: Polity, 2022.

The terms originalism and textualism are of recent vintage, but the methodology they represent can be traced to the beginning of our nation.

Originalism is superior to the common law approach of judges who enact their own policy preferences in their "interpretation" of the law. Originalism is the only legitimate way for a Supreme Court justice to approach the job. As Alexander Hamilton noted in *The Federalist* No. 78, "Courts must declare the sense of the law; and if they should be disposed to exercise WILL instead of JUDGMENT, the consequence would equally be the substitution of their pleasure to that of the legislative body."[31] Supreme Court justices who exercise their will rather than their judgment misuse their judicial power.

Further, common law–style judging by Supreme Court justices weakens our Republic. It takes sovereignty away from the people and places it in the hands of five justices who, by design, have been given political independence. Allowing a majority of the Supreme Court to amend the Constitution or a statute is anti-democratic—particularly in the constitutional context. Legitimately amending the Constitution takes supermajorities of Congress and the states, just as a supermajority of the original thirteen states had to adopt the Constitution in the first place. The Bill of Rights and the Reconstruction Amendments, which recognize and protect our individual rights against the federal and state governments, had to pass this supermajority bar. Allowing five unelected justices to overrule the will of the people as expressed in the Constitution and our laws upends our constitutional system. The fundamental tension that afflicts the current Supreme Court—between fairly interpreting a Constitution that is designed to restrain the majority, on the one hand, and, on the other, falling prey to the temptation to use the Constitution to advance a judge's own preferred policies—has lain at the center of our constitutional history from the very beginning. It is to that history we now turn.

CHAPTER 2

Marshall, Marbury, and McCulloch

The Supreme Court's awesome power to "say what the law is," as Chief Justice John Marshall famously declared in 1803 in *Marbury v. Madison*, was itself a creation of judicial fiat. Read the Constitution from front to back, and you will not find a provision that clearly grants the Supreme Court the power to block an act of Congress or the executive order of a president. In fact, Chief Justice Marshall and his colleagues successfully grabbed a power that would gradually place the Court on the pedestal on which it sits today. But the story of the Court's growing power has not been a happy one: it has suffered from conflict, controversy, and setbacks that have harmed the nation and roiled its politics.

Of the three branches of government, the Constitution places the Supreme Court last. Article I lists the limited authorities of Congress, while leaving the bulk of public power in the hands of the states. Article II sets out the vague but broad executive power that the president wields to protect the nation, to execute the laws, and to guide the administration. Article III vests in the Supreme Court and the lower federal courts "the judicial Power,"

A Book You're Not Supposed to Read

Novus Ordo Seclorum: The Intellectual Origins of the Constitution by Forrest McDonald. Lawrence, Kansas: University Press of Kansas, 1985.

which includes the sole right to decide cases or controversies arising under the nation's laws. Nothing in Article III or any other clause of the Constitution states that the Supreme Court is allowed to overturn the acts of the other branches.

Judicial Review

In *Marbury* the Court deduced this power we now term "judicial review" from the structure, not just the text, of the Constitution. The case grew out of a lawsuit brought by William Marbury, whom President John Adams had appointed to a lowly federal job in his final days in office. Adams signed Marbury's commission, but Adams's secretary of state (one John Marshall) failed to deliver it. When Thomas Jefferson took office in 1801, his secretary of state, James Madison—who had been the primary drafter and defender of the Constitution in 1787–1788—refused to hand over the commission, preventing Marbury from taking office. Madison himself did not believe the Supreme Court enjoyed the power of judicial review; he held the justices in such contempt that he refused even to appear to defend the Jefferson administration in the litigation. Madison and Jefferson were daring Chief Justice Marshall to order them to deliver Marbury's commission, an order they would have refused. Defiance of the Supreme Court by a Jefferson administration that had swept into the White House with large majorities in Congress would have rendered the young Court's authority stillborn.

But instead, Marshall pulled off one of the great feats of political gymnastics in American history. He concluded that Jefferson and Madison were illegally withholding Marbury's commission, but he also found that the Judiciary Act of 1789, which gave the Supreme Court jurisdiction over the case, violated the Constitution. Congress could not give the Court the power to hear more cases than the Constitution permitted, and, Marshall found, the Constitution did not include cases such as Marbury's in its list of those

equal status to the other two branches of government, but a very different job. While Congress may make the laws, and the president enforces them, the federal courts alone decide the cases that arise under them. In deciding a case where one party (in this case Marbury) depends on a federal law and the other party (in this case Madison) depends on the Constitution, a court must choose which form of law should prevail. Supreme Court justices, like any other officers of the government, must obey the Constitution as the supreme law of the land, because it is the highest form of law. As Marshall concluded, the Constitution embodies "the principle, supposed to be essential to all written constitutions, that a law repugnant to the constitution is void; and that *courts*, as well as other departments, are bound by that instrument" [emphasis added].[4]

A Book You're Not Supposed to Read

Commentaries on the Constitution of the United States by Joseph Story. 3 vols. Boston: Hilliard, Gray, and Company; Cambridge: Brown, Shattuck, and Co., 1833.

The Creation of the American Republic, 1776–1787 by Gordon S. Wood. Chapel Hill: University of North Carolina Press, 1998.

Notice that *Marbury*, the very foundation of the Supreme Court's power today, does not claim that the courts can lay sole claim to the right to interpret the Constitution. Instead, Chief Justice Marshall describes it as a duty that applies to all officers of the government. When they enforce the laws, presidents must uphold the Constitution first above any other laws—to do this effectively, they must first understand the Constitution's meaning. Congress must refuse to enact laws that conflict with the Constitution, which requires members of the House and Senate also to understand the Constitution first. And the Supreme Court enjoys the power of judicial review because when it performs its unique function of deciding cases or controversies, it must interpret the Constitution when one of the parties claims it gives him a right. As Marshall emphasized, "It is emphatically the province and duty of the judicial department to say what the law is."[5] But

Marshall could not claim that the Constitution gave the responsibility to interpret the law solely to the courts—it comes naturally to the president and Congress as well.

"Necessary and Proper"

Judicial review's initially weak hold on the political order led the early Supreme Court to exercise its power sparingly. The Court would not block another federal law until the disastrous *Dred Scott v. Sandford* case, which helped bring on the Civil War. Instead, the justices turned their efforts toward the defense of national authorities against the centrifugal forces of the states. The Marshall Court's most important decision during this period, *McCulloch v. Maryland* (1819), upheld the ability of the federal government to create institutions. Where *Marbury* established basic principles of the separation of powers, *McCulloch* did the same with federalism. In its very first year under the new Constitution, Congress had created a national bank that could borrow and lend funds, issue bonds, and handle the federal government's financial operations. The Constitution, however, provided no explicit power to create a bank or any other federal agencies. In fact, during the secret Constitutional Convention, the delegates had rejected Benjamin Franklin's proposal to allow the federal government to create a national university and other proposals to grant monopolies—powers very similar to the creation of a bank.

Democracy and Distrust: A Theory of Judicial Review by John Hart Ely. Cambridge: Harvard University Press, 1980.

Constitutional Fate: Theory of the Constitution by Philip Bobbitt. New York: Oxford University Press, 1984.

Nevertheless, Chief Justice Marshall used the nature and structure of the Constitution to support a reading of the Necessary and Proper Clause to allow the bank. Coming at the end of Congress's enumerated powers in Article I, Section 8, that clause declares that Congress shall have power "to make all Laws which shall be necessary and proper for carrying into Execution the foregoing Powers, and all other Powers vested by this Constitution in the Government of the United States." Marshall argued that the bank helped implement "the great powers" given to the federal government to wage war, to regulate interstate commerce, and to tax, spend, and borrow money. But rather than explain why the bank was necessary to achieve these goals, he instead proposed that the powers granted in the Constitution depended on the circumstances, rather than fixed limits. "The sound construction of the constitution must allow to the national legislature that discretion, with respect to the means by which the powers it confers are to be carried into execution, which will enable that body to perform the high duties assigned to it," he wrote. "Let the end be legitimate, let it be within the scope of the constitution, and all means which are appropriate, which are plainly adapted to that end, which are not prohibited, but consist with the letter and spirit of the constitution, are constitutional."[6] The courts, Marshall concluded, would defer to Congress on whether the means were "Necessary and Proper" to the Constitution's ends.[7]

The importance of *McCulloch* to our constitutional and political order is almost without rival. Thanks to *McCulloch v. Maryland*, Congress could create today's Federal Reserve Bank and, through its sophisticated control of the money supply, its influence over the national economy. Thanks to *McCulloch v. Maryland*, Congress could establish the innumerable agencies that have expanded the federal government beyond any conceivable original design. Thanks to *McCulloch v. Maryland*, Congress could push the role of the federal government into areas unimaginable at the time of the Framing, such as education, welfare, and health care. At an early date in the Supreme Court's history, Marshall introduced into the corpus of constitutional law the idea that the Constitution did not necessarily have a fixed

Supremely Adaptable?

In *McCulloch*, Marshall famously declared that the Constitution was "intended to endure for ages to come, and consequently, to be adapted to the various *crises* of human affairs."[8]

meaning, and that the federal government's powers were not narrowly limited.

Marshall is often considered the greatest justice in the history of the Supreme Court. He was a Virginian who had served as an artillery officer during the Revolutionary War, as a delegate at the Virginia Ratifying Convention, and as a member of Congress. Marshall rose quickly within the Adams administration to become secretary of state from 1800 to 1801 and then chief justice just before Jefferson became president. Marshall was not great simply because he was the longest-serving chief justice (thirty-four years), or the leader of the Court during its infancy, or because he was chief justice during a nationalizing period. We do not think of John Jay (the first chief justice) or Harlan Stone (justice, and then chief justice, who supported the New Deal) as "great." Chief Justice John Marshall deserves his reputation because of his defense—in *Marbury v. Madison*—of the idea of a written constitution that places limits on the government.

Some, Jefferson most of all, have argued that Marshall was nothing more than a partisan Federalist who, after defeat by Jefferson's Democratic-Republicans in the election of 1800, led his party's retreat behind the walls of the federal judiciary. But in *Marbury*, Marshall spurned the opportunity to strike a blow against Jefferson. Instead, Marshall adopted an approach to constitutional interpretation that hewed closely to the constitutional text and structure and made it the judiciary's duty to enforce the written limits on government power.

McCulloch, however, imprinted an expansive reading on the Necessary and Proper Clause that bestowed on Congress powers that the Framers had not contemplated. As Madison wrote in reaction to *McCulloch*, "Those who recollect, and still more, those who shared in what passed in the State conventions, through which the people ratified the Constitution, with respect to the extent of the powers vested in Congress, cannot easily be persuaded that the avowal of such [an interpretation] would not have prevented its ratification."[9] If the Constitution really gave the federal government the powers that *McCulloch* said it did, it would never have been adopted in the first place. *McCulloch* injected the Supreme Court into the partisan politics of the day, and undermined the very concept introduced in *Marbury*, of a Constitution of limited powers.

Interstate Commerce

The third great case in the trilogy of Marshall Court decisions addressed the federal government's power to regulate interstate commerce. Article I, Section 8 of the Constitution contains the principal legislative powers, such as the power to raise the military, declare war, and set rules for intellectual property. Perhaps the most important of these powers for domestic affairs is the Interstate Commerce Clause—with the taxing and spending powers providing perhaps even greater (though indirect) levers of federal influence. In *Gibbons v. Ogden* (1825), the Court considered a New York law that granted a monopoly on steamboat traffic between New York City and New Jersey. Again writing for the Court, Chief Justice Marshall held that the Interstate Commerce Clause applied to more than just goods crossing state borders. Instead, Congress could regulate both goods and services—including navigation and the transportation of people—not just at the time of their interstate travel, but also throughout their journey. The clause said that Congress could regulate commerce "among the several States," and Marshall observed that "the word 'among' means intermingled with. . . . Commerce among the States, cannot stop at the external boundary line of each State, but may be introduced into the interior."[10] And the power was to "regulate," which gave Congress almost complete discretion over that intercourse. With

The Clause That Ate the Constitution?

"Until this Court replaces its existing Commerce Clause jurisprudence with a standard more consistent with the original understanding, we will continue to see Congress appropriating state police powers under the guise of regulating commerce." —Justice Clarence Thomas, concurring in *United States v. Morrison*[11]

this authorization, Congress would eventually, by the time of the New Deal, claim the power not just to regulate goods and services that moved between the states, but virtually all commercial activity in the nation, even if the activity took place entirely within a single state. By the year 2000, Justice Thomas could complain that the Court's expansive reading of the Commerce Clause had allowed the federal government to usurp the basic "police powers" of the states.

CHAPTER 3

From the Civil War to the New Deal

Though it claimed the power of judicial review in *Marbury v. Madison*, the Court did not strike down another federal law for another fifty-four years. Instead, the Court spent the intervening half century preventing states from intruding upon federal prerogatives. *McCulloch* blocked Maryland's tax on the national bank, while *Gibbons* felled a New York law for conflicting with federal control of the waterways. The Court often encountered issues long after the president and the Congress had decided them—*McCulloch* was issued nearly three decades after President Washington had decided the bank bill was constitutional and signed it. The Court did not reach many of the important constitutional issues of the day, such as the structure of the executive branch, the president's conduct of foreign affairs, the scope of Congress's spending power, the management of the territories and their accession as states, and—most dire of all—slavery.

The nation's antebellum leaders had sought to maintain the Union even as slavery drove the North and South apart. The Northwest Ordinance, which the Continental Congress had enacted to govern the first territories, banned slavery entirely. The Framers deliberately avoided using the word "slavery" in the Constitution. Nevertheless, their Constitution allowed the states to protect the terrible institution by giving the federal government no explicit power to regulate it. In fact, insofar as the Constitution touched on slavery at all, it was to give slave states an advantage. Most infamously, the Three-Fifths Clause allowed

It Took a Civil War

In the Reconstruction Era, the Three-Fifths Clause, found in Article I (at Section 2, Clause 3) of the Constitution, was repealed by the Thirteenth and Fourteenth Amendments.

states to count "three fifths of all other Persons" (an oblique reference to slaves, who are never mentioned by that name in the Constitution) for purposes of allocating congressional seats—which meant that Southern states received a boost in their House delegations from the very slave populations that could not vote. That in turn had an effect on outcomes in the Electoral College by giving the slave states more leverage there than the size of their voting populations warranted. Thus the system was skewed in favor of electing pro-slavery presidents. Article IV's Fugitive Slave Clause required states to return any "Person held to Service or Labour in one State, under the Laws thereof, escaping into another."

The Importation Clause allowed Congress to regulate or prohibit the slave trade, but not until 1808. Although the Framers allowed slavery, many of them hoped that slavery would come to a timely end on its own.

Because the Constitution allowed states to protect slavery, the constitutional struggle between the "free soil" North and the unfree South came to a crisis in the territories. Southern leaders believed that slavery had to keep expanding into new lands in order to survive (some of them even had designs on annexing Cuba), while many in the North hoped that confining slavery to the states where it already existed would lead to its eventual demise. Article IV of the Constitution gave Congress the power "to dispose of and make all needful Rules and Regulations respecting the Territory or other Property belonging to the United States." As we have seen, when Congress ratified the 1787 Northwest Ordinance, covering the territory from which Illinois, Michigan, and other states would emerge, it prohibited slavery in the future midwestern states. But as the nation steadily expanded westwards across the Mississippi, free and slave states fought over whether to permit slavery in the new territories. Congress admitted slave and free states in tandem in order to preserve a balance of power in the Senate. In the 1820 Missouri Compromise, for example, Congress admitted Missouri as a slave state and Maine as a free state and then prohibited slavery in other territories north of Arkansas. But the balance of power between North and South eroded as the North's population grew quickly and huge swaths of land came into the possession of the United States after the Mexican-American War ended in 1848. The admission of California into the Union in 1850 tipped the balance of the Senate in favor of the free states. In the Compromise of 1850, and then the Kansas-Nebraska Act of 1854, Congress eventually settled on a principle of "popular sovereignty" that left the slavery question up to the majority of the voters of each territory.

The Worst Decision Ever

After fifty years of deference to the decisions of Congress and the president, however, the Supreme Court thrust itself into the political maelstrom. In *Dred Scott v. Sandford*, the Court struck down the part of the Missouri Compromise that allowed federal regulation of slavery in the territories. By implication, the power of the free soil states in the North and the West to prohibit slavery fell into doubt. Dred Scott had challenged his enslavement because his owner had taken him to Illinois and Minnesota, a free state and free territory, respectively, and then returned with him to Missouri, a slave state. For a 7–2 majority, Chief Justice Taney wrote that African Americans could never become American citizens and that Congress did not have the constitutional authority to restrict slavery in the territories. Despite the Declaration of Independence's recognition of the natural equality of all, the Court held that the Framers would have understood that African Americans "are not included, and were not intended to be included, under the word 'citizens' in the Constitution, and can therefore claim none of the rights and privileges which that instrument provides for and secures to citizens of the United States."[1] According to Chief Justice Taney, slaves fell under the constitutional right to property, and hence the federal government could not restrict their ownership in the territories without denying slave owners who settled there "due process of law." As Lincoln and other members of the new Republican Party would argue, Taney's theory implied that Southerners could bring slaves into the North.

Chief Justice Taney could have decided the case on narrower grounds. He could have held that Dred Scott had no standing to sue or that Missouri law controlled the question of Scott's status. Instead, the Court sought to settle the slavery question once and for all. Chief Justice Taney and his majority thought their opinion would end the political conflict and head off civil war. Fierce opposition to the Kansas-Nebraska Act had led to the Whig Party's demise, the loss of 70 percent of the Democratic Party's House seats in the free states, and the rise of a new anti-slavery political party, the Republican Party, which existed only in the North. The Republican Party asserted that Congress could regulate slavery in the territories—as it had in the Missouri Compromise. Under the leadership of Senator Stephen Douglas, the Democratic Party adopted the South's belief that the territories should be able to choose for themselves, upon becoming states, whether to adopt slavery.

There has been no more woeful moment in the Supreme Court's history than *Dred Scott*. The Court based its holding on ideas of white supremacy. According to Taney, at the time of the Founding, African Americans were "a subordinate and inferior class of beings, who had been subjugated by the dominant race, and, whether emancipated or not, yet remained subject to their authority."[2] Because the text of the Constitution did not prohibit the states or Congress from vesting African Americans with political equality, Taney had to resort to the worst sort of interpretation, claiming that the Framers must have thought that African Americans should remain permanently subordinated to whites—even though they had never said so in any Founding document—and that their unexpressed intentions somehow superseded the constitutional text as written and ratified. (Taney ran roughshod over history: he ignored the facts that some five thousand African Americans had fought for American independence during the Revolutionary War and that by 1800 almost every Northern state had abolished slavery or provided for gradual emancipation. The Massachusetts Supreme Court had ruled slavery to be incompatible with the state's constitution in 1783.) Taney turned his back on the Declaration of Independence's self-evident truth "that all men are created equal, that they are endowed by their Creator with certain unalienable Rights, that among these are Life, Liberty and the pursuit of Happiness." Instead, Taney claimed that the drafters of the Declaration "knew that it [the language about self-evident rights] would not in any part of the civilized world be supposed to embrace the negro race, which, by common consent, had been excluded from civilized Governments and the family of nations, and doomed to slavery."[3] Again, Taney was holding that the unexpressed (supposed) intentions of the Framers pre-empted the plain meaning of the Founding texts that they had written and ratified.

A Book You're Not Supposed to Read

The Unconstitutionality of Slavery by Lysander Spooner. Boston: Bela Marsh, 1845.

Dred Scott was not just bad constitutional interpretation, but bad politics. By foreclosing federal regulation of slavery in the territories, the justices hoped to put an end to the struggle between North and South. They thought the controversy over slavery would evaporate or fade away—the North would come to terms with the existence of slavery and no longer pursue the end of the damnable institution. The justices viewed the North as the aggressors against the constitutional rights of the South. Some politicians of the time also looked to the Court to end the dispute that

The Exception That Proves the Rule?

In *Ex parte Milligan* (1866), a groundbreaking case that was not decided until after the Civil War, the Supreme Court declared it unconstitutional to try civilians before military tribunals as long as civil courts are open.[4] Milligan and two codefendants, all civilians, had been sentenced to hang at a military trial for conspiracy and inciting rebellion.

threatened the Union. Indeed, President James Buchanan, without doubt the worst president in American history, declared *Dred Scott* a welcome resolution of the problem, "'congratulat[ing]' the American people 'upon the final settlement by the Supreme Court of the United States of the question of slavery in the Territories' which 'irrevocably fixed' the issue and put an end to the 'dangerous excitement'"[brackets in the original].[5] But the political controversy did not end. *Dred Scott* neither brought the nation together nor solved the slavery question. In fact, it helped precipitate the bloodiest war in American history, one that killed about six hundred thousand soldiers (still the largest number of deaths in any U.S. conflict) and ripped the country apart. Republicans viewed the Supreme Court as hostile to their cause. Perhaps the Civil War would have come anyway. But *Dred Scott* closed off a route to political compromise and instead compounded the divisions between North and South.

Hostility toward the Supreme Court reached its high point during the Civil War and Reconstruction. Lincoln, as we have seen, conceded in his first inaugural address that Supreme Court decisions should receive "very high respect and consideration," but he also argued that for "the policy of the government, upon vital questions, affecting the whole people . . . to be irrevocably fixed by decisions of the Supreme Court" was incompatible with government by the people.[6] Lincoln did not wait for the Supreme Court to decide whether secession violated the Constitution. Upon the April 1861 firing on Fort Sumter, Lincoln immediately called out the militia, drew money out of the Treasury, ordered a blockade of the South, and launched offensive operations to restore the Union. Chief Justice Taney (in a solo opinion) tried to stop Lincoln by ordering him to release imprisoned Confederate sympathizers. Lincoln ignored him—to date the only time a president has refused to carry out a Supreme Court order. Thereafter, the Court would play little role in the course of the Civil War, other than to affirm, in the *Prize Cases*,[7] the early decisions of Lincoln and Congress at the outset of the war.

Court Packing, Nineteenth Century–Style

The steep dive in the Court's reputation invited political meddling. In 1863 Congress expanded the size of the Court to ten justices to give Lincoln an appointment; when Democrat Andrew Johnson assumed the presidency after Lincoln was assassinated, Congress cut the size of the Court by three. After Ulysses S. Grant won the presidency in 1868, Congress added two justices back to give the Republicans more appointments.

Distrust of the Court made itself evident in the new constitutional amendments that codified the Civil War's result. The Thirteenth, Fourteenth, and Fifteenth Amendments reversed *Dred Scott*, declared that African Americans were citizens, and established the constitutional liberty and equality of all citizens without regard to race. Each of these amendments also included a provision resembling Article I's Necessary and Proper Clause, which gave Congress the power "to enforce" their provisions with "appropriate legislation." The enforcement power signaled that the nation no longer trusted the Supreme Court to defend the constitutional rights of Americans. Instead, the victorious North looked to congressional enactments and executive actions to enforce the end of slavery, the guarantee of equal protection, due process, equal privileges and immunities for citizens, and voting rights.

As the end of Reconstruction brought this dark chapter in the Court's history to a close, the justices embarked on a different cause, this time on behalf of laissez-faire economics. The Civil War had accelerated the nationalization of the American economy and society. Nationwide railroad and telegraph networks helped stitch the Union into a single market.

Industrialization led to the mass production of goods and services and the emergence of large corporations and financial institutions. In response government sought to regulate businesses in new ways, by setting uniform working conditions or requiring common manufacturing standards. The Progressive movement, which had supporters as different as Republican Teddy Roosevelt (in his second run for the presidency in 1912) and Democrat Woodrow Wilson (who beat TR), called for wealth taxes, extensive federal regulation of business and working conditions, support of union organization, agriculture support programs, and social welfare for unemployment, health care, and old age. In the face of these new government interventions, the Court turned to the defense of economic liberties.

Two developments signaled the Court's change in focus.

First, sadly, the Court betrayed the Reconstruction's goal of undoing slavery's legal oppression of blacks. The Reconstruction Amendments had sought to guarantee equal rights for the freedmen by (a) prohibiting slavery (the Thirteenth Amendment); (b) protecting the "privileges or immunities" of all American citizens, requiring the equal protection of all persons under state law, and providing all persons with the right of due process (the Fourteenth Amendment); and (c) declaring the right of male citizens to vote without regard to race (the Fifteenth Amendment). For the first time, the Constitution required states to give equal respect to the individual rights of all persons within their borders. In the *Slaughter-House Cases* (1873), however, a mere five years after the ratification of the Fourteenth Amendment, the Court held that the Privileges or Immunities Clause recognized no substantive individual rights at all. *Slaughter-House* eviscerated the Reconstruction Congress's intent that the freedoms of the Bill of Rights apply to the states as well as the federal government.[8] The Court then left the freedmen to their fate in *Plessy v. Ferguson* (1896), which, like *Dred Scott*, represents one of the most shameful moments in the history of the American judiciary. In *Plessy* the Court approved "separate but equal," which allowed the Southern states to impose a system of racial segregation on blacks despite the language, structure, and clear purpose of the Fourteenth Amendment.[9] *Plessy* ushered in the "Jim Crow" era: by law or custom, Southern states (and some Northern ones) denied the freedmen their civil and political rights for the next sixty years.

A Book You're Not Supposed to Read

Vindicating the Founders: Race, Sex, Class, and Justice in the Origins of America by Thomas G. West. Lanham, Maryland: Rowman and Littlefield Publishers, 2000.

The *Lochner* Era

Having withdrawn from the field of civil rights, for the next half century the Court devoted its energies to defining and defending economic liberties. In the face of the large-scale industrialization and nationalization of the economy, both federal and state governments attempted to regulate corporate activity, working conditions, and labor organization. The Court halted the exercise of such power by both levels of government. With respect to federal power, the Court found that the Constitution withheld from Congress the authority to control activity that occurred wholly within a single state (rather than across interstate borders). In *Hammer v. Dagenhart* (1918), the Court struck down a federal law banning the sale of goods made by child labor. *Hammer* held that Congress could not even regulate the interstate movement of such goods because the actual production had occurred wholly within a state.[10] This decision effectively ruled off-limits any federal role in regulating manufacturing, agriculture, and labor relations.

While the Constitution grants Congress only limited, enumerated authorities, it reserves to the states what is known as the "police power," which allows them to regulate all people and activity within their borders. But when states enacted laws setting working conditions and other health and safety rules, the Supreme Court again balked. The justices' most important

Skepticism Warranted?

Recent scholarship, in fact, bears out the Court's unwillingness to accept the New York legislators' supposedly benevolent motivations. It appears that New York passed the law to suppress competition by non-unionized immigrant bakers who were willing to work longer hours than others.[11]

decision in this vein was *Lochner v. New York* (1905), which came to define this period of the Court's history. *Lochner* struck down a New York State law that prohibited bakers from working more than ten hours per day or sixty hours a week. The Court held that a law mandating maximum hours or a minimum wage "necessarily interferes with the right of contract between the employer and employees" that is part of "the liberty of the individual protected by the Fourteenth Amendment."[12] It rejected arguments that the New York legislature sought to protect the health and safety of bakers or to ensure the quality of their bread. During "the *Lochner* Era," the Court invalidated 184 state laws governing working hours and wages, organized labor, commodity prices, and entry into business.

Lochner has become famous for the dissent by Justice Oliver Wendell Holmes Jr., who accused the justices in the majority of advancing their own laissez-faire values through the guise of interpreting "liberty" in the Due Process Clause. "The Fourteenth Amendment does not enact Mr. Herbert Spencer's Social Statics," Holmes wrote, with reference to a Social Darwinist work of the time. The Constitution "is not intended to embody a particular economic theory, whether of paternalism and the organic relation of the citizen to the state or of *laissez faire*." Whether judges might personally find laws "injudicious," or even "tyrannical," he argued, should have no bearing on the question of whether they conflict with the Constitution.[13] Scholars today continue to debate how far the original Constitution and the Reconstruction Amendments protect the economic liberties of property and contract. But whatever the outcome of that argument, Holmes's dissent continues to stand as a powerful warning against the temptation for the justices to rely upon their personal philosophies or policies rather than the text, structure, and history of the Constitution. His caution became the point of attack for the president and Congress when they next came into major conflict with the Court—thirty years later.

"The Switch in Time That Saved Nine"

The greatest conflict between the Supreme Court and the other branches of the federal government, one that still shapes how today's judges think, came over the 1930s New Deal. Like Lincoln, Franklin Roosevelt took office with the nation beset by crisis. But instead of an impending civil war, Americans faced the worst economy in their history.

> Between the summer of 1929 and the spring of 1933, nominal gross national product dropped by 50 percent. Prices for all goods fell by about a third; income from agriculture collapsed from $6 billion to $2 billion; industrial production declined by 37 percent; and business investment plummeted from $24 billion to $3 billion. About one-quarter of the workforce, 13 million Americans, remained consistently unemployed, and the unemployment rate would remain above 15 percent for the rest of the decade. More than 5,000 banks failed, with a loss of $7 billion in deposits. From the time of the crash in October 1929 to its low in July 1932, the Dow Jones Industrial Average fell more than 75 percent. It was not a problem caused by famine or drought, dwindling natural resources, or crippled production; crops spoiled and livestock were destroyed because market prices were too low.[14]

The causes of the Depression were complex. Little evidence seems to support the claim that the stock market crash triggered the Depression—stock markets have sharply declined since then, most recently in 1987, with no underlying change in economic growth.

> In their classic *Monetary History of the United States*, Milton Friedman and Anna Schwartz argued that a normal recession deepened into the Great Depression because the Federal Reserve mistakenly responded to the banking panic by restricting the money supply. A deflation in prices followed. . . . Others argue that the Great Depression must be understood within the context of the international economy, which witnessed bank failures and recession in Germany and France, defaults on World War I loan and reparation payments, abandonment of the gold standard, and the dumping of agricultural products on world markets.[15]

But many at the time, FDR included, blamed the Great Depression on "economic royalists," the rich, financiers, and speculators.[16] Roosevelt set a precedent for his successors by rushing a torrent of legislation through Congress in his first hundred days in office. The National Industrial Recovery Act (NIRA), the Agricultural Adjustment Act (AAA), and the Banking Act all granted FDR extraordinary economic powers to fight the Depression. Their enactment witnessed the breakdown of the sharp distinction between the executive and legislative branches. The executive branch took the primary responsibility for drafting bills, Congress passed them quickly with a minimum of deliberation (sometimes sight unseen), and then the president and the administrative agencies assumed unprecedented power over the peacetime economy. The AAA, for example, gave the executive the power to dictate the crops to be planted and the prices to be charged. Under the NIRA, agencies enacted industry-wide codes of conduct—often drafted by the industries themselves—governing production and employment. New

Dealers sought to address falling prices for commodities by mandating higher prices, reduced competition, and limited quantities.

These laws dared the justices to block the New Deal. The NIRA did not just attempt to ban a single product or manufacturing process—it placed all industrial production in the nation under federal regulation. The AAA did the same with agriculture, and another law limited coal mining. Laws passed later, such as the National Labor Relations Act and the Public Utility Holding Company Act, set nationwide rules on unions and utilities, while the Social Security Act created a universal system of unemployment compensation and old-age pensions. The New Deal legislation raised immediate constitutional problems under existing Supreme Court precedent. These laws pushed the Constitution's grant of authority to Congress to make laws "to regulate Commerce . . . among the several States" beyond the limits that had been set by the Court. Other laws, such as those enacting new public employment and unemployment relief programs, raised constitutional issues about the national government's taxing and spending authority.

Initially the Supreme Court would have none of it. In the first case examining a New Deal law, *Panama Refining Co. v. Ryan* (1935), an 8–1 majority of the Court invalidated the NIRA's grant of power to the executive branch to set quotas on the interstate transportation of oil. Chief Justice Charles Evans Hughes wrote that the provision unconstitutionally delegated legislative power to the president.[17] The Court went on to strike down three more New Deal laws, with the centerpiece decision a unanimous rejection of the NIRA in *A. L. A. Schechter Poultry v. United States* (the so-called "Sick Chicken Case"). The Roosevelt administration had used its power under the NIRA to prosecute the owners of a New York City–area chicken slaughterhouse for violating federal industry codes. *Schechter Poultry* held that the Constitution prohibited Congress from delegating limitless legislative power to the president, and that Congress could not regulate activity that occurred within a single state. That decision was a shot across the bow of the Roosevelt administration. If the Court kept to its precedent that intrastate manufacturing and agriculture lay outside federal authority, more pillars of the New Deal—perhaps even the whole program itself—might collapse. In pointed language the Court rejected the Roosevelt administration's overarching approach to the Great Depression: "Extraordinary conditions do not create or enlarge constitutional power."[18]

FDR responded with a political attack on the Court that went well beyond anything in the struggles between Marshall and Jefferson or Taney and Lincoln. In an hour-and-a-half press conference, the president declared *Schechter Poultry* to be the most significant judicial decision since *Dred Scott*. *Schechter*'s narrow view of the Commerce Clause was the real threat to the New Deal. If Congress could not regulate the activities of the butchers because they were local in nature, it would be unable to police most other manufacturing or agricultural enterprises. "The whole tendency over these years has been to view the interstate commerce clause in the light of present-day civilization," Roosevelt told the press. "We are interdependent—we are tied together." To Roosevelt, the justices' way of thinking failed to take account of the national character of the economy. "We have been relegated to a horse-and-buggy definition of interstate commerce."[19] FDR considered a variety of proposals: increasing the number of justices (giving the president enough new appointments to change the balance on the Court), reducing the Court's jurisdiction, or requiring a supermajority of justices to declare a federal law unconstitutional.[20] At the same time, FDR and Congress enacted a second wave of New Deal laws, including the National Labor Relations Act and the Social Security Act, which created specialized bureaucracies to handle more discrete areas of the national economy. While the First New Deal vested the president with emergency powers to handle the Depression, the Second New Deal of 1935–1936 promised permanent government intervention in the American economy and society.

Rather than retreat before this second outburst of lawmaking, the Court stuck to its guns. In the spring of 1936, it declared unconstitutional more elements of the New Deal. In *United States v. Butler*, the Court held unconstitutional the AAA's use of taxes and grants to regulate agricultural production. The majority declared that Congress could not use taxes and spending to regulate intrastate agriculture, which lay within the reserved powers of the states.[21] *Butler* threatened the Social Security Act, which used a combination of taxes and spending to provide relief and pensions to the unemployed and elderly. In *Carter v. Carter Coal Co.*, a 5–4 majority struck down a 1935 law that set prices, wages, hours, and collective bargaining rules for the coal industry. The Court found that the production of coal did not amount to interstate commerce and instead also fell within the reserved powers of the states.[22] In another case, the justices attacked the proceedings of the Securities and Exchange Commission as "odious" and "pernicious" and compared them to the "intolerable abuses of the Star Chamber."[23] And *Morehead v. New York ex rel. Tipaldo* found that New York's minimum wage law violated the Due Process Clause, in line with earlier cases in which the Court had found that such laws interfered with the right to contract.[24]

In the space of just two years, the Court had ripped apart the first wave of New Deal laws, and it was threatening to do the same to the second. FDR did not mention the Court in his 1936 re-election campaign, which produced one of the great electoral victories in American history: 523 electoral votes to 8 (the largest advantage ever recorded in a contested two-party election in American history), every state but Maine and Vermont, more than 60 percent of the popular vote, and a Democratic Congress with two-thirds majorities in both House and Senate. Observers legitimately questioned whether the Republican Party would shortly disappear. Fresh off his victory, FDR proposed a restructuring of the Court to eliminate its opposition to the New Deal. On February 5, 1937, he sent Congress a judiciary "reform" bill that would add a new justice to the Court for every sitting

One Vote Away: How a Single Supreme Court Seat Can Change History by Ted Cruz. Washington, D.C.: Regnery Publishing, 2020.

justice over the age of seventy.[25] Because of the advanced age of several members of the Court, Roosevelt's proposal would have allowed him to appoint six new justices. Rather than criticize the Court for its opposition to the New Deal, Roosevelt disingenuously claimed that the elderly justices were delaying the efficient administration of justice.

Despite his electoral success, FDR's Court-packing plan—the first domestic initiative of his second term—suffered a humiliating defeat. Mail and telegrams to Congress went nine-to-one against the plan, and polling showed a majority of the country opposed it. Elements of the New Deal coalition, such as farmers and some unions, attacked the plan early. Senate Republicans unified in opposition shortly after the president announced his proposal, and both conservative and liberal Democrats in the Senate came out against the plan. Various college and university presidents, academics, and the American Bar Association opposed the plan. The coup de grâce was delivered by none other than Chief Justice Hughes, in a letter made public during Senate Judiciary Committee hearings, rebutting point by point FDR's claims that the Court was overworked and that the older justices could not perform their duties. Both liberal justice Louis Brandeis and conservative justice Willis Van Devanter approved the letter, which most historians believe ended the Court-packing plan for good.

Historians and political scientists have argued ever since over whether FDR's defeated proposal still won the war. A week after the Court-packing bill stalled in Congress, the Court upheld a state minimum wage law for women. Two weeks later, the Court upheld the National Labor Relations Act, which had been challenged on the same grounds raised in the "Sick Chicken" and *Carter* cases. This time, in *NLRB v. Jones & Laughlin Steel Corp.*, Chief Justice Hughes led a 5–4 majority in rejecting the doctrine that manufacturing did not constitute interstate commerce. Jones & Laughlin Steel was the fourth largest steel company in the nation with operations in multiple states. As the Court observed, "the stoppage of those operations by industrial strife would have a most serious effect upon interstate commerce." "It is obvious," the Court found, that the effect "would be immediate and might be catastrophic." Henceforth the Court would allow federal regulation of the economy, even of wholly intrastate activity, because of the interconnectedness of the national market. To do otherwise would be to "shut our eyes to the plainest facts of our national life" and to judge questions of interstate commerce "in an intellectual vacuum."[26] It would be sixty years before the Court struck down another federal law based on the interstate commerce power. Shortly after the Court's "switch in time that saved nine"—as the Court's change of course under the threat of FDR's Court-packing plan is known—several opponents of the New Deal retired from the Court. By 1941 FDR had appointed eight of the nine justices and saved his New Deal. In the end, the Court enabled the creation of the Administrative State under which we now live—a topic we pursue below.

CHAPTER 4

Equality before the Law

After its defeat during the New Deal, the Court entered the current age—the age of equality. Turning its back on economic liberties, the Court now devoted itself to the protection of minorities: first as defined by race and religion, then by gender (a "minority" only in a non-numerical sense), and most recently by sexual orientation. Its campaign took two forms. First, the Court sought to enforce the Fourteenth Amendment's mandate that the states as well as the federal government obey the Bill of Rights. Second, it worked to keep the promise of the Civil War and Reconstruction that these freedoms would include all Americans, regardless of race. Unlike in its earlier struggles during the antebellum, Civil War, and early New Deal periods, in this project the Court has often had the support of the majority of the American people, or at least of powerful political coalitions. But as the Court expanded these liberties beyond those rooted firmly in the constitutional text, it became the center of long-lasting legal and political controversy.

Incorporating the Bill of Rights

The Court's mission to read the Bill of Rights as applying against the states began with a fundamental handicap. In the *Slaughter-House Cases*, the Court rejected the Reconstruction Congress's original understanding that the Privileges or Immunities Clause extended the Bill

The Original Meaning of the Fourteenth Amendment: Its Letter and Its Spirit by Randy E. Barnett and Evan D. Bernick. Cambridge: Belknap Press, 2021.

of Rights to the states[1]—a position that the Court still holds today. When the justices began expanding individual rights in the first half of the twentieth century, they had to find another constitutional foundation for "incorporating" the Bill of Rights against the states. They settled upon the Due Process Clause, on the theory that denying certain rights would violate the "fundamental . . . liberties" or "the concept of ordered liberty."[2] Under this theory, known as "selective incorporation," the Court held that the states had to respect political rights. It found that the First Amendment rights of free speech (1925), assembly (1937), press (1931) and exercise of religion (1940) applied to the states, and it also forbade states from establishing religion (1947).[3] Except for a decision forbidding mandatory prayer in public schools,[4] these decisions did not spark controversy, perhaps because these rights truly seemed fundamental to a republican form of government at both the federal and state levels.

But the Court met with far more controversy and opposition when it extended the federal rights of criminal suspects to the states. In a series of famous cases, the Court held that states could not engage in a search without a warrant (*Mapp v. Ohio*, 1961), that they must provide for the assistance of counsel (*Gideon v. Wainright*, 1963), and that police must give warnings to protect the right to remain silent (*Miranda v. Arizona*, 1966).[5] These decisions, and others that applied virtually all the rights contained in the Bill of Rights to the states, came during the chief justiceship of Earl Warren. Thanks to these decisions and the Court's end of segregation (on which more shortly), the Warren Court became a byword for judicial activism.

It may be the case that the original understanding of the Fourteenth Amendment prohibited states from carrying out unreasonable searches and seizures. But in *Mapp v. Ohio*, the Warren Court forced all the states to adopt the "exclusionary rule"—the remedy for an illegal search requires the suppression in court not only of the evidence found in the search, but all the "fruit of the poisonous tree."[6] *Miranda* has a similar effect. Members of the Reconstruction Congress would have understood the Privileges or Immunities Clause to protect the right of a suspect against self-incrimination and the right to a lawyer. Those rights form part of the nation's history and tradition of fair process in criminal cases. But the Warren Court used *Miranda* to dictate warnings that all state and federal police must provide upon an arrest. "You have the right to remain silent. Anything you say can (and will) be used against you in a court of law. You have the right to the presence of an attorney, and if you cannot afford an attorney, one will be appointed for you prior to any questioning."[7] These words are known to every American thanks to crime movies and TV shows. But the words appear nowhere in the constitutional text. In neither *Mapp* nor *Miranda* could the Court show that its ruling had any support in the constitutional text, structure, or history. Instead, the justices seized the opportunity to dictate new rules of law and order throughout the nation.

Don't Impeach Earl Warren!

The Warren Court's reputation for judicial activism is unfortunate in some respects, because some of its decisions—such as its reversal of the Jim Crow system of legalized racial oppression—restored the original understanding of the Constitution. It did, however, deserve its reputation for judicial activism when it went beyond reviving the core meaning of the Reconstruction Amendments.

A similar flaw beset the Court's noble fight for racial equality. The Warren Court's greatest decision—indeed, perhaps the greatest decision in the Supreme Court's history after *Marbury v. Madison*—was *Brown v. Board of Education* (1954). In *Brown*, the NAACP, led by future justice Thurgood Marshall, challenged *Plessy*'s "separate but equal" doctrine, which had allowed Topeka, Kansas, to maintain two sets of schools, one for blacks and

The Warren Court and American Politics by Lucas A. Powe Jr. Cambridge: Belknap Press, 2002.

one for whites. A unanimous Supreme Court held that segregating black and white children in different public schools harmed the former, "even though the physical facilities and other 'tangible' factors may be equal," because segregation "has a tendency to [retard] the educational and mental development" of black children. "In the field of public education the doctrine of 'separate but equal' has no place," Chief Justice Warren wrote. "Separate educational facilities are inherently unequal."[8] Curiously, the Court did not expressly overrule *Plessy*, perhaps out of concern about the response that was sure to come in the South. The Court's attention to politics led to a second misstep in its otherwise admirable fight against racial discrimination. In the follow-up case known as *Brown II* (1955), the justices advised the lower courts that they should oversee desegregation efforts "with all deliberate speed."[9] The implementation was more deliberate than speedy. Southern states engaged in a strategy of "massive resistance" to *Brown* that left schools significantly segregated even into the late 1960s.[10] Historians today conclude that the broader gains of the civil rights movement, as codified in the Civil Rights Acts of 1964 and 1965, not *Brown*, brought about permanent desegregation in the South.[11]

A Book You're Not Supposed to Read

From Jim Crow to Civil Rights: The Supreme Court and the Struggle for Racial Equality by Michael J. Klarman. Oxford University Press, 2006.

The *Brown* decision produced unintended consequences. It sparked broader political and social changes, but also led the Court to overextend itself. *Brown* became the starting point of the Warren Court's campaign to remake American society. It marked a broader quest to promote equality, rather than individual liberty, that would draw the Court into its current controversies. Some of the decisions that followed *Brown*, such as *Reynolds v. Sims* (1964), which established the "one person, one vote" standard, and the 1970s cases leading to full equality for women, have met with broad acceptance.[12] But others have not. A desire to speed desegregation in the 1970s led the Court to approve busing programs that transported children in order to produce some idealized racial mixture in urban schools. Confident in their ability to engineer racial policies, the justices upheld affirmative action programs that consider race in college and university admissions. In 2023 the Court will have the opportunity to correct this last mistake when it issues a ruling on the use of race in admissions by Harvard University and the University of North Carolina.

Beyond the Text

The quest for equality led the justices down a second path that was even more controversial. In addition to protecting racial minorities, the Court embarked on a mission to expand a right to privacy. In sporadic cases stretching back to the 1920s, the Court had blocked state laws interfering with, for example, parental rights over the raising of children. Its decisions on the right to be free of unreasonable searches and seizures, on the right to speech and association, and of religious freedom, also rested in part on the idea that the Constitution protected a zone of privacy. But the Court stepped into a political and legal quagmire when it entered the battles over sexual freedom.

In 1965 *Griswold v. Connecticut* found unconstitutional a state law that forbade adults from using contraceptives. "Would we allow the police to search the sacred precincts of marital bedrooms for telltale signs of the use of contraceptives?" asked Justice William O. Douglas, writing for the majority in *Griswold*. "The very idea is repulsive to the notions of privacy surrounding the marriage relationship."[13] But the Court could not explain how the text,

It's Right There in the Penumbras of the Emanations

The "right to privacy"—let alone the specific right to use contraception—is, to say the least, difficult to locate in the text of the Constitution. But, as Justice Douglas wrote in *Griswold*, "Specific guarantees in the Bill of Rights have penumbras, formed by emanations from those guarantees that help give them life and substance."[14]

structure, or history of the Fourteenth Amendment's Due Process Clause—which requires that the state provide a fair procedure before it deprives a person of "life, liberty, or property"—created these or any substantive rights.

Loosely locating constitutional rights in the Due Process Clause was a fateful choice that would come to haunt the Court. *Griswold* set the Court on a trajectory that led to *Roe v. Wade* (1973) and fifty years of controversy. In *Roe*, Justice Harry Blackmun wrote for a 7–2 majority that the Due Process Clause protected a woman's right to an abortion. Finding that a fundamental constitutional right protected "activities relating to marriage," such as procreation, contraception, family relationships, and child rearing and education, the Court concluded that privacy was also "broad enough to encompass a woman's decision whether or not to terminate her pregnancy." But the Court also recognized that the defendant State of Texas has "[an] important and legitimate interest in protecting the potentiality of human life," in other words, that of the fetus. While claiming that he could not "resolve the difficult question of when life begins," Justice Blackmun balanced the interests of the mother and that of the fetus to reach the Court's holding that a state could prohibit abortion only after the point of viability, or about twenty-eight weeks of pregnancy under the medical technology of that time.[15]

Roe was widely criticized for its legal reasoning, or lack thereof. But perhaps even worse was the Court's seizure of the authority to make a basic decision of public policy from the political process. In one fell swoop, the Court overturned the abortion laws of all fifty states. At the time of *Roe*, thirty states still prohibited abortion at all stages, but about one-third had begun to expand abortion rights. *Roe* replaced the gradual movement of the American people, through their state governments, toward more liberalized abortion policies with one rule created by judicial fiat. Even future justice Ruth Bader Ginsburg commented in 1992 that *Roe* "halted a political process that was moving in a reform direction and thereby, I believe, prolonged divisiveness and deferred stable settlement of the issue."[18] *Roe* came to distort constitutional law and politics, as pro-choice and pro-life groups pressured presidents and the Senate to appoint and confirm justices to the Supreme Court who would advance their favored views on abortion. Judicial confirmation hearings became thinly veiled exercises in interrogating nominees on their views on *Roe*. Presidents, members of Congress, and interest groups came to borrow the techniques of election campaigns and apply them to the judiciary. In 1992 the Court had the opportunity to revisit *Roe* and return the question to the states. Instead, in *Planned Parenthood v. Casey*, three justices—all appointed by Republican, pro-life presidents—issued an extraordinary joint opinion refusing to overturn *Roe* in the name of *stare decisis*: the idea that the Court should obey its past precedents in order to maintain legal stability and enhance respect for the rule of law.

Bad Reviews

In his dissent to *Doe v. Bolton*, the companion case to *Roe v. Wade*, Justice Byron White accused the majority of an "exercise of raw judicial power,"[16] and prominent liberal law professor John Hart Ely famously wrote that the decision was "*not* constitutional law and gives almost no sense of an obligation to try to be."[17]

The Court in *Casey* "call[ed] the contending sides of a national controversy to end their national division" and accept the legitimacy of *Roe*.[19] But instead of tamping down the political conflict over abortion, *Casey* prolonged it for another three decades. (We discuss the Court's eventual decision to overturn *Roe* in 2022 in greater detail in the subsequent chapters.)

The Court's trip into the thickets of the sexual revolution also created an important counterexample to the story of *Roe*. Until the 1990s the Court had long respected the right of states to criminalize homosexual acts. In a 1961 dissent in *Poe v. Ullman*, for instance, Justice John Marshall Harlan characterized "laws forbidding adultery, fornication and homosexual practices" as "deeply pressed into the substance of our social life."[20] Twenty-five years later, in *Bowers v. Hardwick* (1986), the Court held that the right to privacy it had identified in the *Roe* line of cases did not protect homosexual conduct in the bedroom. Laws against homosexuality assumed the same status as laws regarding suicide, euthanasia, or the death penalty—all remained in the hands of the states. But in *Lawrence v. Texas* (2003), the Court rejected *stare decisis* and overturned *Bowers*. According to Justice Kennedy's majority opinion, the Due Process Clause protects the right of gays "to enter upon this relationship in the confines of their homes and their own private lives and still retain their dignity as free persons."[21] But instead of elevating gays to the level of a protected class, such as racial minorities or women, or holding that the right to engage in homosexual acts was a fundamental right, such as speech or religion, the Court declared that state laws interfering with homosexuals' sexual liberty failed the minimal "rational basis" required of all laws. Predictably, the Court proceeded a decade later to strike down laws forbidding gays to marry. In *Obergefell v. Hodges* (2015), Justice Kennedy declared for the majority that the Due Process Clause protected marriage as a fundamental right and that laws against it "burden the liberty of same-sex couples" and "abridge central precepts of equality."[22] Both decisions prohibited states from regulating sexual relations and marriage, which they had controlled under their police powers from the beginning of the Republic.

These decisions made the Court a censor of state laws on the basis of its vision of the proper attitude toward certain social groups. The majority did not respond meaningfully to Justice Scalia's cutting dissent that these decisions threatened traditional state legislation regulating morality. While Justice Kennedy claimed *Lawrence* and *Obergefell* only protected consensual activity that harmed no third parties, Justice Scalia observed that states had long punished similarly "harmless" conduct by adults, such as prostitution, adultery, incest, obscenity, and pornography.[23] The Court escalated a conflict with states that might have represented only outliers in attitudes toward gays, as in *Lawrence*, into a battle with a national popular majority. In 1996 Congress had passed, and President Clinton had signed, the Defense of Marriage Act, which allowed states to refuse to recognize gay marriages. The presidential candidates in 2008 and 2012, Barack Obama, John McCain, and Mitt Romney, took the stand that the Constitution did not protect gay marriage; nominees to the Supreme Court testified to the same understanding. The Court, which admitted that the text and structure of the Constitution did not address gay rights, could do little to show that the nation's history and tradition had developed sufficiently to recognize these as rights that should supplant the states' traditional authority.

A Book You're Not Supposed to Read

What Is Marriage? Man and Woman: A Defense by Sherif Girgis, Ryan T. Anderson, and Robert P. George. 2nd ed. New York: Encounter Books, 2020.

Nevertheless, the nation has changed its attitude toward gay marriage since—perhaps because of—*Obergefell*. Whereas a substantial majority opposed gay marriage as recently as 2010 (in 2004, Americans even opposed it overwhelmingly, 60 percent to 31 percent), by 2019 attitudes had completely reversed (61 percent in support versus 31 percent opposed). Support is even greater among younger Americans: nearly 75 percent of Millennials favor gay marriage, while a majority of those born before 1945 still disapprove.[24] That trend suggests that increasingly broad majorities of the American people would oppose a judicial reversal of *Obergefell*. This seems, in part, to be the impetus behind the Roberts

Court's declaration—which we will consider below—that it can overturn *Roe v. Wade* but leave *Obergefell* untouched. As Mr. Dooley, a famed (and fictional) political pundit of the early twentieth century observed, "The Supreme Court follows the election returns."[25]

PART II

Substantive Due Process, Privacy, and Abortion

CHAPTER 5

Abortion and the Current Supreme Court

This chapter introduces today's Supreme Court, called the Roberts Court after its chief justice, by focusing on *Dobbs v. Jackson Women's Health Organization*. *Dobbs* overturned *Roe v. Wade*, which had found a woman's constitutional right to abortion, and *Planned Parenthood v. Casey*, in which the Court had refused to overturn *Roe* because of its allegiance to past decisions. *Dobbs* sparked unprecedented political controversy even before it appeared on the docket. Partisan conflict over judicial nominations reached new heights with President Donald Trump's three Supreme Court nominees, who decisively altered the ideological balance of the Court. Even while *Dobbs* was still under consideration by the justices, an effort to destroy the Court's institutional independence came to a crescendo. A devastating leak of the draft of Justice Alito's majority opinion invited extreme pressure on the justices—including a foiled assassination plot against Justice Brett Kavanaugh—in a last-ditch effort to force a change in direction. Refusing to bend to political pressure, a majority of the Court overturned *Roe* and *Casey* on June 24, 2022. A five-justice majority found that the text of the Constitution does not provide for a right to an abortion and returned the question to the states.

Politicization, by the Numbers

Until 1965 the Senate confirmed more than half of all nominations to the Supreme Court by voice vote (meaning the senators did not even bother to record their individual votes), and most other nominations passed by comfortable margins. Only about 18 percent of nominees failed. A majority received confirmation votes within ten days of nomination. After 1965, however, waits of more than sixty days have become the norm, with the Senate rejecting about one in four nominees.[1]

Constitutional Cage Match

Controversial Supreme Court decisions since the 1960s, especially *Roe*—and efforts to change the makeup of the Court to overturn those cases—have transformed judicial confirmation hearings into prime-time television spectacles. What had once been routine Senate business has become one of the most dangerous arenas for partisan combat. This should come as no surprise. As the Court has expanded its reach to more social issues of great importance, those who care about those issues have little means to influence national policy except by changing the membership of the Court. *Roe* thrust the Court into the late twentieth- and early twenty-first-century struggles over sexual freedom and gender identity. The primary means for pro-life and pro-choice Americans to achieve their goals on abortion became Supreme Court confirmations. Every time a vacancy opened on the Supreme Court, the fate of abortion seemed to be at stake.

The Trump presidency thrust the clash over Supreme Court appointments into the very center of national politics. In early 2016 Justice Antonin Scalia's death opened a Court vacancy that might have guaranteed the long-term survival of *Roe*, but the Republican Senate majority refused to allow President Obama to appoint a successor. The vacancy put *Roe*, and the Court's future direction, at stake in the 2016 election. Candidate Donald Trump promised to appoint only pro-life justices and even released a list of candidates during the campaign. Hillary Clinton responded by committing, as several of her predecessors had, to nominate only pro-choice jurists to the high court. The Supreme Court became the focus of a presidential election as never before.

Then, in just one term, President Trump had the remarkable opportunity to fill three vacancies to the Supreme Court, more than either President Obama or President Clinton had in their two-term presidencies. The specific vacancies themselves would prove critical. Justice Scalia's passing in 2016 and his replacement by Justice Neil Gorsuch did not change the 5–4 majority that continued to support *Roe*. But with Justice Anthony Kennedy's retirement two years later, the last of the authors of the *Casey* plurality left the Court. Justice Ruth Bader Ginsburg's death in 2020 gave President Trump the opportunity to replace the Court's champion of women's rights and its most stalwart defender of *Roe*.

The Makeup of the Court Today

President Trump's three nominees—Gorsuch, Kavanaugh, and Amy Coney Barrett—are cut from the same cloth. All three served as judges on the federal Appeals Courts with impeccable academic credentials. They all served as clerks to Supreme Court justices themselves (each justice hires four clerks, usually a few years out of law school, who are top-performing students in their graduating classes). Most important, all three were well-known conservatives who received the support of groups such as the Federalist Society and the Heritage Foundation. All three were also young, at least by judicial standards, and could expect to serve on the Supreme Court for two or even three decades.

The first Trump appointee, Neil Gorsuch, hailed from Colorado, where his family name adorns fancy ski-clothing stores. He grew up in Washington, D.C., graduated from Columbia University and Harvard Law School, and served as a law clerk to a federal Appeals Court judge in Colorado and then to Supreme Court Justices Byron White and Kennedy. After a few years at a boutique law firm, Gorsuch served in the U.S. Justice Department before President George W. Bush appointed him to the Tenth Circuit Court of

Appeals in Denver. He served there for eleven years before President Trump nominated him to the Supreme Court in 2017 at the age of forty-nine. Although Gorsuch was eminently qualified for the position, and his addition would have no effect on the Court's ideological balance, the Senate confirmed him by a vote of only 54–45.

The second appointee, Brett Kavanaugh, had spent his life and career in Washington, D.C. After going to the same high school as Gorsuch (though two years ahead), Kavanaugh graduated from Yale College and Yale Law School. He clerked for an Appeals Court judge in California and then for Justice Kennedy. He then took the first of several political positions when he served in Ken Starr's independent counsel investigation into President Bill Clinton, which ultimately led to the second impeachment in American history. After several years in private practice, Kavanaugh joined the White House staff of President George W. Bush, who appointed Kavanaugh to the federal Appeals Court in Washington, D.C. President Trump nominated him to the Supreme Court in 2018, and the Senate confirmed him by a 50–48 vote at the age of fifty-three.

The third Trump nominee to the Court, Amy Coney Barrett, did not come from government and Washington, D.C., as Gorsuch and Kavanaugh did, but instead from the academy. After graduating from Rhodes College and Notre Dame Law School, she clerked in the D.C. Circuit Court of Appeals and then for Justice Antonin Scalia. After a few years of private practice, she returned to Notre Dame to teach law. Ultimately holding an endowed chair, Barrett wrote primarily on interpretation and the federal courts. President Trump appointed her in 2017 to the Court of Appeals in Chicago before nominating her at the age of forty-eight to replace Justice Ginsburg. The Senate confirmed her 52–48 just eight days before the 2020 presidential election.

The extreme opposition to these nominees reveals *Roe*'s distortion of the constitutional system. All three had outstanding credentials and backgrounds and had achieved distinction in their careers. A Republican president and Senate that had run on a platform of choosing conservatives for the bench elevated them. Opponents of Justice Gorsuch launched ridiculous accusations, such as claims of plagiarism in his Ph.D. dissertation and biased statements as a young law student. Compared to Kavanaugh, however, Gorsuch had it easy. Kavanaugh's opponents tried to block his confirmation with accusations that he had committed sexual harassment or even rape as a high school and college student. Pro-choice protesters interrupted his hearings repeatedly, spent hundreds of thousands of dollars on television ads warning that his confirmation would sound *Roe v. Wade*'s death knell, and even sent over a thousand coat hangers (symbols of self-administered abortions) to Republican senator Susan Collins of Maine, one of the critical votes for his confirmation. Barrett's nomination encountered challenges, too. Democrats insinuated that she was motivated more by religion than by fidelity to the law—Senator Dianne Feinstein had said at the hearing on Barrett's nomination to a federal Appeals Court that "the dogma lives loudly within you."[2] She became the first Supreme Court justice in 150 years to be confirmed on a purely party-line vote.

The three Trump justices joined a Court with a tenuous majority in favor of abortion rights. John Roberts has served as chief justice since 2005, when President George W. Bush appointed him to replace William Rehnquist. Roberts graduated from Harvard College and Harvard Law School, clerked for the justice he would replace, and went on to several important legal positions in the Reagan-Bush White House and Department of Justice. He became one of the top Supreme Court advocates before President George W. Bush appointed him to the D.C. Circuit in 2003, and then the Supreme Court. Chief Justice Roberts has led the Court in expanding religious freedom, striking down the government's use of race, and limiting the federal government's regulatory powers. But as the chief justice, Roberts has also displayed concern for the institutional independence of the Court. His desire to keep the Court at a remove from political controversies apparently (according to uncontradicted media reports) led him to supply the fifth vote to uphold President Obama's national health care plan in 2012.[3] He has also flipped positions on abortion. While he voted to uphold a partial-birth abortion ban in 2007 and dissented from a 2016 decision blocking Texas' regulation of abortion doctors, he flipped positions and joined a liberal majority in 2020 to block those very same regulations when enacted by Louisiana.[4]

To the chief justice's right sits Clarence Thomas, the Court's most senior justice and the leader of its conservative bloc. Raised in rural Georgia, Thomas graduated from the College of the Holy Cross and from Yale Law School. He began his career as a lawyer in the Missouri attorney general's office, practiced in a corporate general counsel's office, and then joined the staff of Senator John Danforth in Washington, D.C. President Reagan appointed him to head the civil rights office of the Department of Education and then the Equal Employment Opportunity Commission. President George H. W. Bush named him to the federal Appeals Court in Washington, D.C., in 1990, before elevating him to the Supreme Court to replace Justice Thurgood Marshall a year later. Thomas's confirmation foreshadowed the bitter partisan fights to come. It appeared that his appointment would shift the balance of the Court against *Roe*, and pro-choice opponents to his nomination responded first by attacking his interest in natural rights, and then by presenting Anita Hill's claims of sexual harassment. After dueling prime-time testimony in which Thomas categorically denied Hill's accusations, the Senate voted to confirm 52–48, the closest Supreme Court confirmation vote up to that time. In his three decades on the Court, Thomas has become known for his fidelity to interpreting the Constitution based on the original understanding held by the Founders and for his disregard for *stare decisis*.

President George W. Bush's second appointment to the Supreme Court, Samuel Alito, has proven to be far more conservative than Chief Justice

Roberts. Raised in New Jersey, Alito graduated from Princeton and Yale Law School. He clerked for the federal Appeals Court in Philadelphia before joining the Justice Department during the Reagan administration. President Ronald Reagan appointed him as U.S. attorney for New Jersey and then named him to serve as a judge in the federal Appeals Court where he had once clerked. Fifteen years later, President George W. Bush nominated him to replace Justice Sandra Day O'Connor. At that time the Court had five other justices who supported *Roe v. Wade*, so Alito's appointment did not alter the balance of the Court on abortion. In addition to *Dobbs*, Alito has made his mark with opinions expanding religious freedom and with his defense of tradition and historical practice in constitutional interpretation.

My Grandfather's Son: A Memoir by Clarence Thomas. New York: Harper Perennial, 2008.

With Trump's three appointees added to these three justices—admittedly of varying degrees of conservativism—who were already on the Court, the pro-life wing of the Supreme Court could claim five or six likely votes. The members of this conservative majority focus their attention on the text, structure, and original understanding of the Constitution and reject the more free-wheeling approach to interpretation of the 1960s and 1970s. This majority has coalesced around overruling *Roe*, opposing the government's resort to race, and curbing the power of the administrative agencies. But the conservative justices differ in their varying attitudes toward precedent, or the doctrine of *stare decisis*, which counsels courts to stick with the reasoning and outcome of earlier decisions—even when they are wrong. Concerned about the Court's political standing, Chief Justice Roberts shows a willingness to obey earlier cases, even when he had personally dissented from the initial decision, because he wishes to avoid the impression that politics drives judicial outcomes.[5] At the other end of the spectrum, Justice Thomas believes that deferring to past decisions when they are wrong elevates judges above the Constitution itself—a reasonable attitude for an African American who grew up under the racial segregation permitted by *Plessy v. Ferguson*. How far the conservative majority will allow past decisions to cabin its commitment to enforcing the original understanding of the Constitution will dictate the course of American constitutional law for the next decade.

These conservatives face a depleted liberal wing of the Court. Harry Blackmun, John Paul Stevens, Sandra Day O'Connor, Anthony Kennedy, and David Souter, though all appointed by Republicans, became part of the Court majorities that defended *Roe* and the right to privacy and transformed gay marriage into a fundamental right. They joined progressive justices such as Clinton appointees Stephen Breyer and Ruth Bader Ginsburg—and before them the famous William J. Brennan and Thurgood Marshall (appointed by Eisenhower and Johnson, respectively)—in the belief that federal judges should interpret the Constitution expansively, even creatively, to protect a broad set of federal rights and to expand the power of the federal government at the expense of the states. But as judicial politics became a more central subject for electoral politics, presidents searched for judges with more certain views, and Senates placed judicial nominees under greater scrutiny. With President Trump's three appointments to the Supreme Court, the phenomenon of conservative judges who "grow in office" toward progressivism is coming to an end. And based on their youth, the conservative justices should hold a majority on the Court for at least the next decade.

With Justice Stephen Breyer's 2022 retirement, Justice Sonia Sotomayor became the most senior member of the progressive bloc on the Court. Appointed by President Obama at the age of fifty-five, she was the third woman, and first Hispanic, to join the Court. She grew up in the Bronx, New York, graduated from Princeton University and Yale Law School, and went on to serve as an assistant district attorney in New York City;

They Grew in Office

While Republican presidents since the time of Nixon have appointed a greater number of Supreme Court justices than Democratic presidents, several of their nominees drifted—or rushed—to the progressive wing.

Sotomayor is the only current justice with significant prosecutorial experience. She served as a judge on the federal District and Appeals Courts in New York before her nomination to the Supreme Court (and Senate confirmation by a 68–31 vote) in 2009. In replacing David Souter, Sotomayor did not change the ideological balance of the Court; she voted with Justices Breyer and Ginsburg about 90 percent of the time. In her written opinions, she has defended the government's use of race in affirmative action and voting rights and has joined impassioned criticisms of the Court's cases expanding religious and gun rights.

President Obama's second appointment to the Court, Elena Kagan, is the only current justice who had no previous judicial experience. Her background instead involved a mixture of academic and government positions. She grew up in New York City and graduated from Princeton University and Harvard Law School. She then clerked for liberal judges Abner Mikva of the D.C. Circuit and Justice Thurgood Marshall of the Supreme Court. After a short time in private practice, Kagan joined the University of Chicago law faculty, where she met lecturer Barack Obama. She joined the Clinton White House and eventually became deputy director of the Domestic Policy Council. After the end of the Clinton administration, she joined the Harvard Law School faculty and succeeded to the deanship. In 2009 President Obama appointed her solicitor general, the government's advocate before the Supreme Court (sometimes known as "The Tenth Justice"), and then nominated her to the Supreme Court the following year. In her confirmation hearings, she famously declared—invoking the method of interpretation long promoted by Justice Scalia—that "we are all originalists,"[6] and she was confirmed by a 64–37 vote. Nonetheless, she votes consistently with the liberal wing of the Court—about 90 percent of the time—and she has devoted much of her efforts to defending the Administrative State from a skeptical Roberts Court.

Ketanji Brown Jackson is the third member of the Court's liberal wing. President Biden campaigned on the promise that he would nominate the first African-American woman to the Court, and he kept that promise. (We disagree with politicians' practices of pre-emptively limiting the pools for prominent positions to those of certain races or genders.) Raised in Miami, Florida, Jackson graduated from Harvard College and Harvard Law School and then clerked for a federal Appeals Court and Justice Breyer on the Supreme Court. She went into private practice, worked for the government sentencing commission, and then took a unique path to the Court—she became a public defender, representing criminal suspects who could not afford their own lawyers. President Obama appointed Jackson to the federal District Court in Washington, D.C., and then President Biden appointed her to the Court of Appeals, where she served for only a year before her elevation to the high court in 2022 to replace the justice for whom she had clerked over twenty years before. While she had little time to develop a full record of appellate opinions, she testified before the Senate that the "Constitution is fixed in its meaning," that it is not a living document, and that originalism provides a valuable approach to its interpretation.[7] On the other hand, she has specifically refused to define natural rights or to include them in her constitutional thinking. Her progress through the Senate highlighted the level of acrimony that has come to characterize the confirmation process. The Judiciary Committee refused, by tie vote, to recommend her to the full Senate, which confirmed her by a vote of 53–47. While Justice Jackson could surprise those who expect her to follow in the footsteps of Justices Breyer and Ginsburg, it is unlikely that she will stray far from the progressive wing of the Court.

Reconsidering *Roe*—and Everything Else

It was in this environment that the issue of abortion came back before the Supreme Court in the 2021–2022 term. Abortion elicits different approaches to the Constitution, conflicting understandings of the Court's place in American politics, and divergent theories about the role of judges. Under the Warren Court approach to constitutional interpretation, which still echoes in Kennedy's mysticism over abortion and gay marriage, the Supreme Court has steadily added more and more important social issues to its docket. Every time it claims constitutional power over another social issue, it deprives the people's elected representatives in our statehouses or in Congress of the ability to determine the policies that govern. As it increasingly resembles a legislature, the Court has steadily become more political. Anyone who cares deeply about abortion, gay marriage, race, religion, or speech can achieve policy changes only by influencing the appointment of justices to the Supreme Court, not by working to win elections. Naturally the decisions of the justices on these issues will be seen as political, rather than legal, in nature. It was only a matter of time before the political tactics of campaigns, lobbying, and legislation jumped

She Doesn't Hold These Rights to Be Inalienable

From Ketanji Brown Jackson's written answers to questions from the Senate Judiciary Committee:

[QUESTION] 15. Please explain, in your own words, the theory prevalent among members of the Founding Fathers' generation that humans possess natural rights that are inherent or inalienable.

[KETANJI BROWN JACKSON] RESPONSE: The theory that humans possess inherent or inalienable rights is reflected in the Declaration of Independence, which states: "We hold these truths to be self-evident, that all men are created equal, that they are endowed by their Creator with certain unalienable Rights, that among these are Life, Liberty, and the pursuit of Happiness."

[QUESTION] 16. Do you hold a position on whether individuals possess natural rights, yes or no?

[KETANJI BROWN JACKSON] RESPONSE: I do not hold a position on whether individuals possess natural rights.[8]

Slouching towards Gomorrah: Modern Liberalism and American Decline by Robert H. Bork. New York: ReganBooks, 2003.

across First Street, Washington, D.C., from the Capitol to the Court.

Some observers will argue that the unleashing of these political Furies has polarized the justices. Political polarization has clearly struck a blow to the workings of the other branches. And there is no doubt that the justices bear deep disagreements. But they are not the same divisions that drive partisan competition between the Republican and Democratic Parties. Instead, the conservative and liberal wings of the Court disagree over deeper issues, such as whether judges should interpret the Constitution based on its original understanding or in line with contemporary views. (Originalism can lead to progressive results, such as recent Court decisions that have expanded the rights of criminal suspects to jury trials; and "living constitutionalism" could produce conservative results, such as allowing a greater respect for freedom of speech and association.) The justices also disagree deeply about the proper role of the federal government, with originalists generally in favor of tougher enforcement of the limits on the powers of the national government, and of a stricter observance of the separation of powers between the president, Congress, and the courts. Progressives generally allow for a freer federal hand in domestic affairs and more experimentation in the workings of the government. Because it is not possible in this short book to provide a comprehensive review of every area of constitutional significance, we focus on three major cases the Court decided near the end of its 2021–2022 term: one on abortion (*Dobbs*), one on guns rights (*Bruen*), and one on the Administrative State (*West Virginia v. EPA*). Then, in our conclusion, we take a look at both the Court's past and its likely future: we will examine, first, the role of precedent, and second, the Court's growing interest in restoring more traditional forms of separation of powers and federalism.

CHAPTER 6

The Leak

Mississippi State Department of Health officer Thomas Dobbs asked the Supreme Court, which heard the case in December 2020, whether Mississippi could ban all abortions after fifteen weeks of pregnancy. Under *Roe*, as reaffirmed in *Planned Parenthood v. Casey*, states could regulate abortions after the point of fetal viability, so long as they did not place an undue burden on a woman's right to choose. But before viability, which occurs at about twenty-two to twenty-three weeks into pregnancy, the Court had held that the Constitution's Due Process Clause protects a virtually unrestricted right to an abortion. In early May 2022, someone leaked a draft opinion (dated February 10, 2022, and authored by Justice Samuel Alito), overturning *Roe* and returning abortion policy back to the states (and, more disputably, to Congress).

Politics by Other Means

The leak of the *Dobbs* opinion was just the latest escalation in the use of political tactics against the Court. No draft of a Supreme Court opinion had ever before leaked to the press; indeed, it is difficult to recall any leak of a full or a draft opinion occurring at any federal court. Leaking, even of the most sensitive classified information, is all too common at the White House, cabinet agencies, and Congress. (American officials, for example, leaked in

The Sweet Mystery of Life

"At the heart of liberty is the right to define one's own concept of existence, of meaning, of the universe, and of the mystery of human life."[1]—the notorious sentence from Justice Kennedy's opinion in *Planned Parenthood v. Casey* that has been widely mocked as the "sweet mystery of life" passage

spring of 2022 that the United States had provided Ukraine with the intelligence necessary to sink the *Moskva*, the flagship of the Russian Black Sea Fleet, and to target Russian generals in the field.) But the judiciary has been the exception to the rule.

The *Dobbs* leak prompted more political pressure tactics. It appears that the leaker had meant to spark exactly that result—increasing outside pressure on the justices to change their minds and keep *Roe* alive. Pro-abortion groups immediately held protests at the homes of Chief Justice Roberts and Justice Kavanaugh and published the home addresses of the five justices in the *Dobbs* majority—the aforementioned Kavanaugh, along with Thomas, Alito, Gorsuch, and Barrett. Federal marshals had to set up twenty-four-hour armed security for the justices and their homes. A month later, an armed twenty-six-year-old California man appeared at Justice Kavanaugh's home in the middle of the night. Police foiled the assassination attempt.

Pro-abortion advocates resorted to these methods because they understood that the fate of *Roe v. Wade* rested in the hands of the justices rather than the political process. Liberal justices Ruth Bader Ginsburg, Stephen Breyer, Elena Kagan, and Sonia Sotomayor had voted in lockstep to strike down virtually any effort by the states to regulate abortion. But it was Justice Kennedy, whom Kavanaugh replaced, who had provided the fifth vote to keep abortion rights alive. His strained efforts to conjure forth a right to abortion from a spare constitutional text had given birth to confused, even mystical definitions of privacy. Kennedy created a jurisprudence of subjectivity, where the Court could find rights whenever it wanted if some favored group felt its "own concept of existence" was threatened.

Not Even Trying

The great liberal legal scholar John Hart Ely called *Roe* "a very bad decision," and not because he disagreed with it on policy grounds. Rather, he viewed *Roe* as "bad because it is bad constitutional law, or rather because it is *not* constitutional law and gives almost no sense of an obligation to try to be."[2]

Back to the Text

Dobbs is important, and not just for ending this constitutional mysticism. With the three Trump justices, the Roberts Court halted the misguided adventure into the world of non-textual, judicially created rights. For the last half century, progressives have turned to the Supreme Court to win what politics denied them. The Court embedded the sexual revolution in the Constitution and "found" new progressive rights for privacy, dignity, and sexual orientation.

While the Left welcomed *Roe*'s result, some of its more serious thinkers worried about the Court's reasoning and its embrace of a political role. Ruth Bader Ginsburg, for example, criticized *Roe* before she joined the Court. She argued that the right to abortion should be grounded in equal protection, not privacy, and that abortion would have been better protected in the long term by state-by-state adoption rather than by the Court's imposition of its will from on high.[3]

A Book You're Not Supposed to Read

Tearing Us Apart: How Abortion Harms Everything and Solves Nothing by Ryan T. Anderson and Alexandra DeSanctis. Washington, D.C.: Regnery Publishing, 2022.

Legal conservatives waged a fifty-year campaign to overturn *Roe* not because they were obsessed with abortion. They opposed *Roe* for politicizing the Supreme Court, abusing the Constitution, and short-circuiting democracy to advance a left-wing moral vision. The theory of *Roe*—that the Due Process Clause, which speaks only to processes owed by the government before it deprives anyone of life, liberty, or property, also provided "substantive" protection for an unenumerated right to "privacy"—led inevitably to *Obergefell*, which overrode all state laws regulating gay marriage. According to Justice Kennedy, substantive due process included a constitutional right to marry someone of the same sex despite the policies of approximately two-thirds of the states. Justice Kennedy's vacuous reasoning did not disappoint: "The Constitution promises liberty to all within its reach, a liberty that includes certain specific rights that allow persons, within a lawful realm, to define and express their identity."[4]

The subjectivity of this approach invites the Court to replace our elected representatives in making policy on every claim of individual rights. Under *Roe* and *Casey*, every federal and state abortion regulation had to go to the Supreme Court, which aggrandized its power first by constitutionalizing abortion and then by creating a vague test that drove every important case to its docket. *Dobbs* leaves these decisions to the states. States can define an unborn child as a person and bring him or her within the protections of the criminal laws that protect life. The Court would allow those states to criminalize abortions that kill an unborn child. Some states will follow this path, and some will not. *Dobbs* also allows states to keep or make abortion legal. By overturning *Roe*, *Dobbs* allows states more space to articulate and defend their interests in abortion or in fetal life.

The Court Steps Back

The outcome of a single Supreme Court case is not the point. Conservatives, even those in the pro-life movement, must observe a distinction between law and politics. More important than whether Dobbs or Jackson Women's Health won the case are the Court's legal principles and reasoning. Recognizing that constitutional interpretation remains a fundamentally legal enterprise, rather than just another arena for political contest, remains crucial if the government is to obey the written Constitution. Alexander Hamilton declared in *Federalist* No. 78 that "courts must declare the sense of the law; and if they should be disposed to exercise WILL instead of JUDGMENT, the consequence would equally be the substitution of their pleasure to that of the legislative body."[5] Supreme Court justices that impose their will instead of using their judgment usurp the powers that the Constitution reserves to the elected branches and the states.

Allowing a Supreme Court majority to cross the line from law to policy—no matter how worthy the policy—is fundamentally anti-constitutional. An errant Supreme Court decision effectively amends the Constitution, because Congress and the states cannot overturn the justices through simple legislation. Only two-thirds of Congress and three-quarters of the states can change the constitutional text, just as a supermajority of nine of the original thirteen states was required to adopt the Constitution in 1788. Our constitutional system will be turned upside down if five justices can overrule the will of supermajorities of the American people as expressed in the text of the Constitution.

Lincoln too warned that "if the policy of the government, upon vital questions, affecting the whole people, is to be irrevocably fixed by decisions of the Supreme Court . . . the people will have ceased . . . to be their own rulers. . . ."[6] But Lincoln did not propose defiance of the Supreme Court, even though he and the Republican Party defined themselves in opposition to the atrocious *Dred Scott* decision—and though he would go on to refuse to carry out a Supreme Court justice's order to release imprisoned Confederate sympathizers. Instead, he argued that the president and Congress must enforce the judgment of the Court, but should refuse to apply the dicta of the case (in *Dred Scott*, that blacks could not be citizens) more broadly to other circumstances. Lincoln believed that the other branches were entirely within their rights to contest the Court over the meaning and principles of the Constitution. The other branches can use their own powers—judicial appointments, taxing and spending powers, executive enforcement of the law—to persuade the justices to correct their errors. Lincoln understood that respecting the institution of the judiciary as one of the three coequal branches of government remained central to the Constitution's separation of powers. Properly limited to interpreting the law, the judiciary, in Hamilton's words, will remain the "least dangerous [branch] to the political rights of the Constitution."[7] But if it does not husband its limited powers, according to Hamilton, the Court will not have the institutional "fortitude" to stand up to the majority when the Constitution demands it—to protect the right of the unpopular to speak and organize, of religious minorities to worship, or of criminal suspects to a fair trial.[8]

The *Dobbs* leak threatened to breach this fundamental line between law and politics. It made the Court an object in the arena of electoral politics—and of threatening protests, and even of an assassination attempt. But it also threatened to turn the Court's internal operations in a political direction. If leaks become the norm in important cases, clerks could begin disclosing the Court's internal arguments and votes, the changing coalitions around different drafts, and even the thought processes of individual justices. Justices might take explicit political factors into account in their decisions. Court decisions might no longer result from legal reasoning and persuasion, but from the openly political arts of interest groups, coalitions, and logrolling. If the justices begin to act in an openly political manner, the American people could rightly ask whether citizens should pay any special deference to the Supreme Court in the interpretation of the Constitution. And the president and Congress, which attract more practiced and experienced politicians, might redouble their efforts at pressuring the Court. While open efforts to politically pressure the Court have remained rare in our history (FDR's Court-packing plan, President's Obama's efforts to save his health care law), in recent years progressives have floated proposals to expand the size of the Court, heavily regulate the justices' "ethics," and tamper with the procedures for appearing before the Court. If the Court appears to be operating politically, not legally, these efforts may be futile no more.

CHAPTER 7

Overruling *Roe*: The *Dobbs* Decision

Justice Alito's opinion in *Dobbs* has come under withering criticism from abortion rights supporters. The main line of attack is the claim that *Dobbs* introduces a radical approach to constitutional rights that, followed to its logical conclusion, would eventually doom gay marriage, contraceptives, interracial marriage, and even parental control over children. But these criticisms rest on a progressive understanding of the Constitution that has come unmoored from the document's text, history, and structure. *Dobbs* easily parries the progressive thrust, but it remains a modest opinion, advancing no alternative theory of rights.[1]

Not So Radical

Dobbs's critics accuse the majority of radicalism. But *Dobbs* rejects *Roe* for reasons that distinguished liberal scholars have shared. Abortion does not appear anywhere in the constitutional text. To assert, as *Roe* does, that a right to abortion lurks somewhere in the Fourteenth Amendment guarantee that "no State shall . . . deprive any person of life, liberty or property, without due process of law" is to twist words beyond their meaning. Due process, by its very terms, addresses the procedures that the government must follow, not the substantive rights it must recognize. While the Second Amendment, for example, guarantees the right to possess a firearm, the Due Process Clause only requires the state to follow fair procedures

Abortion and Divorce in Western Law: American Failures, European Challenges by Mary Ann Glendon. Cambridge: Harvard University Press, 1987.

when it limits that right (as when a legislature bars felons from possessing guns). Even if abortion rests within the understanding of "liberty," the Fourteenth Amendment allows states to deprive persons of their liberty so long as they receive fair process. To believe in "substantive" due process, as liberal scholars and judges do, is to entertain a contradictory definition, such as dry water or dark light.

In the second step of its argument, *Dobbs* rejects any idea that precedent, history, or tradition adds abortion to a list of other rights not enumerated in the text but nonetheless so "fundamental" as to deserve constitutional protection.[2] The twentieth-century Supreme Court not only held that the Fourteenth Amendment "incorporated" most of the Bill of Rights against the states but also identified a few rights that are "deeply rooted in history and tradition" and essential to our "scheme of ordered liberty."[3] In upholding the right of individual Americans to possess firearms, the Court (Justice Scalia writing for the majority in *District of Columbia v. Heller*) relied on the Second Amendment, but it also reviewed history and found that a large majority of states that had ratified the Fourteenth Amendment in 1868 also had laws protecting the right to keep and bear arms.[4] The Court has also long recognized the freedom of parents to raise and educate their children without government interference,[5] a right not enumerated in the Constitution.

History, however, also explains why the justices have refused other rights entry into the constitutional canon. In *Washington v. Glucksberg*, the Rehnquist Court held that euthanasia did not count as a "liberty interest" protected by the Fourteenth Amendment because it was not "objectively, deeply rooted in this Nation's history and tradition."[6] A similar analysis has turned aside efforts to limit or even end the death penalty.[7] *Dobbs* carefully explains why this same logic requires the Court to reject a constitutional right to abortion. Before, after, and at the time of the ratification of the Fourteenth Amendment, Anglo-American law treated abortion as a crime. Even by the time of *Roe*, most states regulated abortion and did not recognize it as a fundamental right.[8]

The Null Set

"Until the latter part of the 20th century, there was no support in American law for a constitutional right to obtain an abortion," Justice Alito concluded in *Dobbs*.[9] Zero. None.

Opening a Can of Worms

Liberal critics pounced on this historical analysis. They argued that the same logic would also reject a right to interracial marriage and gay marriage, which fall under a larger right to "privacy" that goes unmentioned in the Constitution but has long received some judicial protection. "The thrust of the decision and the dramatic and radical approach it takes to interpreting the Constitution's unenumerated rights, narrowly and stingily, will not depend on the tone," said Harvard law professor Laurence Tribe. "The opinion, whether it's delivered in a velvet glove or not, is going to be an iron fist. The court is really announcing that it's laying down the gauntlet with respect to rights like those recognized in Lawrence v. Texas, in terms of sexual intimacy, and Obergefell v. Hodges, in terms of the right to marry."[10]

Tribe has a point. If the Court were to address all claims of unenumerated rights by asking (a) whether the constitutional text grants the right, and, if not, (b) whether history and tradition support such a right, the case for gay marriage or homosexual sex would begin to crumble. Alito distinguishes these cases on something like John Stuart Mill's harm principle: that individuals should have the freedom to act as they wish, so long as they do not harm third parties. *Dobbs* suggests that the rights to marry, to use contraceptives, and to gay marriage and sex do not hurt un-consenting others.

"What sharply distinguishes the abortion right from the rights recognized in the cases on which *Roe* and *Casey* rely," Alito says, is the fact that "abortion destroys what those decisions call 'potential life' and what the law at issue in this case regards as the life of an 'unborn human being.'" There is no wide historical consensus that abortion is an individual right; to the contrary, Alito observes, states had long regulated abortion. Even half a century after *Roe*, twenty-six states filed briefs in *Dobbs* to challenge the existence of the right.[11]

Alito's promise not to touch gay marriage or contraception, however, has the flavor of an *ipse dixit*—he won't because he says he won't. His opinion does not provide a reason grounded in a theory of the Constitution to explain why *Roe* must fail while these other unenumerated rights survive. In this respect, *Dobbs*—despite the claims of liberal commentators—adopts a relatively modest stance. At its core is a claim not about individual rights so much as about the political process. *Dobbs* says that the Constitution does not take a position on many questions about freedom and liberty, beyond those in the plain text of the Bill of Rights and the Reconstruction Amendments, but instead leaves those issues up to the states or Congress. "It is time to heed the Constitution and return the issue of abortion to the people's elected representatives," Alito writes. He quotes Justice Scalia's dissent in *Casey*, which made the strongest case for letting politics decide: "The permissibility of abortion, and the limitations, upon it, are to be resolved like most important questions in our democracy: by citizens trying to persuade one another and then voting."[12] *Dobbs* does not innovate. It merely restates the main line of argument developed over decades by conservative jurists, led by Scalia and Judge Robert Bork: the Constitution creates a governing system that privileges positive law—law made by legislatures—rather than unwritten law provided by sources external to the written text. The Scalia-Bork approach takes the Constitution as neutral on most moral questions and favors judicial restraint so that Americans acting through their legislatures can give the answers.

This positivist approach puts the majority in the difficult position of explaining why voters should decide the question of the right to abortion but not to gay marriage or sexual privacy. All lack a foundation in the constitutional text and all involve conduct that states had historically prohibited or widely regulated. It is here that *Dobbs* could have gone further to preserve some scope for unenumerated individual rights even as it rejected *Roe*. One promising path would have relocated such freedoms from the "substantive due process" purportedly found in the Due Process Clause to the Privileges or Immunities Clause just before it in the Fourteenth Amendment, which declares: "No State shall make or enforce any law which shall abridge the privileges or immunities of citizens of the United States." If the plain text of any constitutional provision protects unenumerated rights, it is the Privileges or Immunities Clause. Note how its language echoes the language of the First Amendment, which declares that "Congress shall make no law . . . abridging the freedom of speech, or of the press." Abolitionists and the radical Republicans who led Congress in the Civil War and Reconstruction believed that "privileges or immunities" included a series of individual rights, chief among them the right to be free and to keep the fruits of one's labors. Perhaps the original meaning of the Privileges or Immunities Clause protected a nineteenth-century version of a right to privacy, so long as its exercise did not harm others. More modestly, it may have included traditional, widely recognized customary rights regarding marital privacy and parental responsibility. Unfortunately, the Supreme Court turned the Privileges or Immunities Clause into a dead letter in the deeply flawed 1873 *Slaughter-House Cases*.[13] Justice Clarence Thomas—who, interestingly, as senior justice in the *Dobbs* majority, could have kept the *Dobbs* opinion but instead assigned it to Alito—used his separate opinion in *Dobbs* to renew his call for a revival of the Privileges or Immunities Clause.[14]

The Declaration versus the Constitution

Appeals to the Declaration of Independence were too much for the late Justice Scalia, who once wrote dismissively, "If you want aspirations, you can read the Declaration of Independence.... There is no such philosophizing in our Constitution."[15]

Justice Thomas Weighs In

Justice Thomas's decision to assign the main opinion was a classic Holmesian (as in Sherlock, not Oliver Wendell) case of the dog that did not bark. Although Thomas and Alito typically align on the outcome of cases, Thomas's jurisprudence differs from Alito's in important ways. Beyond Thomas's expansive views about the Privileges or Immunities Clause, he is the one justice who anchors his constitutional analysis in the natural law tradition (natural law as Thomas Aquinas understood it, and the modern natural rights tradition best expressed by that other Thomas—Jefferson—in the Declaration of Independence). Justice Thomas, nearly alone among modern justices, cites the Declaration as an authoritative source of guidance in constitutional analysis.

Justice Thomas joined *Dobbs* with a concurrence that made his more expansive view of individual rights plain. "Because the Due Process Clause does not secure *any* substantive rights, it does not secure a right to abortion," he explains [emphasis in the original]. Substantive due process is "particularly dangerous," he argues, because judges can use it to elevate their own preferences over those of the American people. The "exaltation of judicial policymaking" not only led to *Roe*, but distorted constitutional law more broadly and has produced terrible results. As Justice Thomas notes, *Dred Scott* relied on substantive due process to prohibit the regulation of slavery in the territories. For this reason Justice Thomas would go further than the majority. "In future cases, we should reconsider all of this Court's substantive due process precedents, including *Griswold*, *Lawrence*, and *Obergefell*," Justice Thomas writes. "Because any substantive due process decision is 'demonstrably erroneous,' ... we have a duty to 'correct the error' established in those precedents."[16] Critics have exaggerated Justice Thomas's concurrence as a threat to eliminate any right to privacy in the Constitution. Instead, he argues that the Court should examine "whether other constitutional provisions guarantee the myriad rights that our substantive due process cases have generated." According to Justice Thomas, the Court should naturally look to the Privileges or Immunities Clause, where the text of the Constitution does guarantee the rights of all American citizens, as the source of unenumerated constitutional rights.[17]

Abortion has always been a profoundly moral issue, as even Justice Blackmun's incoherent opinion in *Roe* recognized.[18] By anchoring the reversal of *Roe* in an analysis that the "right" to abortion cannot be "objectively, deeply rooted in this Nation's history and tradition," *Dobbs* sidesteps the fundamental moral dimension and omits any consideration of whether the Court can or should consider any aspect of natural law (which is also part of our history and tradition, no matter how much law schools may wish to ignore it). Returning the issue to the states for persuasion and deliberation by elected representatives may be good politics—more on that below—and a stable settlement at the Court. But this settlement is unlikely to stick for the long haul.

The Post-*Dobbs* Landscape

The pro-life movement has long compared *Roe* to *Dred Scott*, and the parallel goes beyond the denial of rights to life and liberty to a certain class of human beings. Ironically, the post-*Dobbs* prospect of determining the law and policy of abortion through majority rule in the states echoes the position Stephen Douglas took in the 1850s—that slavery in the territories and new states should be a matter of local popular sovereignty. "I don't care whether slavery is voted up or down," Douglas famously said. Like the unborn today, slaves did not get a vote on the question. Lincoln,

Dred Scott and the Problem of Constitutional Evil by Mark A. Graber. Cambridge: Cambridge University Press, 2008.

unlike most practicing politicians willing to compromise on many hard questions, wouldn't bend on this point, because no one "has a right to do wrong."[19]

Pro-lifers need not settle on a definitive answer about when human life begins to believe that extending the protection of the law to the unborn is not a matter that should be left up to shifting majorities. Justice Thomas has illuminated the next step of the journey by demanding that the Court locate those unenumerated rights elsewhere than the Due Process Clause. His view does not—yet—command five votes on the Court. But Thomas has started the conversation that could make natural law a basis for constitutional judgment in the future. His concurrence is part of the process of democratic persuasion on constitutional values, akin to Justice John Harlan's famous dissent in *Plessy v. Ferguson*, which argued against all racial classifications in our law. The Court may have removed itself from the issue for the time being, but sooner or later the problem is likely to be forced upon it again, unless our political branches amend the Constitution in an attempt to terminate a political struggle that will not end soon.

The outcry over *Dobbs* is partly inspired by the fear that overruling *Roe* may well upend more than just *Roe*. *Dobbs* may represent a watershed moment in American judicial politics and constitutional thought by potentially restoring balance between the three branches of government that conservatives have long sought. However, the aftermath may also disappoint more aggressive conservative intellectuals who seek to replace liberalism's tottering foundations with a communitarian version of the common good.

The logic of *Dobbs* effects a subtle reversal of the Left's use of the Court as an engine for social change. In the wake of *Brown v. Board of Education*, liberals increasingly saw the judiciary as an engine to drive policy ends that they could not gain through the normal political process. Chief Justice Earl Warren and a bench filled with liberal-minded justices were happy to embrace this activist mode. "Rights" were created left and right (but mostly left)—*Roe*'s right to abortion in 1973, but extending, in recent years, to the discovery of the heretofore unknown right to same-sex marriage. *Dobbs* aims to close the judiciary as a manufacturing plant for unending "rights."

A Book You're Not Supposed to Read

Common Good Constitutionalism by Adrian Vermuele. Medford, Massachusetts: Polity, 2022.

In the wake of *Dobbs*, suddenly it is the Left that has turned against the Supreme Court. It is hard to deny that the opposition has arisen to a Court that now has a majority of Republican-appointed justices committed to originalist principles. Progressives have demanded that President Biden and congressional Democrats expand the size of the Supreme Court—seemingly oblivious to the fate of FDR's Court-packing plan—and consider term and age limits on the justices. Conservatives, meanwhile, are not full-throttle defenders of the Court: they have long held a far more skeptical attitude toward the Court's claim of supremacy in interpreting the Constitution. Nevertheless, the Court deserves a robust defense—not because of its recent decision on abortion, but because it stands as a valuable institutional limit on simple majority rule.

The political response to *Dobbs* has brought the progressive attitude toward the Constitution and the Court into clear focus. Progressives are taking unprecedented measures against the justices because of their specific votes on abortion, regardless of the logic or reasoning of their opinion. More broadly, liberals have long supported or attacked the Court based on how its decisions affect the interests of the groups—minorities, women, environmental organizations—that make up their political coalition.

Dress Code

To the Left, the only difference between a judge and a politician is that politicians don't get to wear robes.

Progressives mostly treat law and facts as smoke and mirrors. They don't want courts to interpret the law, but rather to make policy. Their excuses are the inherent malleability of language and the rapid changes in society and the economy. To them judges enjoy raw political power to determine society's winners and losers. President Obama gave away the game when he said he was looking for judges with "empathy."[20] President Biden followed suit by declaring he would only consider African-American women for his first Supreme Court pick. For progressives, the racial identity of the judge predicts his or her future voting patterns: the race of the nominee is a proxy for the future judge's positions on unions, racial minorities, criminal suspects, and so forth. If the law is simply another means to achieve desired policies denied to them through electoral politics, and there is no real difference between law and politics, progressives predictably will resort to political tactics—leaks, protests, threats, and interest group pressure—to exert influence on the courts.

Dobbs may represent not an end to the contentious politics of abortion, but the beginning of a new and more intense phase of that bitter controversy. While the *Dobbs* majority may hope that overruling *Roe* will lower the political temperature around abortion by removing it from the control of the federal judiciary and placing it with the political branches in the fifty states, the likelihood is that the issue will still heat up in several ways. The centripetal forces of American politics may return the issue again to Washington, D.C., and the Supreme Court may well be dragged back into the fray, whether it wants to be or not. Abortion has been treated as a constitutional right for so long that there hasn't been much sustained thought given to how "returning the issue to the states" is likely to play out. As long as the issue was thought to be confined to the judiciary, legislators could avoid making clear decisions and taking actual votes. Now, office holders will no longer be able to posture on the issue.

Back to the States, the People, and Congress

First, there will now be pitched battles in state legislatures over statutes regulating abortion. Any deep-blue states that don't already have permissive abortion statutes on the books from the pre-*Roe* era (New York, Illinois, and California, for example) will surely move to enact them, while deep-red states will do the reverse. States in the middle will likely see bitter fights for control of the legislature that may repeat themselves every election cycle. It should not be assumed that the politics of abortion will be stable even in deep-red or deep-blue states, as some Republicans who generally profess to be pro-life may balk at proposed abortion restrictions (such as banning abortion as near the moment of conception as possible), and some pro-choice Democrats may balk at late-term or taxpayer-subsidized abortion. There's an additional wild card for pro-choice Catholic Democrats. Consider the recent decision of San Francisco's archbishop Salvatore J. Cordileone to deny Communion to House Speaker Nancy Pelosi because of her pro-choice views.[21] If this practice spreads to other Catholic prelates around the country, it will not only give pause to pro-choice Catholic politicians, but also inflame the "separation of church and state" debate.

Second, attempts to settle abortion policy won't be confined to legislatures. The twenty-six states that have an initiative and referendum process will likely see ballot initiative campaigns that will seek to fix statutory law. Less than two months after the *Dobbs* decision, Kansas voters rejected a "Value Them Both" amendment to their state constitution that would have overturned a state Supreme Court decision that had found a right to abortion in the Kansas Constitution. Some initiatives will even seek to amend state constitutions in a pro-life or pro-choice direction. Some states that have rights to privacy explicitly included in their constitutions will see the issue brought into state courts. The state-by-state variation in judicial outcomes will raise afresh the problem of judicial lawmaking—and may propel the matter back to the U.S. Supreme Court in unpredictable ways.

We are likely entering a new period of greater instability and conflict over abortion. Two factors guarantee this messy result. First, unlike in the pre-*Roe* era, when abortion politics were slowly heating up but not yet the focus of significant organized efforts on both sides, today there are well-established (and well-funded) pro-life and pro-choice organizations that will mount highly visible campaigns and lobbying efforts at every level of government. There is also a second and more important reason the politics and law are likely to be unstable: the cognitive dissonance of public opinion about abortion. A *Wall Street Journal* poll taken shortly after *Dobbs* found that a majority opposed overturning *Roe*.[22] But there has seldom been an issue about which survey results depend so heavily on the wording and presentation order of the questions. Subsequent polls found majorities opposing late-term abortion, or supporting the general proposition that abortion can or should be regulated after about fifteen weeks[23]—the very limit that was set by the state law upheld in *Dobbs*.

The basic reason for this cognitive dissonance is that many people don't like to think through the consequences of believing that abortion ends a human life—as even many pro-choice survey respondents believe—while at the same time they think abortion should be legal. As long as the issue rested with the Supreme Court it wasn't necessary to resolve these incompatible principles. The key to the outcome of the new phase of abortion politics will be old-fashioned democratic persuasion. Beneath the surface of ambiguous opinion is an interesting fact: while the rate of abortion soared after *Roe*, for more than two decades now the abortion rate has been steadily declining.[24] Fewer pregnant women seem to want to have abortions.

Finally, there is going to be intense political pressure for Congress and the executive branch to weigh in on the issue. Indeed, both have jumped into the fray already: Congress has considered a bill to codify *Roe* on a nationwide basis, and the Biden administration has issued administrative "guidance" to federally funded hospitals in states where abortion is now illegal to threaten them with the loss of financial aid if they do not perform "emergency" abortions.[25]

One aspect of *Dobbs* that might tempt Congress to snatch the issue back from the states is Justice Alito's argument that a right to abortion cannot be rooted in the history and traditions of the nation. The past doesn't have to control the future, after all. History does not prevent a twenty-first-century Congress from attempting to support abortion rights—or, with a different political party in control, to discourage them. New laws, however, would have to come at the issue sideways. Despite Democratic efforts of late, the Constitution does not permit Congress to directly overturn a Supreme Court decision. In *City of Boerne v. Flores*, for example, the justices confronted the Religious Freedom Restoration Act of 1994, which had sought to reverse an earlier Court decision (*Employment Division v. Smith*) that had narrowed religious freedoms.[26] Before *Smith*, the Court had subjected laws that burdened religious freedom to a strict scrutiny test, under which most laws fail. But with Justice Scalia writing, the *Smith* Court had held that it would uphold a "neutral law of general applicability" (such as the drug control law at issue in the case) even if it burdened the free exercise of religion (the smoking of hallucinogenic peyote as part of a Native American religious ceremony).

Congress had claimed that it had the power to restore the earlier, broader understanding of religious freedom via the Religious Freedom Restoration Act (RFRA) under Section 5 of the Fourteenth Amendment, which states that "the Congress shall have the power to enforce, by appropriate legislation, the provisions of this article." "This article" refers to the Fourteenth

Amendment itself, in particular to its Equal Protection and Due Process Clauses, which have served as the fount of most of the important judicially recognized individual rights that apply against the states. Under this power Congress claimed it could restore religious freedom to its pre-*Smith* status and require any law that burdened the right to satisfy strict scrutiny again. The Court struck down the RFRA. "Legislation which alters the meaning of the Free Exercise Clause cannot be said to be enforcing the Clause. Congress does not enforce a constitutional right by changing what the right is," Justice Kennedy wrote for the Court. The power to determine the scope of rights under the Fourteenth Amendment, the *Boerne* Court found, rested in the hands of the Supreme Court, not Congress.[27] *City of Boerne* dooms any congressional effort to directly overrule *Dobbs*.

In a failed May 2022 effort to codify *Roe*, Senate Democrats claimed authority to establish a national rule on abortion under the Interstate Commerce Clause. The Commerce Clause has indeed provided Congress with the authority to establish federal rights beyond those recognized in the Constitution. Many of the most important federal rights have resulted from congressional, rather than judicial, action. Congress, for example, used the Commerce Clause to enact the Civil Rights Act of 1964, which prohibits racial and gender discrimination in employment and travel. Congress can regulate activity that does not cross state borders, the Court has held, if the activity is commercial in nature and, in the aggregate, has a substantial effect on national markets. Under this logic the Court has upheld federal drug convictions for the possession of small amounts of marijuana on the ground that such small amounts effectively snowball into large impacts on the national market for drugs. Under that same theory, Congress could require doctors to offer abortion as part of its regulation of the health care industry. A Republican Congress relied on the same power to regulate interstate commerce when it enacted a ban on partial-birth abortions, which the Supreme Court upheld in *Gonzales v. Carhart* (2007).[28]

A Commerce Clause–based abortion bill, however, would still run into constitutional difficulties. *Carhart* held that a federal ban on partial-birth abortions did not run afoul of *Roe v. Wade* and *Planned Parenthood v. Casey*—a holding rendered unnecessary now by *Dobbs*.[29] But it did not reach the question of whether Congress had the authority to directly regulate the entire medical profession. In other cases, however, the Rehnquist and Roberts Courts have limited the Commerce Clause's command over non-economic activity. In *United States v. Lopez* (1995), the Court struck down a law that had prohibited carrying guns in school zones because gun possession was not truly commercial in nature. The Court forbade Congress from invading the states' authority over general criminal law under the guise of regulating commerce.[30] In *United States v. Morrison* (2000), the Court invalidated the Violence Against Women Act, which had made gender-motivated violence that crossed state borders illegal. Again, the Court found that the federal government had unconstitutionally used the Commerce Clause to intrude into the states' prerogative over criminal law.[31] The Court could view a bill codifying *Roe*, in the face of *Dobbs*, as a similar federal invasion of the states' traditional control over the medical profession or crime.

Despite these limits the Constitution does provide Congress with indirect means to influence abortions. A Congress intent on preserving *Roe* could use the very same powers that it used to create Obamacare: the Taxing and Spending Clauses. Congress could, for example, provide vouchers to pregnant women to travel to states where abortion is legal, or even subsidize the performance of abortions. It could purchase and ship abortion pills. It could require federal and private health insurance policies to reimburse abortion-related expenses. More controversially, Congress could even cut federal health care funds for states and hospitals that refuse to perform abortions—though those states and hospitals would argue in their defense that federal spending restraints cannot force them to violate state law.

The Tempting of America: The Political Seduction of the Law by Robert H. Bork. New York: Touchstone, 1990.

Dobbs does not mean that our nation's struggle over abortion will end, only that it will move to a different, more political, arena. But as progressives threaten to bring Congress's powers to bear, they should keep in mind that constitutional powers do not run in one direction only. Any power that a Democratic Congress might use to codify *Roe* nationwide is a power that a Republican Congress could use to ban abortion nationwide. Any spending cuts directed at hospitals and states that refuse to carry out abortions could become, in the hands of a Republican Congress, cuts aimed at states that allow abortion. *Dobbs* encourages both pro- and anti-*Roe* forces to focus their efforts on a state-by-state contest that takes advantage of our nation's federalism, but they are likely to find the allure of a uniform national solution irresistible.

Returning abortion and other moral issues to the political process will result in a diversity of policies. Our federal system already allows such differences on matters of life and death, such as the death penalty or euthanasia. The states, and the people, will become more responsible—leading us in the direction of a more robust democracy rather than the increasingly fragile one we have today. In *Dobbs*, the Court took the first step toward restraining itself and repairing both the legal and political defects of its privacy jurisprudence. The best way for the Court to stay out of politics is for the Court to stay out of politics.

PART III

Gun Control or Gun Rights?

CHAPTER 8

Heller: The Court Takes Up the Second Amendment

Few subjects are as controversial and polarizing in contemporary America as guns. The statistics about gun-related deaths and injuries are appalling. Violent crimes—murders and homicides in particular—are regularly committed with guns. Moreover, guns need not be used in crimes to be lethal: they are frequently used in suicides, and they are the cause of many serious accidents. Children especially may be at risk if guns are left within their reach at home. And the sheer number of guns in circulation terrifies many.

On the other hand, the breakdown of law and order in many of our major cities, including two that have been defendants in civil cases before the Supreme Court—Washington, D.C., and Chicago—has terrified many law-abiding citizens who wish to protect themselves, their families, and their homes by carrying guns in crime-infested neighborhoods or keeping them accessible in their homes. During the riots that shook the nation in summer of 2020, urban and suburban dwellers overwhelmed gun dealers and

Outnumbered by Our Weapons

According to reporting by Bloomberg, there are 393.3 million firearms in America, or 120.5 for every resident of the country, making the United States the "only country with more civilian-owned firearms than people."[1]

What Makes America Different

"Besides the advantage of being armed, which the Americans possess over the people of almost every other nation, the existence of subordinate governments, to which the people are attached, and by which the militia officers are appointed, forms a barrier against the enterprises of ambition, more insurmountable than any which a simple government of any form can admit of. Notwithstanding the military establishments in the several kingdoms of Europe, which are carried as far as the public resources will bear, the governments are afraid to trust the people with arms." —James Madison, *The Federalist* No. 46 (1788)[4]

"The right of the citizens to keep and bear arms has justly been considered, as the palladium of the liberties of a republic; since it offers a strong moral check against the usurpation and arbitrary power of rulers; and will generally, even if these are successful in the first instance, enable the people to resist and triumph over them." —Justice Joseph Story, *Commentaries on the Constitution of the United States* (1833)[5]

exhausted their supplies with demands for self-defense weapons. Handguns in particular are the weapon of choice for many, especially the elderly and infirm: they are small, easily transported, readily concealed in the home or on the person, and not difficult to handle and fire against an attacker. And, of course, guns have recreational uses in sports and hunting. Moreover, the effectiveness of gun control in reducing lethal violence or curbing crime is highly questionable. Even stringent gun regulations may not significantly reduce murder rates,[2] and some of the most atrocious recent instances of gun-related mass murders have occurred in jurisdictions with rigorous gun controls.[3]

Three Groundbreaking Cases

The Supreme Court is not expected, or even allowed, to enter this vehement policy debate. But it *is* expected to decide constitutional questions, even if its judgments are certain to be politically unpopular in many quarters. And, after almost seventy years of silence on the Second Amendment, the Court began speaking about the Second Amendment again in 2008. In this and the next two chapters, we examine a trilogy of recent Supreme Court Second Amendment opinions, all of them landmarks of constitutional law. The first is *District of Columbia v. Heller* (2008); the second is *McDonald v. City of Chicago* (2010); and the third, decided only at the end of the Court's 2021–2022 term, is *New York State Rifle & Pistol Association v. Bruen* (2022).[6] We have four main objectives in view.

First, we aim to describe succinctly but accurately the justices' opinions in the cases, offering our own evaluation of the quality of the reasoning in each. Gun control is an important matter both of public policy and of constitutional law, and it deserves careful consideration.

Second, we will use the justices' various styles of argument to illustrate different methodologies for interpreting the constitutional text. One method, dominant in all three of these Second Amendment cases, is to search for the "original public meaning" of the text. This approach attempts to discover how reasonable citizens would have understood the text at the time when it was proposed, debated, and ratified. An alternative method is to look for the "original intent" behind the text: the intention of those who drafted the text and proposed it to the people for ratification. The difference between these two methods is that there may well be a difference between what the text *means* and what those who drafted it *intended* to accomplish. For example, the *language* of the Equal Protection Clause of the Fourteenth Amendment would have barred racial segregation in the public schools, but those who drafted the language may not have intended it to have that effect.[7] A third interpretative method derives from the "living constitutionalism" associated with the Progressive movement and its latter-day heirs.[8] This method seeks to align the Court's decisions with contemporary needs and values. The dissenting justices in these cases, though willing to take account of original meaning or intent, have tended to base their reasoning on policy considerations rather than on constitutional text or historic practices.

Third, we consider the source of constitutional rights. The right to keep and bear arms (whatever it may mean) is an *enumerated* right, squarely

Twenty Years, One Convert?

Justice Thomas has been arguing that the incorporation of rights against the states should be grounded in the Privileges or Immunities Clause, not in "substantive due process," since his dissent in the *Saenz v. Roe* case in 1999.[9] Finally, in 2019, in *Timbs v. Indiana*, Justice Neil Gorsuch signaled that he may be willing to accept Thomas's Fourteenth Amendment incorporation jurisprudence: "As an original matter, I acknowledge, the appropriate vehicle for incorporation may well be the Fourteenth Amendment's Privileges or Immunities Clause, rather than, as this Court has long assumed, the Due Process Clause.... But nothing in this case turns on that question, and, regardless of the precise vehicle, there can be no serious doubt that the Fourteenth Amendment requires the States to respect the freedom from excessive fines enshrined in the Eighth Amendment."[10]

located in the text of the Constitution. The right to an abortion, by contrast, is not textually enumerated. That does not mean that there is no such constitutional right, though the absence of a textual reference to it might point that way. As we have seen, the Court has often held (and we agree) that there are some unenumerated constitutional rights. Indeed, in the Ninth Amendment, the text of the Constitution declares the existence of such rights. But the Court should be cautious about discovering or inventing unenumerated rights. For example, does the Constitution really place the unenumerated right of freedom of contract on the very same plane as the enumerated right to freedom of speech? The Court once thought so; it no longer does.

One problem, as we have seen, has been to identify the source of unenumerated rights. For almost a century and a half, the Court has said that the primary or sole source of such rights is the Due Process Clause of the Fourteenth Amendment—a theory that, as we saw above, Justice Clarence Thomas has criticized as implausible. Below we explain Justice Thomas's theory, advanced with learning and power in the *McDonald* case, that the true source of unenumerated rights is the Privileges or Immunities Clause of the Fourteenth Amendment. While Thomas has not yet persuaded the other justices to accept his view, we think that over time the Court may gradually come to it.[11]

Fourth, and finally, we will look at what these Second Amendment cases say about how the Roberts Court will assess claims to constitutional rights, whether enumerated or unenumerated. The Court seems likely to weight historical practices and traditions heavily in making those judgments. It will look for patterns of legislation, custom, and widespread practice in deciding whether an alleged right exists and, if so, what types of state regulation are permissible. Contemporary regulations do not have to match historical antecedents perfectly, but the Court will require them to be analogous. For example, in *Bruen*, the Court signaled its willingness to uphold a state ban on carrying handguns in "sensitive" places, such as a courtroom, because a pattern of similar state regulation extends back for decades or even centuries to pre-revolutionary America and England. But the Court was not willing to allow the New York State legislature to ban the storing or carrying of handguns anywhere in Manhattan because the legislature deems the entire island to be a "sensitive place." We expect that what is true of gun control will be true of other forms of state regulation, such as restrictions on "morning-after" pills that can be used as abortifacients. States that restrict the sale of such drugs may defend their prohibitions as akin to historic bans on abortion; women who wish to use such drugs may argue that the right to obtain and use contraceptives or other medications is entrenched in American law and practices. In deciding among rival arguments, the gun rights cases, especially *Bruen*, will be models.

The First Major Second Amendment Case in Seventy Years

The first of the Court's three main recent Second Amendment cases was *District of Columbia v. Heller* (2008). Only once before, in *United States v. Miller* (1939), had the Court issued a major Second Amendment decision—and that was nearly seventy years earlier.[12] If *Heller* did not exactly write on a clean slate, therefore, it wrote on a slate that had plenty of room. And by any standard, it was a landmark case.

Before the Court in *Heller* was a set of gun control laws enacted by the District of Columbia. The most important of these was the district's general prohibition on the possession of handguns. D.C. had made it a crime to possess unregistered firearms, and registration of a handgun within the district was (in most cases) prohibited. Further, no person was allowed to carry an unlicensed handgun, though the chief of police could issue licenses for one-year periods. Finally, the district required residents to keep lawfully owned firearms, such as registered long guns, unfunctional in most places, including their homes, even when the weapons were needed for self-defense. The plaintiff was a district special police officer, authorized to carry a handgun while on duty, who sought an injunction against the district's ban on registering handguns and relief from its licensing requirements insofar as they forbade carrying unlicensed firearms within his home.

The District of Columbia was a federal defendant. Though Congress had delegated its powers to the District of Columbia government, in effect granting it home rule, Congress has plenary power over the district under the Constitution. That mattered because under *Barron v. Baltimore*, an 1833 decision by Chief Justice Marshall, the Bill of Rights applied only to the federal government and not to the states.[13] As we have seen, that constitutional limitation was changed by the Fourteenth Amendment. But as of 2008 the Court had still not decided whether *all* the amendments in the Bill of Rights, including the Second Amendment, were applicable to the states as well.

The *Heller* Court split 5–4 over the constitutionality of the district's gun controls. In an opinion authored by Justice Scalia, the Court struck down the ban on handguns and the requirement to keep guns at home disabled. Four justices dissented in two separate opinions, one by Justice Stevens and the other by Justice Breyer, though all four dissenters joined both of those opinions.

The interest of the case lies as much in its methodology as in its substance. Justice Scalia's method was to apply a form of "originalist" interpretation to the Second Amendment. He looked to the original *public meaning* of that amendment, saying that "we are guided by the principle that the Constitution was written to be understood by the voters; its words and phrases were used in their normal and ordinary as distinguished from technical meaning" [internal quotation marks omitted].[14] Scalia's approach had a distinguished pedigree, traceable back to James Madison.

A Precedent for Judging by the Original Meaning

In the 1791 House debate over Secretary of the Treasury Alexander Hamilton's proposal to incorporate a national bank of the United States, Representative James Madison, an opponent of the bank, outlined a set of interpretative rules to guide the search for the meaning of constitutional provisions (in that case, primarily the meaning of the Necessary and Proper Clause of Article I). High on Madison's list of rules was recourse to "contemporary and concurrent expositions," which would provide "a reasonable evidence of the meaning of the parties." Madison illustrated his rule by quoting from the "explanations in the State [ratifying] Conventions," together with the "explanatory declarations and amendments accompanying the ratifications of the several States." Such materials provided "evidence of the sense in which the Constitution was understood and adopted."[15]

Though he reached quite a different conclusion, Justice Stevens's dissent also sought to follow an "originalist" approach, though he seems to have been more concerned with the original *intent* of those who framed the amendment, as opposed to its ordinary public *meaning* at the time it was proposed and ratified, as was Justice Scalia. Most originalists now take the latter view, but the search for original *intent* has able supporters.

Justice Breyer also dedicated part of his opinion to the origins and background of the amendment. But the weight of his dissent was on the reasonableness of the district's *policy* of gun control. These divergent approaches led the Court to two very different interpretations of the Second Amendment. For the majority the Second Amendment protected an individual right to possess a handgun for traditionally lawful purposes, including for self-defense within the home. For the dissenters, the Second Amendment had a far narrower field of application: it protected only the right to possess and carry a firearm *in connection with service in the militia.* And although the "militia" at the time the Second Amendment was adopted consisted essentially of every able-bodied adult male citizen, the "militia" nowadays is a much more limited class: those who serve in their states' National Guard. Hence, for the dissenters, there is either no constitutionally protected right to keep a handgun even in the home or to use it even in self-defense, or, if there *is* such a right, it can be outweighed by the government's interest in public safety (an interest the dissenters thought particularly powerful in crowded urban areas such as the District of Columbia).

The analysis of the majority opinion by Justice Scalia begins with the text of the Second Amendment, which reads: "A well regulated Militia, being necessary to the security of a free State, the right of the people to keep and bear Arms, shall not be infringed."

How to Understand the Preamble—and the Militia

It is immediately obvious that the text has two parts: a preamble ("A well-regulated Militia, being necessary to the security of a free State") and an operative part ("the right of the people to keep and bear Arms, shall not be infringed"). That linguistic structure poses hard interpretative questions: What is the effect of the preamble, and what is its relationship to the operative clause?

Justice Scalia argued that in eighteenth-century legal usage, a preamble might serve to disambiguate the operative clause of a law, but in general "does not limit or expand the scope of the operative clause."[16] Moreover, since Scalia found the operative part of the amendment unambiguous, he concluded that the preamble has little or nothing to add to its interpretation.

For Justice Stevens, in contrast, the preamble "sets forth the object of the Amendment and informs the meaning of the remainder of its text."[17] Stevens too cited eighteenth-century sources—notably, state Declarations of Rights—in support of his view. The matter is difficult: certainly some eighteenth-century lawmakers, including Anti-Federalists, took the view that the *Constitution's* preamble expanded, or threatened to expand, the powers of Congress enumerated in Article I. The Anti-Federalist writer Brutus, for instance, maintained that because "the great objects [of the Constitution] are declared in this preamble in general and indefinite terms. . . . The inference is natural that the legislature will have an authority to make all laws which they shall judge necessary for the common safety, and to promote the general welfare. This amounts to a power to make laws at discretion: No terms can be found more indefinite than these."[19] If a constitutional preamble can be understood to *expand* the scope of a clause, it can surely be taken to *limit* its scope. Moreover, preambles can set out the overall purpose of the operative provisions to which they are annexed; and the Supreme Court has taken the *purpose* of a constitutional clause as a guide to its meaning.

A Well Regulated Militia

"Should one fifth, or one eighth part of the men capable of bearing arms, be made a select militia, as has been proposed, and those the young and ardent part of the community, possessed of but little or no property, and all the others put upon a plan that will render them of no importance, the former will answer all the purposes of an army, while the latter will be defenceless. The state must train the militia in such form and according to such systems and rules as Congress shall prescribe: and the only actual influence the respective states will have respecting the militia will be in appointing the officers."

—*Letters from the Federal Farmer to The Republican* (1787)[18]

After arguing that the Second Amendment's preamble should not be taken to limit the right protected by the amendment, Scalia turned to the question, Who are the *holders* of the right to keep and bear arms? The amendment speaks of "the right *of the people*." Who are "the people?

Comparing the Second Amendment to other constitutional clauses that safeguard the rights of (or say are retained by) "the people"—the First, Fourth and Ninth Amendments—Scalia justifiably concluded that all such instances "unambiguously refer to individual rights, not 'collective' rights, or rights that may be exercised only through participation in some corporate body." Moreover, he reasoned, the amendment's reference to "the people" is broader than a reference to that subset of the people who composed "the militia"—in colonial America, those "who were male, able bodied, and within a certain age range."[20]

"A Pre-Existing Right"

Next up is the meaning of the substance or operative part of the amendment: the right "to keep and bear arms." Reviewing the historical evidence, Scalia concluded that the phrase "'keep arms' was simply a common way of referring to possessing arms, for militiamen *and everyone else"* [emphasis in the original]. Likewise, he found that to "bear arms" was understood to refer "to carrying [arms] for a particular purpose—confrontation." "In numerous instances [of eighteenth-century usage], 'bear arms' was unambiguously used to refer to the carrying of weapons outside of an organized militia." These instances, Scalia noted, included two Founding-era state Declarations of Rights (Pennsylvania and Vermont) that specifically mentioned a "right to bear arms" in defense *both* of the state *and* of oneself.[21]

Scalia argued that his textual interpretation is "strongly confirmed by the historical background of the Second Amendment, which he maintained "codified a *pre-existing* right" [emphasis in the original]. That pre-existing right traces back to the English Glorious Revolution of 1688, which overthrew the Catholic King James II and led to the accession of his Protestant daughter Mary and her Dutch Protestant consort William to the throne. Shortly afterwards, William and Mary agreed to the Declaration of Right, swiftly codified as the English Bill of Rights, which promised—albeit only as against the Crown, not as against Parliament—that "the subjects which are Protestants may have Arms for their Defence suitable to their Conditions, and as allowed by Law." This English provision was "the predecessor to our Second Amendment" and, "by the time of the founding, the right to have arms had become fundamental for English subjects."[22] The English conception reached legally trained eighteenth-century Americans through the work of Sir William Blackstone, whose influence on the Framers was profound: in 1999 the Court said that Blackstone's works "constituted the preeminent authority on English law for the founding generation."[23] Blackstone interpreted an English subject's right to possess arms as a "natural right" and as "the right of having and using arms for self-preservation and defence."[24]

Guns for Thee but Not for Me

"The late King James the Second, by the assistance of divers evil counsellors, judges and ministers employed by him, did endeavour to subvert and extirpate the Protestant religion and the laws and liberties of this kingdom. . . . By causing several good subjects being Protestants to be disarmed at the same time when papists were both armed and employed contrary to law." —English Bill of Rights (1689)

Finally, Scalia's opinion for the Court pivots back to the amendment's preamble. He notes that after the ratification of the original, unamended Constitution, many Americans feared that Congress might use its enumerated powers in the Militia Clauses to disarm the state militias (which the Constitution gave Congress the power to "organize"), and that many also believed that the preservation of (armed) state militias was desirable because they "might be necessary to oppose an oppressive [federal] military force if the constitutional order broke down." In consequence of these political pressures, the Second Amendment was adopted. Scalia therefore found it "entirely sensible" to think that "the Second Amendment's prefatory clause announces the purpose for which the right was codified: to prevent elimination of the militia." But, he insists, "the prefatory clause does not suggest that preserving the militia was the *only* reason" for the amendment [emphasis added]. Though its "*codification*" in a written Constitution may have been for that purpose, self-defense, rather than preserving the militia, "was the *central component* of the right" so codified [emphasis in the original].[25]

To fully grasp Scalia's argument requires attention to the distinction between the "militia" as the adult male able-bodied citizenry and the "organized" militia, meaning an armed body selected from that larger population and placed under military discipline and command. He believed that the Second Amendment's preamble refers to the former, not the latter. He argued that if "the Second Amendment right is no more than the right to keep and use weapons as a member of the organized militia . . . if, that is, the *organized* militia is the sole institutional beneficiary" of the Second Amendment, then the amendment "does not secure the existence of a 'citizens' militia' as a safeguard against tyranny."[26] In other words, interpreted that way, the amendment could not serve the purpose that called it into existence. This is so because "Congress retains plenary authority to organize the militia, which must include the authority to say who will belong to the organized force." And Congress did, in fact, exclude a part of the otherwise eligible population—free black males—in the first Militia Act of 1792. In other words, on the view Scalia rejects, "the Second Amendment protects citizens' right to use a gun in an organization from which Congress has plenary authority to exclude them."[27] If the underlying purpose of the amendment was to preserve a potential armed counterweight to congressional abuses, then the amendment was poorly designed to do that. But if the people, as individual citizens, each possessed the right (as against the federal government) to keep and bear arms, then Congress could not disarm the state militias—because doing so would entail disarming some or all citizens.

Although unsympathetic critics have accused Scalia's *Heller* opinion of "faux originalism,"[28] we contend that it is a model of true originalism—specifically of the "original meaning" rather than the "original intent" kind. It exhibits three characteristic features of the "original public meaning" variety of originalism. First, it conscientiously reads the text in light of the meaning that ordinary Americans at the time would have understood. Second, it traces the history of the text back through the legal documents that shaped its development, and it places the text in the context of documents roughly contemporaneous with it that expressed a similar idea. Third, it attempts to show that an alternative reading of the text, though perhaps admissible on the surface, would defeat the conceded purpose for which the text was adopted.

This is *not* to say that Scalia's interpretation of the Second Amendment was *correct* (though it is certainly defensible). One prominent scholar of the Second Amendment (in a book published at about the same time as *Heller*) concluded that "it is difficult to know with precision how the Second Amendment was understood by the vast majority of Americans at the time it was proposed. In all likelihood there was no single original understanding. . . ."[29] We have already seen one plausible criticism of Scalia's reasoning (as to the effect of preambles). Furthermore, the drafting history of the amendment reveals that some state proposals to include a specific reference to the right of individual self-defense in the amendment's text were rejected (though the effect of that omission is debatable). It may also be that the Federalists who drafted the Second Amendment in Congress hoodwinked the American public; they may have crafted an amendment that did *not* serve the Anti-Federalists' aim of preserving a force of armed citizens whom the states could mobilize to resist federal tyranny. Indeed, textualism might arguably lead to that conclusion, if a "well-regulated" militia refers only to an "organized" militia!

Amend the Second Amendment!

"Emotional claims that the right to possess deadly weapons is so important that it is protected by the federal Constitution distort intelligent debate about the wisdom of particular aspects of proposed legislation designed to minimize the slaughter caused by the prevalence of guns in private hands."
—retired justice John Paul Stevens, *Six Amendments: How and Why We Should Change the Constitution* (2014)[30]

The Dissents

We turn next to Justice Stevens's dissent. It is safe to say that Justice Stevens was not a fan of the Second Amendment. After retiring from the Court in 2010, he wrote a book in which he called for rewriting it: *Six Amendments: How and Why We Should Change the Constitution.* Unsurprisingly, his proposed rewrite tracked his *Heller* dissent.

Stevens began by stressing the *purpose* of the Second Amendment: "It was a response to concerns raised during the ratification of the Constitution that the power of Congress to disarm the state militias and create a national standing army posed an intolerable threat to the sovereignty of the several States." In view of that core purpose, the amendment's failure specifically to refer to a "right to possess and use guns for nonmilitary purposes like . . . personal self-defense" is critical. The amendment's silence on that means that "there is no indication that the Framers of the Amendment intended to enshrine the common-law right of self-defense in the constitution."[31]

Stevens relied on the amendment's preamble to show that "the preservation of the militia" was "the Amendment's purpose." He cited the language of several contemporaneous state Declarations of Rights and statutes that "highlight the importance members of the founding generation attached to the maintenance of state militias." Two of the Declarations of Rights—Pennsylvania's and Vermont's—were distinctive in that they *did* refer to the right to use firearms in self-defense. "The contrast between those two declarations and the Second Amendment reinforces the clear statement of purpose announced in the Amendment's preamble [and] confirms that the Framers' single-minded focus in crafting the constitutional guarantee 'to keep and bear arms' was on military uses of firearms."[32]

Arguing from the limiting effect of the preamble and the amendment's omission of any reference to self-defense, Stevens maintains that "the 'right to keep and bear arms' protects only a right to possess and use firearms in connection with service in a state-organized militia." He then reasons that "the absence of any reference to civilian uses of weapons tailors the text of the Amendment to the purpose identified in its preamble."[33]

Stevens further argues that the various state proposals for constitutional amendments that led to the drafting of the Second Amendment usually embedded the phrase "keep and bear arms" "within a group of principles that are distinctly military in meaning." An exception was the amendment proposed by New Hampshire, which characterized the right "in more clearly personal terms."[34] (New Hampshire had proposed to say, "Congress shall never disarm any Citizen unless such as are or have been in Actual Rebellion.")[35] Other efforts to specify self-defense as a purpose of the amendment had been rejected in Pennsylvania and Massachusetts. When the state proposals were submitted to Congress, Representative James Madison was tasked with drafting a version for Congress to consider. Madison's first draft "omitted any mention of nonmilitary use or possession of weapons"—a fact that for Stevens is "strikingly significant." Madison's draft was therefore debated and modified in Congress but, again, no language regarding self-defense was included in the final product.[36]

We might explain the difference between Scalia's and Stevens's interpretations in this way. For Scalia, the Second Amendment means, in substance, something like this:

> A well regulated Militia [that is, the entire body of armed, able-bodied adult male citizens], being necessary for the security of a free State, the right of the people [as individuals] to keep and

> bear Arms [for all traditionally lawful purposes, including lawful self-defense] shall not be infringed.

And as an implied corollary:

> Congress cannot disarm the state militias, which are formed from the armed, able-bodied adult male citizenry of the people of the states.

For Stevens the Second Amendment means, in substance, something like this:

> A well regulated [that is, organized] Militia [consisting of a subset of armed, able-bodied adult male citizens], being necessary for the security of a free State, the right of the people to keep and bear Arms [when serving in the militia] shall not be infringed.

With the implied corollary:

> Congress may regulate or prohibit the possession or carrying of weapons by all persons not members of, or (in its judgment) not eligible to become members of, the organized militia; Congress may also regulate or prohibit the possession or carrying of weapons by anyone for any non-militia-related purpose, including self-defense within the home.

We are not offering a judgment about the merits of these competing readings; we are more concerned with illustrating how different originalist methodologies can work. But we would observe that Stevens's originalist arguments, though forceful, suffer from a serious difficulty. What effect should be given to the amendment's silence about the right of individual self-defense? Silence could be taken to mean that the Second Amendment does *not* protect such a right (as against Congress). Alternatively, silence might mean that the language of the amendment, especially its reference to "the right *of the people*," was originally considered comprehensive enough to include the possession and use of firearms for that purpose. Consider that the draft amendment that Madison prepared for Congress had made a specific reference to conscientious objectors: it had stated that "no person religiously scrupulous of bearing arms, shall be compelled to render military service in person."[37] Congress deleted that clause before sending the amendment back to the states for ratification. What did *that* omission mean? That Congress retained the power to conscript conscientious objectors (then, notably, the Quakers) into military service? That under the unamended Constitution, Congress had no such power anyway, so that an amendment for that purpose was unnecessary? Or that *another* proposed amendment—what eventually became the First Amendment's "Free Exercise of Religion" Clause—would cover that situation and bar Congress from drafting Quakers and other religious pacifists? It is hard to say: the *intent* behind the elimination of the proviso is elusive. As Justice Gorsuch was to say a few years later in *Ramos v. Louisiana* (2020), commenting on the first Congress's decision to reject a proposed draft of the Sixth Amendment, "rather than dwelling on text left on the cutting room floor, we are much better served by interpreting the language Congress retained and the States ratified."[38]

Another possibility—not raised either by the *Heller* majority or the dissenters—is that the amended Constitution would protect the right to keep and bear arms in self-defense in *another* provision—not the Second Amendment, but the Ninth, which declares that "the enumeration in the Constitution, of certain rights, shall not be construed to deny or disparage others retained by the people." On this theory the dissenters' reading of the Second Amendment would be basically correct: it has a civic purpose and preserves a traditional right of a *political* character. The right of armed self-defense, by contrast, was considered to be a fundamental natural right—though not "civic" or "political". But over the centuries that natural right had been modified by the common law courts and was subject to some degree of legislative regulation. (For instance, as Blackstone explained it, the right of personal self-defense included a duty to retreat whenever possible.)[39] So understood, the right of personal self-defense could arguably have fallen within the Ninth Amendment's ambit—an unenumerated but constitutional right.

Justice Breyer's dissent recapitulated some of the originalist themes sounded by the other justices. But the more important part of his opinion developed and applied a test for courts to follow in reviewing Second Amendment claims. Without meaning to deprecate Breyer's opinion, we would characterize it as a very sophisticated form of "living constitutionalism"—a methodology that is usually, and rightly, contrasted with "originalism."

Breyer's proposed test was designed to be used even on the assumption that one goal of the Second Amendment was to "help assure citizens that they would have arms available for purposes of self-defense." "Even so," Breyer argued, "a legislature could reasonably conclude that [a challenged gun control law] will advance goals of great public importance, namely, saving lives, preventing injury, and reducing crime." If the legislature can make that showing, then the task of the reviewing court is to determine whether the challenged law "imposes a burden upon gun owners that seems proportionately no greater than restrictions in existence at the time the Second Amendment was adopted."[40] Otherwise put, reviewing courts should inquire "whether the statute burdens a protected interest in a way or to an extent that is out of proportion to the statute's salutary effects upon other important governmental interests. . . . Any answer would take account both of the statute's effects upon the competing interests and the existence of any clearly superior less restrictive alternative.'"[41] Call this "interest-balancing inquiry" the proportionality test. It is fairly evident that much or most gun control would pass this proportionality test, and would therefore be held to be constitutional. Indeed, in Breyer's view, even the district's law, which effectively prevented D.C. residents from possessing handguns, was constitutional—and if it was, what gun control measure would not be?

Crisis of the Two Constitutions: The Rise, Decline, and Recovery of American Greatness by Charles R. Kesler. New York: Encounter Books, 2021.

Living Constitution, Dying Faith: Progressivism and the New Science of Jurisprudence by Bradley C. S. Watson. Wilmington, Delaware: ISI Books, 2009.

A Right like Any Other

The courts would surely not use Breyer's proportionality test in evaluating claims challenging governmental infringement of other enumerated constitutional rights. If it were used, the scope of the Bill of Rights, and of other constitutional provisions protecting individual rights, would be sharply contracted. Consider, for example, the Court's 1977 decision in *National Socialist Party of America v. Village of Skokie.* A group of American Nazis had planned to parade through the streets of Skokie, Illinois—a township that happened to have many Jewish inhabitants who had survived the Holocaust. The marchers intended to wear Nazi uniforms, display the swastika, and distribute pamphlets or exhibit materials inciting hatred against Jews and non-whites. The township obtained an injunction from the state courts to halt the march. The Supreme Court reversed the injunction and required the state court to hear the Nazis' free speech appeal without delay, thus leaving open the possibility that the Nazis would be allowed to march.[42]

It is far from clear that the case would have come out the same way if the Court had applied a proportionality test to the Nazis' First Amendment claim. First, the township certainly had important interests at stake, including preserving the peace, reducing the risk of violent clashes between marchers and protesters, preventing the intentional infliction of emotional harm on Holocaust survivors, their families, and other residents, and thwarting incitements to hatred of Jews and other minorities. Second, the Nazis' competing interest was in expressing an ideology through speeches and gestures that are without political value. And third, there was no "clearly superior, less restrictive alternative"[43] for the village of Skokie to prevent the threatened injuries than to block the march. The Nazis might have sought another venue (in fact, they had) in which to stage their parade. Rather than attempting to "balance" these competing interests, the Court decided that the balance had *already* been struck by the Free Speech Clause of the First Amendment. The Court continues to follow this approach in more recent free speech cases, such as *Snyder v. Phelps* (2011).[44]

If that is how the Court decides First Amendment claims, what justifies the adoption of such a very different standard in Second Amendment cases? Breyer's proportionality test would have marginalized the Second Amendment, placing it on a lower level than other enumerated rights. We would have a two-tiered Bill of Rights.

CHAPTER 9

McDonald: Incorporating the Second Amendment

Our review of the next Second Amendment case, *McDonald v. City of Chicago* (2010), has a different focus from our analysis of *District of Columbia v. Heller* in the last chapter.[1] Coming just two years after *Heller*, *McDonald* addressed an issue that *Heller* had left open: Did the Second Amendment apply to state and local governments in the same way it applied to the federal government?

McDonald was in other respects mainly a rematch between the two judicial coalitions that had fought out *Heller*. Again, it was a 5–4 decision, with the more conservative members of the Court, here led by Justice Alito, prevailing in striking down the challenged gun control regulations, and the more progressive members, led again by Justices Stevens and Breyer, voting to uphold them. What made *McDonald* significantly different from *Heller* is that it brought the Court's "incorporation" doctrine to the fore.

Recall that in *Barron v. Baltimore*, the Marshall Court had ruled that the Fifth Amendment's Takings Clause (which prohibits the government from taking private property without paying just compensation) did not apply to the conduct of a state or local government. In light of *Barron*, the rights enumerated in the first eight amendments to the Constitution in the Bill of Rights were held inapplicable to the states. To be sure, state constitutions, statutes, or common law decisions might apply the equivalents of those protections. But when they did, it was a matter of state law, not of the federal Bill of Rights.

The Fourteenth Amendment

The Civil War and Reconstruction changed that. There was a prevalent feeling that the war necessitated major alterations in the constitutional design of the Union, especially with regard to federalism. After the Civil War, three constitutional amendments were adopted that radically changed the structure of the original Constitution. In the Thirteenth Amendment, the United States abolished slavery and empowered Congress to take enforcement action against it. In the Fourteenth Amendment, the people confirmed the citizenship of the African-American population, endowed all American citizens with an array of civil rights, and granted Congress enforcement powers. (At the time, the term "civil rights" had a narrower meaning than currently, and it did not include such political rights as the right to vote.) In the Fifteenth Amendment, the people prohibited discrimination in voting on the basis of race, and again empowered Congress to enforce this rule. As a result, African-American males (though as yet no females of any race) were enfranchised.

Section One of the Fourteenth Amendment was in some ways the engine of the entire scheme. It reads, "All persons born or naturalized in the United States, and subject to the jurisdiction thereof, are citizens of the United States and of the State wherein they reside. No State shall make or enforce any law which shall abridge the privileges or immunities of citizens of the United States; nor shall any State deprive any person of life, liberty, or property, without due process of law; nor deny to any person within its jurisdiction the equal protection of the laws."

In its first sentence, relating to citizenship, the amendment overruled that part of the *Dred Scott* decision saying that African Americans could never—even if emancipated or born free—be citizens of the United States. In the Civil Rights Act of 1866, Congress had sought to establish that "all persons born in the United States" were "citizens of the United States" regardless of race or color. But the Citizenship Clause of Section One of the Fourteenth Amendment settled the matter once and for all.

The meaning of the next sentence of Section One of the Fourteenth Amendment was before the Court in *McDonald* (as it had often been before). Purely as a textual matter, that language was directed at *the states*, forbidding them to "make or enforce" certain kinds of laws. Right away, the language signaled an abridgement of the states' rights that had existed before the Civil War. Two kinds of protected individual rights, and two classes of rights-holders, were identified. First, "citizens of the United States" (including of course those whose citizenship was created or confirmed by the preceding Citizenship Clause) were protected from state action with regard to their "privileges or immunities." Second, "persons"—including citizens and noncitizens alike—were protected against state actions that deprived them of life, liberty, or property "without due process of law" or that denied them "the equal protection of the laws."

The language chosen here clearly reflected provisions in the original Constitution. As we have seen, the phrase "privileges or immunities" in the Fourteenth Amendment seemed to allude to the Privileges and Immunities Clause of Article IV (though the change from "and" to "or" indicated that it might have a broader scope). And the Fourteenth Amendment's Due Process Clause echoed the Due Process Clause of the Fifth Amendment in the Bill of Rights (which, under *Barron*, had been restricted to the federal government).

What was the original meaning of this language? What purposes was it designed to serve?

Many contemporaries who had lived through the war and Reconstruction and participated in the drafting and ratification of the Fourteenth Amendment believed that it accomplished several things. Their views of the amendment's effects have substantial support in current legal scholarship (though the scholarly debate remains extremely active).[2] The consensus is that the amendment did at least the following:

1. It overruled *Barron v. Baltimore* and "incorporated" all the rights enumerated in the Bill of Rights—that is, it made those enumerated rights applicable to the states. Moreover, this incorporation required national uniformity: the rights applied in the same way to state action as to federal action. This was done by way of the language referring to the "privileges or immunities of citizens of the United States"; thus, the "incorporated" rights protected only those who were citizens.
2. It also held certain *unenumerated* rights to be among the "privileges or immunities" of citizenship. In the first instance, these included the rights that Congress had mentioned in the Civil Rights Act of 1866. Primarily, those were rights respecting the making and enforcement of contracts and the holding of property. Despite emancipation the former Confederate states had been denying these rights to their African-American populations. Congress passed a bill to combat these discriminatory measures, but Lincoln's successor, President Andrew Johnson, vetoed the bill, in part on constitutional grounds. It was not clear that Congress had the constitutional power in 1866 to enact legislation so deeply intrusive into domestic state affairs. In any event, Congress overrode Johnson's veto. And Section One of the Fourteenth Amendment (and, specifically, the "privileges or immunities" language) confirmed the possession of these rights.
3. It also confirmed that citizens possessed *other* unenumerated rights besides the property and contract rights identified

in the Civil Rights Act. How these rights were to be identified was not made clear. But they could reasonably be thought to include basic rights long embedded in the common law or entrenched in the constitutions, statutes, or customs of the states. So one might point to the right to raise a family and educate one's own children, as upheld in the 1925 case of *Pierce v. Society of Sisters*.[3] Of relevance to *McDonald*, these unenumerated rights could also embrace the right to keep and carry firearms for the purpose of self-defense.

4. Finally, Section One provided certain protections for noncitizens as well as for citizens: the rights not to be deprived of life, liberty, or property without due process, and the right to the equal protection of the laws.

On this understanding, Section One of the Fourteenth Amendment accomplished a very great deal. It radically restructured the federal system, significantly narrowed the pre–Civil War scope of states' rights, expanded the citizen body to include those whom the war had liberated from slavery (together with their descendants) and endowed all American citizens with an array of rights that would safeguard them against local oppression and that they would carry with them wherever they moved in the Union. In particular, Section One—through the Privileges or Immunities Clause—was understood to incorporate, in full, the rights enumerated in the first eight amendments to the Constitution as against the states. Coupled with Section Five, which accorded Congress broad power to enforce those guarantees, Section One expressed a noble vision whose codification in the Constitution was worth the horror and destructiveness of the Civil War. In this understanding, the Privileges or Immunities Clause was the centerpiece.

The *Slaughter-House Cases*, Substantive Due Process, and Privileges or Immunities

That conception of the Fourteenth Amendment was swiftly rejected by the Supreme Court. In a close 5–4 decision in the *Slaughter-House Cases* (1873), the Court eviscerated the Privileges or Immunities Clause. In the *Slaughter-House* majority's view, the privileges or immunities of American citizenship reduced to a handful of relatively unimportant rights (and, moreover, rights with which the states were unlikely to interfere), such as the right to travel across state lines in order to visit the nation's capital, or the right to the federal government's diplomatic protection while overseas.[4] And while *Slaughter-House* at least left the door open to a more expansive account of the privileges or immunities of federal citizenship, the cases that followed soon after closed that door.[5] If *Slaughter-House* was mistaken (as we think it was), it was an enormous constitutional setback. And the Court's Fourteenth Amendment jurisprudence has still not fully recovered from it.

Despite that momentous reversal, the Court over time increasingly recognized the radical implications of the Fourteenth Amendment's Section One, especially for individual rights. Although the Privileges or Immunities Clause had been designed to carry most of the freight, the Court gradually began to discover that individual constitutional rights—both enumerated and unenumerated—were enfolded within that section's Due Process and Equal Protection Clauses. Specifically, it began to hold, in a piecemeal, case-by-case fashion, that the Fourteenth Amendment's Due Process Clause had incorporated discrete provisions of the Bill of Rights as against the states (though the scope of the right and the remedies for its violations might be different when federal action was challenged). This process came to be called "selective" or "partial" incorporation. The Court also began to discern constitutionally *unenumerated* rights within the rubric of the Due Process Clause—most controversially, the right to an abortion. Thus the Due Process Clause came to take up most of the slack that was left after

Slaughter-House all but annulled the Privileges or Immunities Clause.

As we pointed out in our discussion of *Dobbs*, these Court-made doctrines were (and are) highly problematic. For one thing, what is their textual footing in the Constitution? The Due Process Clauses of the Fourteenth and Fifth Amendments refer, on their face, to *procedural* rights, not to substantive ones. What justified the Court in injecting momentous substantive rights into what look like guarantees of procedural regularity and lawfulness? And how could the Court explain *selective* incorporation in a satisfactory way?

Every Jot and Tittle

It would seem that a central project of the Fourteenth Amendment was to nationalize and standardize the Bill of Rights, ensuring that citizens would have exactly the same set of basic rights under both federal and state legal systems—what Justice Stevens derisively called "jot by jot" incorporation.[6] But if incorporation were to be partial or selective, what *test* could the Court use to decide which rights were in and which were out?

The Court struggled for decades with these difficulties—and the *McDonald* case is just a recent round in that struggle. Some justices—notably, Hugo Black, a long-serving justice appointed by President Franklin D. Roosevelt—had sought to cut the Gordian knot. In a strong dissent in *Adamson v. California* (1947), Black did not urge reconsidering the *Slaughter-House Cases*; instead, he argued that the Fourteenth Amendment's Section One as a whole had incorporated the Bill of Rights, without specifying in which clause. The Court had rejected Black's position (which was much more coherent than its own) and continued to evolve its path-dependent substantive due process jurisprudence.[7] But recent legal scholarship has put extreme pressure on the Court to revisit its earlier jurisprudence, reconceptualize or reject the doctrines of substantive due process and selective incorporation, revitalize the Privileges or Immunities Clause, and even lay *Slaughter-House* to rest.[8] Justice Thomas's concurring opinion in *McDonald*—easily the most interesting opinion in the case—powerfully advocated that approach.

Although he wrote for himself alone, Justice Thomas's bold concurrence in *McDonald* may be a portent of things to come on the Court.[9] While both the plurality opinion by Justice Alito and the dissenting opinions addressed the case by asking whether the right to keep and bear arms was sufficiently "fundamental" to be incorporated and applied to the states by way of the Fourteenth Amendment's Due Process Clause, Justice Thomas instead reviewed the challenged regulations under the Fourteenth Amendment's Privileges or Immunities Clause. In brief, Thomas (1) relied on an "original public understanding" of the Privileges or Immunities Clause to (2) establish that the Second Amendment had been incorporated against the states (3) by way of the Privileges or Immunities Clause and not the Due Process Clause. His reasoning led him to same conclusion that the plurality had reached: the Second Amendment was "fully applicable to the States." But, he maintained, he had taken "a more straightforward path" to that conclusion, "one that is more faithful to the Fourteenth Amendment's text and history."[10]

First, Thomas's methodology: Thomas declared that the Court's objective should have been "to discern what 'ordinary citizens' at the time of the ratification would have understood the Privileges or Immunities Clause to mean."[11] According to Thomas, "When interpreting constitutional text, the goal is to discern the most likely public understanding of a particular provision at the time it was adopted."[12] That method permitted him to consider statements made by members of Congress in debates leading up to, during, and even shortly after the amendment's ratification, as well as other historical materials. But consulting the congressional debates was not undertaken with a view to discovering the "intent" of the amendment's drafters or proponents in Congress. Rather, "statements by legislators can assist . . . to the extent they demonstrate the manner in which the public used or understood a particular word or phrase," particularly if the legislator's remarks were widely disseminated to the public.[13]

Second, in light of that view of the relevance of the congressional process of drafting and debating the amendment, Thomas gave weight to three major speeches given during the congressional debate over the Fourteenth Amendment by two very prominent members of Congress involved in its framing. Of these three speeches, the most important was that by Senator Jacob Howard (though the two earlier speeches, by Congressman John Bingham, were similar in tenor). Howard introduced in the Senate a draft of the amendment that Bingham had modified from his original version and then shepherded through the House. The version that Howard presented included the text of the Privileges or Immunities Clause that was eventually adopted. Howard explained to his Senate colleagues that the Constitution recognized "a mass of privileges, immunities, and rights, some of them secured . . . *by the first eight amendments of the Constitution*" [emphasis added].[14] If ratified, Howard stated, Section One would "restrain the power of the States and compel them at all times to respect *these great fundamental guarantees*" [emphasis added].[15] Section One would impose "a general prohibition upon all the States, as such, from abridging the privileges and immunities of the citizens of the United States." And in specifying what those privileges and immunities were, Howard explicitly included the Second Amendment "right to keep and to bear arms."[16] Howard's speech was widely reported in the major newspapers of the period. Thomas was surely right in considering it to be powerful evidence that, in its original public meaning, the Privilege or Immunities Clause was understood to incorporate the Bill of Rights, and thus the Second Amendment. The congressional debates were only one source among several that pointed to that conclusion.

Third, Thomas argued that it was bizarre to look to the amendment's Due Process Clause, rather than to its Privileges or Immunities Clause, as the basis for incorporating some or all of the Bill of Rights. For one thing, he made the textual point that it "strains credulity" to think that "a constitutional provision that guarantees only 'process' before a person is deprived of life, liberty, or property could define the substance of those rights."[17] Second, he noted that the ratification record lent no support to that view of the Due Process Clause. "Any serious argument over the scope of the Due Process Clause must acknowledge that neither its text nor its history suggests that it protects the many substantive rights this Court's cases now claim it does."[18] Finally, he argued that the "fiction" that the Due Process Clause had a significant substantive component was "dangerous" because it lacked any "guiding principle to distinguish 'fundamental' rights that warrant protection [and incorporation] from nonfundamental rights that do not." That way lay radical judicial subjectivity and arbitrariness. Thomas affirmed that "the original meaning of the Fourteenth Amendment offers a superior alternative [to the Court's substantive due process analysis], and that a return to that meaning would allow this Court to enforce the rights the Fourteenth Amendment is designed to protect with greater clarity and predictability."[19]

Our summary here does incomplete justice to the subtlety and richness of Thomas's lengthy opinion. We have not considered his discussion of the question whether the incorporation of the Second Amendment means that no state can categorically *deny* the right to arms to any of its citizens, or merely that it can deny that right to its citizens provided only that it does so in a nondiscriminatory way. But we hope to have said enough to convey the power of his originalist method.

Thomas noted, but did not attempt to decide, several important questions that his approach to the Privileges or Immunities Clause would pose. For instance, did the clause subsume enumerated rights—like the right to *habeas corpus*—that did not fall within the Bill of Rights? Was *every* provision of the Bill of Rights incorporated against the states, including those that seemed designed to protect the rights of *states* rather than of individuals, such as the Establishment Clause? Did the clause subsume any *unenumerated* rights and, if so, what were they? If the Second Amendment was incorporated by way of the Privileges or Immunities Clause, and the latter was in terms designed for *citizens*, did noncitizens have a constitutional right to keep and bear arms? Would the Court undermine many of its past substantive due process decisions if it reassessed them under the Privileges or Immunities Clause?

Thomas correctly answered that the Court did not need to address and decide those questions in the case before it. Moreover, with considerable intellectual honesty, Thomas seemed well prepared to follow the logic of his position wherever it led. If it meant overturning existing precedents, or creating surprising new ones, so be it. Like the philosopher Arthur Schopenhauer, Thomas seems to think that logic is not like a taxicab: you can't tell it to stop whenever you want to get off.

CHAPTER 10

Bruen: Do You Need a "Special Need" to Carry a Gun?

The last case in the Court's twenty-first-century trilogy on gun rights is *New York State Rifle & Pistol Association v. Bruen*, decided in June of 2022, just one day before *Dobbs*. This was the Court's first major pronouncement on the Second Amendment in twelve years. Much litigation over gun rights had occurred in the lower courts after *Heller* and *McDonald*, and the Court clearly felt that further guidance on the subject was necessary. As the Court saw it, several of the lower courts had misinterpreted *Heller* by applying a far too lenient approach to state gun control legislation. The Court declared a tougher standard of review and applied it to a New York statute that denied law-abiding residents licenses to carry handguns publicly without a "special need for self-defense distinguishable from that of the general community."[1]

Heller itself had noted that the right to keep and bear arms was not absolute but, like any right, subject to limitations. Among these are reasonable restrictions on carrying concealed firearms, disqualifying felons and the mentally ill, and prohibiting firearms in sensitive places. *Bruen* provided the Court with an occasion to illuminate the scope of such permissible limitations.

Bruen also enabled the Court to clarify the historical method for analyzing Second Amendment claims that it had deployed in *Heller* and *McDonald*. In an opinion by Justice Thomas, the Court struck down the statute by a 6–3 majority.[2] Justice Breyer was once again in dissent, with a repeat of his argument that the benefits of much gun control legislation outweighed the infringement on Second Amendment rights.[3] Justice Alito added a short, pointed concurrence that emphasized the narrowness of the Court's holding and that took a scalpel to Breyer's policy-laden dissent.[4] Justice Kavanaugh, joined by the chief justice, wrote a concurrence that underscored the limited scope of the Court's holding.[5] And Justice Amy Coney Barrett, also concurring, drew attention to two significant methodological issues that remained unresolved.[6] The split between conservative and progressive justices that had emerged in *Heller* and *McDonald* reappeared, but the conservatives had been reinforced by the addition of Justice Barrett to the Court after the death of Justice Ruth Bader Ginsburg.

A "Special Need for Self-Protection"

New York's "Sullivan Law," which originated in the early 1900s, effectively made it impossible for most of the state's residents to carry a gun outside the home, even for self-defense. The state criminalized the possession of unlicensed firearms, whether inside or outside the home. It did, however, permit those who wanted to carry a firearm outside the home to obtain a license to carry a concealed pistol or revolver in public places—but only if the license applicant could show "proper cause" to be allowed to do so. And self-defense, as such, was not considered a "proper cause." Rather, the applicant would need to prove (usually, to a judge or police official) a "special need for self-protection." As Justice Alito noted, the state made it extremely hard to prove such a special need.[7] At oral argument New York's solicitor general was asked whether the state would issue a carry permit to someone who worked at night, who had to walk home through dark and crime-infested streets, and who explained that she wanted to carry a gun on her way home because there had been a lot of muggings in the area. The solicitor general replied that, "in general," no. To demonstrate a "special need," the applicant would have to prove more—that she had been *singled out* for attack. And a discretionary decision by the local licensing officer to deny a permit was rarely overturned in court.[8]

Bitter Clingers

"So it's not surprising then that they get bitter, they cling to guns or religion or antipathy toward people who aren't like them or anti-immigrant sentiment or anti-trade sentiment as a way to explain their frustrations." —Barack Obama (2008)[9]

Although New York was not alone in requiring a permit to carry a handgun in public, the vast majority of states (forty-three) were "shall issue" jurisdictions, meaning that licensing officials had no discretion to deny a permit once applicants had met certain objective threshold requirements. New York, five other states, and the District of Columbia were "may issue" jurisdictions, giving licensing officials discretion to deny concealed-carry licenses even if the applicant satisfied statutory criteria, so long as those officials decided that the applicant had not demonstrated "proper cause."[10]

Thomas began his constitutional analysis for the Court by defining the correct standard of review. That standard required a reviewing court to apply two tests. First, does the Second Amendment's "plain text" cover the individual conduct in question? If it does, then the Second Amendment "presumptively" protects that conduct. The Court found that the gun owners in New York easily satisfied that test: they were law-abiding citizens—members of "the people"—who sought to carry concealed handguns outside the home for the purpose of lawful self-defense (but without showing a "special need"). Given the Court's reading of the text of the Second Amendment in *Heller* and *McDonald*, it was incontrovertible that the text covered them.

But that merely created a *presumption* that the challengers had a constitutional right that had been denied by the state. Presumptions can be overcome. So, a second test had to be applied, and here the burden of proof was on the regulators: "The government must demonstrate that the regulation is consistent with this Nation's historical tradition of firearm regulation." If the government makes that showing, its gun control regulation stands; if not, the challenger prevails. To make that showing, the government would have to appeal to history. In particular, the government's attempt at justification had to meet two "relevant metrics": (1) Did its regulation impose a "comparable burden" on the right to keep and bear arms as historical regulations had? And (2) was that regulatory burden "comparably justified"?[11]

In laying down these tests, the Court rejected other standards of review that had been suggested by some of the lower courts. The standard that New York supported—commonly known as "intermediate scrutiny"—bore a close resemblance to the "proportionality" test from Justice Breyer's earlier dissents. On this approach, if the Second Amendment's text and history were deemed inconclusive, a reviewing court would have to ask whether the government could show that the regulation was "substantially related to the achievement of an important governmental interest." Essentially, this is a "means-end" test. It readily led the lower courts to conclude, for example, that the Second Amendment right was "limited to self-defense in the home" and did not extend to public places (such as dangerous neighborhoods). The Court rejected this relaxed, pro-regulatory, and manipulable standard, insisting instead that "the government must affirmatively prove that its firearms regulation is part of the historical tradition that delimits the outer bounds of the right to keep and bear arms."[12]

The Right to Self-Defense

How did the Sullivan Law fare under the Court's history-based test? After a lengthy and detailed review of the history, the Court concluded that New York had failed to show that its regulation was "consistent" with historical practice:

> We conclude that respondents have not met their burden to identify an American tradition justifying the State's proper-cause requirement. The Second Amendment guaranteed to all Americans the right to bear commonly used arms in public subject to certain reasonable, well-defined restrictions. Those restrictions, for example, limited the intent for which one could carry arms, the manner by which one carried arms, or the exceptional circumstances under which one could not carry arms, such as before justices of the peace and other government officials. Apart from a few late-19th-century outlier jurisdictions, American governments simply have not broadly prohibited the public carry of commonly used firearms for personal defense. Nor, subject to a few late-in-time outliers, have American governments required law-abiding, responsible citizens to demonstrate a special need for self-protection distinguishable from that of the general community in order to carry arms in public. [Internal citations and quotation marks omitted.][13]

Justice Alito offered a useful "succinct summary" of what the Court had and had not held:

> The key point [in *Heller*] . . . was that "the people," not just members of the "militia," have the right to use a firearm to defend themselves. And because many people face a serious risk of lethal violence when they venture outside their homes, the Second Amendment was understood at the time of adoption to apply under those circumstances. The Court's exhaustive historical survey establishes that point very clearly, and today's decision therefore holds that a State may not enforce a law, like New York's

> Sullivan Law, that effectively prevents its law-abiding residents from carrying a gun for this purpose.
>
> That is all we decide.[14]

Justice Kavanaugh also noted the limits of the *Heller*, *McDonald*, and *Bruen* holdings. He stated that *Bruen* did not affect the "shall issue" licensing schemes found in forty-three states: these states, he wrote, could continue to enforce their laws. (Presumably, Kavanaugh believed that "shall issue" laws had the requisite historical validation.) The "may issue" states like New York could continue to require licenses for carrying handguns for self-defense, provided that they used "objective licensing requirements" like those of the forty-three states. Kavanaugh tracked *Heller* (and, indeed, the majority opinion in *Bruen* itself) in pointing out that the Second Amendment, while not "a regulatory blank check," was also not "a regulatory straitjacket." There were important boundaries to the amendment's protections, including (for example) state prohibitions on carrying handguns into "sensitive" places.[15]

Predictably, some of the reactions to *Bruen* were extremely hostile. New York State was among the first to denounce the decision and to enact broadened gun control regulation. State Attorney General Letitia James argued that the Court had not struck down the state's licensing requirements for handguns in their entirety; that the Court had seemed to endorse many of the licensing requirements (for example, fingerprinting, background checks, and so forth) common to New York and "must issue" states; that carrying in "sensitive places" might be prohibited; that "unusual weapons" were "subject to further restrictions"; that "carrying guns with unlawful intent" might be prohibited; and that private property owners might be authorized to ban guns on their property. She also noted that New York governor Kathy Hochul had recently signed legislation, adopted at a special session of the state legislature, to strengthen gun control regulations by characterizing additional public settings as "sensitive places," by adding new eligibility requirements for applicants seeking a concealed-carry permit, and by imposing new storage and other safety requirements.[16]

Meanwhile, just hours after *Bruen* was issued, the U.S. Senate, by a 65–33 vote, passed the Bipartisan Safer Communities Act, a significant piece of gun control legislation. The Senate bill swiftly passed the House and was signed into law. Among other things, the new federal act provided funding to states to enact and implement so-called "red flag" laws and closed the so-called "boyfriend loophole" in prior law.[17]

Whether these and other state and federal gun control laws will survive judicial review under *Bruen*'s standards is difficult to predict. In a separate concurring opinion in *Caniglia v. Strom*, a 2021 Fourth Amendment case involving a warrantless police seizure of handguns within a home, Justice Alito had been careful to note that the Court's decision in that case did not affect "the so-called 'red flag' laws that some states are now enacting." Alito explained that these laws "enable the police to seize guns pursuant to a court order to prevent their use for suicide or the infliction of harm on innocent persons." Alito observed that Fourth Amendment challenges to such "red flag" laws were likely.[18] So now are Second Amendment challenges. Unless states can establish that their red flag laws are analogous to traditional gun control legislation, those laws may well fail to satisfy *Bruen*.

Concluding Observations

We conclude this chapter on the Second Amendment with two observations—one about federalism and the other about originalism.

A recurring theme in the criticism of these cases is that the Court does not give sufficient leeway to federalism. It is obvious that the histories, cultures, and laws of the various states, localities, and regions throughout the country reflect different values about gun rights and gun control. One

Local Rules Shouldn't Always Rule

In *Plessy v. Ferguson* (1896), the case upholding the state-sanctioned segregation of whites and blacks in public accommodations, the Court found that racial segregation was "reasonable"—and the test of "reasonableness" was custom. It was customary in the South of that period (and elsewhere in the Union) to segregate Americans along racial lines.[19] But the custom was a terrible one, and the laws embodying and maintaining it were unconstitutional. Federalism cannot provide a justification for Jim Crow laws.

would not expect to find the same views about gun rights in California and Texas, in populous urban areas and rural places, in New England and the South. In view of these differences, would not the constitutional virtues of federalism show to best advantage if the Court refrained from imposing a uniform standard for gun rights across the nation?

We are sympathetic to federalism, but we cannot agree. If the Framers and Ratifiers of the Fourteenth Amendment really meant to apply the Second Amendment to the states (as the Court found), then the Court has no choice but to enforce a uniform national standard. Moreover, judicial tolerance of regional and local variations is by no means always wise.

Our second point concerns originalism. In *Bruen*, Justice Thomas quotes *Heller*: "Constitutional rights are enshrined with the scope they were understood to have *when the people adopted them*" [Thomas's emphasis].[20] This seems to mean that the scope of a constitutionalized right can neither expand nor contract from the point of ratification onward: the right is, so to say, freeze-framed. But both enumerated and unenumerated constitutional rights are usually rooted in Anglo-American common law. One of the chief virtues of the common law is its very flexibility, adaptability, and capacity to change as circumstances seem to require. Does the constitutionalization of a common law right mean an end to its capacity to adapt?

This question has a direct and obvious bearing on the interpretation of such *enumerated* rights as the Eighth Amendment's ban on cruel and unusual punishments, which is anchored in the common law tradition.[21]

But it also affects the interpretation of *unenumerated* constitutional rights such as (let us assume for the sake of argument) the right of marital privacy upheld in *Griswold v. Connecticut* (1965). *Griswold* struck down a state law (anachronistic even at the time) that prohibited married couples from using artificial contraceptives. The Court gave a number of poor reasons for its decision, but missed the most tenable one—that the right of marital privacy in sexual matters was entrenched in the common law, and had been constitutionalized as against state interference through the Privileges or Immunities Clause of the Fourteenth Amendment.[22]

PART IV

The Supreme Court and the Administrative State

CHAPTER 11

The "Living Constitution" and the Fourth Branch

It is obvious that the American constitutional system no longer works as it was designed to do: the textbook account of separation of powers does not come close to describing the way our government actually functions. What is often called the "Fourth Branch" of the government—the federal bureaucracy or the "Administrative State"—has taken its place alongside Congress, the president, and the courts. In practice this branch has displaced Congress as the principal lawmaking power in the government, regulating in intrusive detail many aspects of our private lives: mandating vaccines, booster shots, and masks for adults, children, and even infants; causing home mortgage interest rates to rise or fall; setting rules for security screening at airports; regulating high school athletics programs and college students' sexual conduct; conducting background checks on those wanting to buy handguns; deciding whether new medications for cancer will be available in drug stores; and prescribing whether baby formula made in Europe can be sold in the United States. When presidents and politicians try to persuade the public to comply with administrative mandates, they often urge us to "follow the science"—meaning, obey the instructions of the purportedly neutral and disinterested technical "experts" who are said to populate the federal bureaucracy.[1] Perhaps, as some of its defenders argue, the Administrative State is "essential to promoting the common good in contemporary society; that it does far more good than harm; that it is a clear reflection of democratic will; and that it is entirely legitimate on constitutional grounds."[2]

But to the Supreme Court in 2006, one agency, at least, was behaving like an "enlightened despot."[3] And that, to say the least, is a widely shared view.

How did it come to this?

Government by Technocracy

A series of presidents and Congresses agreed over the course of several decades to construct an Administrative State at odds with the Spartan separation of powers of the original Constitution. Government by experts emerged during the Progressive Era with Presidents Teddy Roosevelt and Woodrow Wilson, was the focus of the pivotal presidential election of 1912, and then became permanent under President Franklin D. Roosevelt's New Deal. It metastasized under President Lyndon Johnson's Great Society and President Richard Nixon's expansion of environmental and economic laws. It reached high points with President Obama's national health care program and the federal and state measures to combat the COVID-19 pandemic. From 2020 through 2022, the government not only pumped trillions of dollars into the economy to keep it afloat, it also ordered lockdowns of that same economy and restricted the movements and activities of society as a whole in the tiniest detail. The government stopped most interstate travel, prevented many businesses from operating in person, closed down churches, barred landlords from evicting tenants, attempted to force all private employees to be vaccinated, and discharged military personnel who refused the vaccines.

One of the dirty secrets of Washington, D.C., is that all three branches of government have cooperated in the creation of this vast state. Government by experts requires three major alterations to the Framers' establishment of a Congress that passes the law, a president that executes the law, and courts that resolve disputes under the law. In contrast to that vision, today's vast government requires that Congress transfer its lawmaking power to agencies, that the experts in those agencies operate independently of the control of the president, and that judges defer to the decisions of those agencies.

For much of the last seventy-five years, justices of the Supreme Court of both conservative and progressive bent blessed this new technocracy by refusing to limit the lawmaking powers that Congress could transfer to the agencies, preventing presidents from exercising the power to control or remove bureaucrats, and requiring the lower courts to exercise light-to-no review of agency decisions. Each branch of government benefits from this regime: Congress no longer has to take stands on many controversial issues; the executive branch gains more power over policy (though presidents themselves also become more responsible), and the courts avoid clashes with the political branches over power-transfers that both of those branches want to make—and spare themselves from having to develop technical and scientific expertise of their own.

As with abortion and the right to bear arms, however, the Supreme Court announced a sharp change of course in 2022. In *West Virginia v. EPA*, Chief Justice Roberts led six conservative justices in blocking the Biden administration's effort to impose a global warming plan on the nation's entire electricity grid. On the basis of the Court's "major questions doctrine," the majority in that case rejected Biden's argument that Congress's broad delegation of power to the EPA in the Clean Air Act in the 1970s and 1990s gave the administration the power to create a nationwide climate control program for all power plants.[4] *West Virginia* followed other Roberts Court cases that have given presidents more power to fire the heads of independent agencies,[5] which allows the White House to place some bureaucrats under the direct control of the only nationally elected officers in Washington (the president and vice president). The Court made clear that it was bringing to an end the era when Congresses and presidents could agree to vast delegations of power to the agencies. It began what may become a decades-long project to keep Congress and the executive within their constitutional lanes.

Establishing Paternity

If James Madison is called "the Father of the Constitution," then Woodrow Wilson deserves to be considered "the Father of the Living Constitution."

To describe the intellectual and political environment that brought the Supreme Court's nondelegation doctrine to the point of revival would carry us far beyond the compass of this short book. But we must take at least brief notice of the influence of the Progressive movement on the climate of ideas in which the Court worked throughout the twentieth century. In particular, we must sketch out the constitutional ideas of Woodrow Wilson before we discuss the rise of the Administrative State and the Court's response in *West Virginia v. EPA*.

A "New Constitution"

Wilson was both an academic and a politician—a professor, and later president, of Princeton University, and later the governor of New Jersey and president of the United States. Wilson's deep and lasting influence, therefore, can be ascribed not only to the quality of his thought but also to his ability to dominate the nation's discourse and steer its policy.

Wilson himself, like many other distinguished American public intellectuals in the late nineteenth and early twentieth centuries (the philosopher John Dewey and the historian Charles Beard are other examples), was deeply influenced by two currents in European thought: the historicism of the Prussian philosopher G. W. F. Hegel and a version of the evolutionary theory of the English scientist Charles Darwin (to which Wilson gave a racialized interpretation). Wilson saw history as continually evolving into higher and better forms—hence his "Progressivism." In his article "The Study of Administration" (1887), he divided the "constitutional histories of the chief nations of the modern world" into three successive periods. Those nations began in a period of "absolute rulers, and of an

More than a Dime's Worth of Difference

"The Progressive Party believes that the Constitution is a living thing, growing with the people's growth, strengthening with the people's strength, aiding the people in their struggle for life, liberty and the pursuit of happiness, permitting the people to meet all their needs as conditions change. The opposition believes that the Constitution is a dead form." —Albert Beveridge, keynote address to the Progressive National Convention in 1912[6]

"You have been nominated because you stand preeminently for certain fixed and essential principles which the Republican Party maintain. You believe in preserving the constitutional Government of the United States. You believe in the rule of law rather than the rule of men. You realize that the only safety for nations, as for individuals, is to establish and abide by declared principles of action. You are in sympathy with the great practical rules of right conduct that the American people have set up for their own guidance and self-restraint in the limitations of the Constitution—the limitations upon governmental and official power essential to the preservation of liberty and justice. You know that to sweep away these wise rules of self-restraint would be not progress, but decadence." —Senator Elihu Root notifying President Taft of his nomination as the Republican candidate for president in 1912[7]

administrative system adapted to absolute rule." They then ascended to a second and higher stage "in which constitutions are framed to do away with absolute rulers and substitute popular control, and in which administration is neglected for these higher concerns."[8] That was the stage in which our 1787 Constitution was framed. The third and highest period was that "in which the sovereign people undertake to develop administration under [a] new constitution."[9] Elsewhere Wilson summarized his perspective: "The period of constitution-making is passed now. We have reached a new territory in which we need new guides, the vast territory of *administration*."[10]

Making It Up as We Go Along

"As the life of the nation changes so must the interpretation of the document which contains it change, by a nice adjustment, determined, not by the original intention of those who drew the paper, but by the exigencies and the new aspects of life itself." —Woodrow Wilson, *Constitutional Government in the United States*[11]

Wilson argued for a "new constitution" in which separation of powers would be replaced with a separation between "politics" and "administration." He rejected the Framers' separation of powers on two main grounds—it was inefficient, and it allowed for too much popular democracy. Although the Constitution may have been appropriate for a period when "the functions of government were simple," it had become obsolete in a period that required a new "science of administration" that took account of new "difficulties of governmental action."[12]

In an early critique of separation of powers in his *Congressional Government: A Study in American Politics* (1887), Wilson found it to be "manifestly a radical defect in our federal system that it parcels out power and confuses responsibility as it does. The main purpose of the convention of 1787 seems to have been to accomplish this grievous mistake."[13] He predicted that separation of powers and its accompanying checks and balances would lead over time to the demise of the American regime: "No living thing can have its organs offset against each other, as checks, and live."[14]

Wilson contrasted the alleged inefficiency of the American constitutional system with the vigor and effectiveness (as he saw it) of bureaucratic "administration." In his "Study of Administration," he wrote that "administration is everywhere putting its hands to new undertakings. The utility, cheapness, and success of the government's postal service, for instance, point towards the early establishment of governmental control of the telegraph system. . . . Seeing every day new things which the state ought to do, the next thing is to see clearly how it ought to do them."[15]

Wilson's exaltation of the efficiency of administration and his corresponding aversion to separation of powers interlocked with his high regard for the qualities of "expert" administrators and a corresponding devaluation of popular sovereignty and universal suffrage. Granting "large powers and unhampered discretion" to unpolitical administrators was "indispensable."[16] Concentration of power in the same hands was desirable, provided those were expert hands: "There is no danger in power, if only it be not irresponsible. If it be divided, dealt out in shares to many, it is obscured; and if it be obscured, it is made irresponsible. But if it be centred in heads of the [civil] service and in heads of branches of the service, it is easily watched and brought to book."[17] Civil servants' tenure protections, salaries, non-partisanship and professionalism, not fear of political retribution or the voters' ire, would ensure their good conduct and objective judgment.

Wilson went still further, insisting that administration, to be efficient, had to possess sweeping discretionary powers: "*[T]he functions of government are in a very real sense independent of legislation*, and even constitutions, because [they are] as old as government and inherent in its very nature. *The bulk and complex minuteness of our positive law*, which covers almost every case that can arise in Administration, *obscures for us the fact that Administration cannot wait upon legislation*, but must be given leave, or take it, to proceed without specific warrant in giving effect to the characteristic life of the State."[18]

At a minimum this is a demand that Congress not write laws in "bulk and complex minuteness," but instead delegate vast discretionary powers to administrators. But Wilson was also suggesting that administrators do not need even broad legislative delegations in order to act, but should be considered free, in the name of "giving effect to the characteristic life of the State," to act without legislative authorization at all ("Administration cannot wait upon legislation"). As we shall see, Wilson's view that administration can and should act without "specific warrant," *or even with no warrant at all*, reverberates through our current political debates on matters such as global warming and carbon emissions.

Inefficiency was not Wilson's only objection to separation of powers; he also questioned the doctrine of popular sovereignty on which it rested. In both his private and public writings, Wilson, as Justice Thomas has observed, displayed a "deep disdain for the theory of popular sovereignty."[19] In his diary Wilson wrote that "universal suffrage is at the foundation of every evil in this country."[20] In his marginal notes on John Richard Green, he implied that "the principle of universal suffrage" was inconsistent with "those principles of government . . . which have secured personal freedom and political liberty" in the United States.[21] Wilson's skepticism about popular sovereignty and universal suffrage stemmed not only from a low estimate of the mental capacities of ordinary Americans but also from his hostility towards the country's growing racial diversity. In his article "The Study of Administration," he wrote, "To know the public mind of this country, one must know the mind, not of Americans of the older stocks only, but also of Irishmen, of Germans, of negroes. In order to get a footing for new doctrine, one must influence minds cast in every mould of race, minds inheriting every bias of environment, warped by the histories of a score of different nations, warmed or chilled, closed or expanded by almost every climate of the globe."[22]

Elsewhere he concluded that ordinary people "do not often possess" the "discriminating judgment" and "fullness of information" required to make sound judgments on public policy.[23] Hence, "The people should not govern; they should elect the governors: and these governors should be elected for periods long enough to give time for policies not too heedful of transient breezes of public opinion."[24]

In place of the Constitution's inefficient and outmoded separation of powers, Wilson had originally proposed a form of cabinet government modeled on the British parliamentary system. (By the late nineteenth century, the unwritten British Constitution had merged the executive, headed by the prime minister, into the legislature.) But eventually Wilson came to consider that solution unsatisfactory. Congress was too preoccupied with local and sectional interests, too attuned to the voters, and too willing to accept muddled compromises: it could not act for the nation as a whole. He envisaged instead an American constitutional system divided between "politics" and "administration."

On the political side of that division, he arrived at the conception of the president as a "Leader" who would identify the popular will (though not by way of the older, more deliberative constitutional forms) and seek to guide it (one might say "nudge" it) down the path of historical progress. But at the same time, Wilson recognized that the president, no less than Congress, was accountable to the voters; and Wilson wanted administrators to be insulated from "politics." "Politics" could only contaminate and distort their expert and unpolitical judgment of what society needed.

Reflecting this dilemma, Wilson's highly personalized vision of the presidency involved a president at once exceptionally strong and exceptionally weak. In any case, Wilson's presidency is not the office that the Framers designed.

On the one hand, Wilson saw the president as (potentially at any rate) larger than the office and unbounded by the constraints the Constitution imposes on it. "Governments are what politicians make them," he wrote.[25] The president is "at once the choice of the party and of the nation" and "the only party nominee for whom the whole nation votes. . . . No one else represents the people as a whole, exercising a national choice." He is the "spokesman for the real sentiment and purpose of the country."[26] So viewed, the president can claim to embody the will of the people, and to be entitled to implement it, even if Congress has not authorized (or has forbidden) the president to do what he intends. Since the president is elected with a national "mandate," he is empowered to act without reference to Congress. On the

The President Who Would Not Be King: Executive Power under the Constitution by Michael W. McConnell. Princeton: Princeton University Press, 2020.

other hand, an unpolitical bureaucracy must be able to act independently of presidential (that is, political) interference. Its "expertise," not direct or indirect accountability to the voters, underpins its legitimacy and justifies it in exercising its broad powers. In any case, Wilson argued, the president is incapable of exerting executive power effectively. The bureaucracy is just too large, and its tasks are too complex, for the president to oversee it. Thus, he wrote that the president simply "cannot execute the laws."[27] The president's new role as "Leader," moreover, required him to attend to politics and eschew administration. He "is becoming more and more a political and less and less an executive officer."[28] The price of obtaining political leadership of the nation is that the formal powers of the presidency drain away from him and seep into—dare we say?—the Swamp.

The cynic (or is it the realist?) in us wants to say that Wilson's conceptions of the presidency, of Congress, and of the Administrative State have prevailed, and provide a true account of the government we live under today.

Delegation

The growth of the Administrative State that Wilson envisaged was made possible only by the massive and unrelenting transfer of power from the people's elected representatives in Congress to federal agencies within the executive branch. That transfer of power has been going on for decades and shows little sign of slowing. But it violates the principle of separation of powers, which is a fundamental feature of the original constitutional design. To be sure, even in the Founding period, there were vigorous debates over whether Congress could delegate any of its powers to the executive (or judicial) branches and, if so, which powers and to what extent. The Supreme Court played no role in those debates until 1825, when Chief Justice John Marshall handed down the *Wayman v. Southard* decision.[29]

The early debates hovered between two poles. On the one hand, there were powerful reasons to doubt whether the Constitution permitted any delegation at all. If Article I, Section One of the Constitution granted the power to legislate, it was argued that grant of power was *exclusive*: Congress must exercise all of its enumerated powers *itself*, and it could not delegate the choice of how to exercise them to another branch. On the other side, it was obvious that Congress could not, in general laws, prescribe rules for every conceivable contingency. Aside from practicality, moreover, there were reasons to think that the executive was *institutionally* better equipped to make at least some decisions.

These opposing views clashed in, for example, vigorous congressional debates in the 1790s over post offices and postal roads—debates that featured James Madison, along with other leading lights, including the tough-minded Federalist and future Speaker of the House Theodore Sedgwick. Madison and his allies argued, in substance, that Congress could not delegate to the president (or to his subordinate, the postmaster general) the authority to decide where post offices were to be located and where postal roads should run. Detailed and laborious though the task might be, Congress had to make those decisions itself. To delegate that decision-making power to the executive would, in their view, be a violation of separation of powers. Sedgwick and his party took the opposite view: Congress might have to lay down a general principle or broad policy directive for the executive to follow in making those decisions, but once it had set the policy it could constitutionally delegate the implementation of that policy to the other branch. The Federalists argued that the executive possessed better quality information about the country's needs, that it could take a national outlook on these questions while members of Congress were likely to have only blinkered local perspectives, and that it could reach decisions without the haggling, vote-trading, and compromise-brokering that characterizes the legislative process. Those early debates have effects that are still with us today.

Even to the present, the Supreme Court affirms that Congress may not transfer its lawmaking power to another branch. Indeed, statements to this effect are frequent in the Court's opinions. For example, In the *Gundy* case (2019), Justice Kagan—the leading defender of the Administrative State now on the Court—quoted the 1825 *Wayman v. Southard* decision in support of the principle that Congress may not delegate its legislative powers: "Article I of the Constitution provides that '[a]ll legislative Powers herein granted shall be vested in a Congress of the United States.' §1. Accompanying that assignment of power to Congress is a bar on its further delegation. Congress, this Court explained early on, may not transfer to another branch 'powers which are strictly and exclusively legislative.'"[30]

The Court has said the same thing on many other occasions. In *INS v. Chadha* (1983), the Court affirmed that "the Constitution sought to divide the delegated powers of the new Federal Government into three defined categories, Legislative, Executive, and Judicial, *to assure, as nearly as possible, that each Branch of government would confine itself to its assigned responsibility*" [emphasis added].[31] In his powerful dissent in the 1989 *Mistretta* case, Justice Scalia wrote that "except in a few areas constitutionally committed to the Executive Branch, the basic policy decisions governing society are to be made by the Legislature. Our Members of Congress could not, even if they wished, vote all power to the President and adjourn *sine die*."[32]

The Court's reluctance to allow delegation in these cases is supported by powerful evidence from the writings of the Framers and their predecessors in our constitutional tradition. In *The Federalist* No. 48, Madison wrote that there is agreement "on all sides" that "the powers properly belonging to one of the departments ought not to be directly and completely administered by either of the other departments."[33] Looking further back into the legal and political tradition behind the U.S. Constitution, the English philosopher John Locke emphasized that one branch cannot delegate away its power to another:

> The *Legislative cannot transfer the Power of Making Laws* to any other hands. For it being but a delegated Power from the People, they, who have it, cannot pass it over to others. The People alone can appoint the Form of the Commonwealth, which is by Constituting the Legislative, and appointing in whose hands that shall be. And when the People have said, We will submit to rules, and be govern'd by *Laws* made by such Men, and in such Forms, no Body else can say other Men shall make *Laws* for them; nor can the people be bound by any *Laws* but such as are Enacted by those, whom they have Chosen, and Authorised to make *Laws* for them. The power of the *Legislative* being derived from the People by a positive voluntary Grant and Institution, can be no other, than what that positive Grant conveyed, which being only to make *Laws,* and not to make *Legislators,* the *Legislative* can have no power to transfer their Authority of making Laws, and place it in other hands.[34]

At the same time, however, you do not have to think very hard to realize that Congress cannot legislate all the way down to the ground level: the devil is, as they say, in the details. Congress can and should make significant policy decisions for the nation—it is *designed* for that purpose. But it cannot be expected to provide with exquisite granularity for every contingency that may arise in administering a statute. Even in the early Republic, when federal administration was vastly leaner and simpler than it is now, Congress grasped the necessity of delegating some of its lawmaking powers. But which powers, and how far? Can it, for example, delegate the power to lay and collect taxes? To define crimes, as well as to prosecute them? To decide when an emergency has arisen sufficient to warrant the suspension of the writ of *habeas corpus*? To declare war? Once the door to delegating congressional power was opened, how wide would it be allowed to swing? Could Congress, as in Justice Scalia's *reductio ad absurdum*, simply delegate all its lawmaking power to the president and then pack its bags and go home?

The answer that the Supreme Court developed over the decades came to be known as "the delegation doctrine"—and also, confusingly, as "the nondelegation doctrine." The Court's doctrine seemed to be (and perhaps originally was) a sensible compromise between two extreme and unworkable positions. In a nutshell the delegation doctrine attempted to distinguish congressional delegations that were constitutionally permissible from those that were not. The crucial test was whether, in giving some discretionary authority to the executive branch to make rules and regulations, Congress had delineated the specific policy that the executive had to implement. So, Congress sets the policy, the executive carries it out. The executive is empowered to make decisions that are legally binding on the citizens—decisions that may deprive them of life, liberty, or property—just as if it *were* Congress. But Congress must have reined in the executive by providing an "intelligible principle" to guide its implementation of Congress's legislation. If the intelligible principle was too vague or open-ended, then the delegation would be void. If it were very narrow and specific (like, say, a delegation of the power to decide on the size, shape, and color of postage stamps), it would be constitutionally valid, but perhaps not very useful.

It would take us too far off course to recount the history of the delegation doctrine. (Justice Gorsuch does that in his elegant dissent to *Gundy*.[35]) Instead we will fast-forward to the (near) present, to ask what the Court has made of the doctrine. And the answer will be that it has used it to enable the creation of the Administrative State.

In 2001, in an opinion authored by Justice Scalia, the Court offered a broad overview of the law of delegation as it had evolved to that point. Unanimously the Court held, "In a delegation challenge, the constitutional question is whether the statute has delegated legislative power to the [executive] agency. Article I, § 1, of the Constitution vests '[a]ll legislative Powers herein granted . . . in a Congress of the United States.' This text permits no delegation of those powers" [Scalia's brackets and ellipsis].[36]

That was boldly stated. And yet, also echoing precedent, Scalia said that the Court has *permitted* delegations as long as Congress supplies an "intelligible principle" to guide the executive's implementation of the statute. But then, cutting to the heart of the matter, Scalia had to admit that throughout its entire history, the Court has hardly ever struck down a statute for failing to incorporate an "intelligible principle." Only twice, in fact. And both of those occasions were in 1935, before the New Deal was fully under way.[37]

In practice the Court has left Congress free to delegate its powers away, with only the sketchiest of limitations.

And Congress has done exactly that.

For example, even though the power to tax is placed first among the powers of Congress enumerated in Article I, Section 8, and even though

The Golden Mean

Like Goldilocks's porridge, delegation had to be not too hot and not too cold but just right to pass constitutional muster.

The Exceptions That Prove the Rule

"In the history of the Court we have found the requisite 'intelligible principle' lacking in only two statutes, one of which provided literally no guidance for the exercise of discretion, and the other of which conferred authority to regulate the entire economy on the basis of no more precise a standard than stimulating the economy by assuring 'fair competition.' See *Panama Refining Co.* v. *Ryan*, 293 U. S. 388 (1935); *A. L. A. Schechter Poultry Corp* v. *United States*, 295 U. S. 495 (1935)."
—Justice Antonin Scalia in *Whitman v. American Trucking Associations, Inc.*[38]

Ahead of His Time

Cole Porter wrote the lyrics to his wonderful song *Anything Goes* in 1934. As far as the delegation doctrine goes, he was just a little ahead of his time.

taxation plainly involves private rights, the Court held in the 1989 *Skinner v. Railway Labor Executives' Association* case that Congress could delegate away the power to tax.[39] A delegation from Congress permitting the attorney general to designate a drug as illegal for purposes of criminal drug enforcement if doing so was "necessary to avoid an imminent hazard to the public safety" was upheld in the 1991 *Touby v. United States* case. (This, despite the fact that Congress had left "imminence," "necessity," and "hazard" undefined.)[40] In *Lichter v. United States* (1948), the Court upheld a delegation authorizing agencies to recoup "excessive profits" made by defense contractors in wartime, even though the statute provided no metric for determining how much profit was "excessive."[41] *American Power & Light Co. v. SEC* (1946) allowed Congress to delegate to the Securities and Exchange Commission the authority to modify the structure of holding company systems to prevent them from being "unduly or unnecessarily complicate[d]" and to ensure that they do not "unfairly or inequitably distribute voting power among security holders."[42] In *New York Central Securities Corp. v. United States* (1932), the Court ruled that the Interstate Commerce Commission could exercise delegated power over railroad consolidations provided only that it acted in the "public interest."[43]

The Court's liberality in allowing delegations of Congress's legislative power has allowed the people's elected representatives to duck responsibility for making hard political choices. And unlike members of Congress, executive branch bureaucrats who essentially legislate under the name of "regulation" do not have to run for re-election and face the voters. Thus the longer-term effect of Congress's irresponsibility has been to enervate the institution and to weaken the electorate's control over the ways in which we are governed.

When Ambition Doesn't Counter Ambition

Madison and other Framers seem to have been wrong in thinking that the three branches of government would engage in unrelenting power competition, each determinedly seeking to prevent the powers that the Constitution had assigned to it from being usurped by the other branches. In *The Federalist* No. 51, Madison argued that "the great security against a gradual concentration of the several powers in the same department, consists in giving to those who administer each department, the necessary constitutional means, and personal motives, to resist encroachments of the others. . . . Ambition must be made to counteract ambition."[44] Some legal scholars have identified the flaw in Madison's reasoning as the failure to realize that an initial assignment of legal responsibilities and powers may be altered by voluntary exchanges, and that in certain circumstances (in, that is, the absence of what economists call "transactions costs") powers will therefore pass from the branch that values them less to the one that covets them more.[45] The nondelegation doctrine can be seen as a judicial device to preserve the Constitution's initial assignment of powers and to prevent Congress and the executive from engaging in such power exchanges. Unfortunately, the Court itself has been apt to shirk its own responsibility to police the other branches.

Consider this example: The Occupational Safety and Health Act of 1970 created the Occupational Safety and Health Administration and delegated power to that agency to promulgate "occupational safety and health" standards, defined as standards that are "reasonably necessary or appropriate to provide safe or healthful employment."[46] Where toxic materials and harmful physical agents are concerned, the agency must also "set the standard which most adequately assures, to the extent feasible, on the basis of the best available evidence, that no employee will suffer material impairment of health or functional capacity."[47] The statute lays down policy objectives that are in manifest tension with one another: it combines "an

A Book You're Not Supposed to Read

The Administrative State before the Supreme Court: Perspectives on the Nondelegation Doctrine edited by Peter J. Wallison and John Yoo. Washington, D.C.: AEI Press, 2022.

absolute-sounding, no-employee-left-behind goal"[48] with an apparent concern for cost considerations in its "feasibility" language. Congress provided no direction to the agency as to which priority should count for more. Key legislators had disagreed over the criteria the agency was to use in setting its safety and health standards, and instead of trying to strike the balance between more and less stringent criteria themselves, they handed the problem off to the agency with indeterminate language. "That gave every member something to crow about and left the actual policymaking to the . . . agency."[49]

After Congress had thrown the ball into its lap, the agency took the position that no "safe" exposure level to carcinogens could be determined, and that it was therefore required to set an exposure limit at the lowest technologically feasible level that would not impair the viability of the industries regulated. When the agency's position came to the Court for review in *Industrial Union Department v. American Petroleum Institute* (1980), four justices agreed with it, four disagreed with it, and only one (Justice Rehnquist) questioned the statute as an invalid delegation of power.[50]

The Court's laxity in policing Congress has led to the concentration of *all* constitutionally distinct powers in the hands of certain executive agencies—an outcome that the Framers considered the very essence of tyranny. Congress has empowered agencies to promulgate legally binding regulations with penalties for violating them attached (a lawmaking power), to enforce those regulations through legal actions (an executive power), and to have their claims adjudicated in-house by administrative law judges.[51] The principle of separation of powers has been as thoroughly eviscerated as Woodrow Wilson wished for it to be.

CHAPTER 12

Is It Too Late?

Is there any chance that the original design of the Constitution could be restored? In the foreseeable future, might the Supreme Court enforce the separation of powers principle more vigorously against the sweeping delegations of Congress's powers that have made the Administrative State possible? Some analysts have given up hope, saying that the original premises of the Constitution cannot be reinvigorated. Charles Murray of the American Enterprise Institute (AEI), for one, believes that "the Constitution's power to limit government cannot be restored." Murray agrees that "the Constitution is not altogether dead, and the Supreme Court can still make a big difference in national life." But while "a few key Supreme Court decisions" could make "significant improvements," Murray believes that the overall effect would be marginal: "It's one thing to circumscribe the continued expansion of the power of the federal government and quite another to reduce the legal limits of that power; one thing to make regulatory agencies more cautious about using their regulatory power and quite another to remove their power to make those regulations."[2]

Beyond Repair

According to Charles Murray, the "limits on the federal government have been broken in ways that cannot be mended."[1]

Murray may well be right. Under Chief Justice Roberts, Supreme Court decisions overturning major federal laws are infrequent. On average, the Roberts Court has invalidated about two acts of Congress a year—and only one notable provision of landmark federal statutes every two years. This is about the pace of the New Deal Court after 1937, when the Court took a deferential attitude in reviewing congressional legislation.[3] That is not to say that the Roberts Court has always treated major acts of Congress gently. In the 2010 *Citizens United* case, the Court struck down the prohibition in the McCain-Feingold campaign finance reform act on corporate spending for campaign advertising near an election. The Court dismantled the Defense of Marriage Act (DOMA) in two steps: in 2013, it ruled that DOMA's definition of "marriage" for purposes of federal law was invalid, and in 2015, it held that bans on same-sex marriage were unconstitutional.[4] Nonetheless, the 2012 *Sebelius* case, in which the chief justice provided the decisive fifth vote to uphold the individual-mandate provision of the Obamacare statute, seems more in character for the Roberts Court thus far.[5] To a considerable extent, Supreme Court decisions in *any* period depend for their acceptance on the underlying support of strong political coalitions; and ours is a "fractured Republic"[6] in which no recent coalition has proven to be both durable and dominant. It is questionable (at best) whether a political coalition in this country has been (or can be) formed in support of dismantling the Administrative State, or even of forcing Congress to oversee bureaucratic policy-making more diligently. Moreover, there are inevitable time lags between the emergence of new, dominating coalitions on the political scene and changes in the Court's personnel: even after Franklin Roosevelt won a landslide victory in 1932 (and an even bigger victory in 1936), it was some years before he was able to fill enough vacancies to ensure that the Court would sympathize with the New Deal program.

The Major Questions Doctrine and the Clear Statement Rule

Still, there are signs that the federal courts, and some individual Supreme Court justices, are getting restive. If the Roberts Court is willing to take any steps to dismantle the Administrative State, we would expect its first steps to be incremental and cautious. The Court is likely to prefer holding its finger to the wind to see where it is blowing than to try to bring down the entire edifice of the Administrative State in a few swift strokes.[7] The Court's decision in *West Virginia v. EPA*—written by Chief Justice Roberts and handed down on the last day of the momentous 2021–2022 term—signals that that is exactly what the Court is most likely to do. And even before *West Virginia*, the Roberts Court had taken some cautious steps, in a pair of cases concerning the "independent" agencies, to bring the Administrative State into alignment with the Constitution.[8]

West Virginia blocked the EPA's effort to leverage its statutory authority to limit pollution produced by single power plants into wholesale control over the nation's entire electric grid. The decision stalled the Biden administration's aggressive plan to drive the nation toward unreliable renewable energy sources in the name of combating global warming.[9] The Court's new conservative majority took a step in arresting—but not reversing—the apparently inexorable growth of the Administrative State. The decision marks a rare victory in the long war to restore accountability and transparency to the exercise of power by the bureaucracy. But other victories in battle will be needed if the war is to be won.

West Virginia v. EPA raised fundamental questions about the power of federal agencies. Could the bureaucracy reinterpret a vague fifty-year-old statute to authorize sweeping new powers over large sectors of the economy, ones that Congress could not have imagined when it first wrote the law? The Clean Air Act undoubtedly gives the EPA power to limit pollution from single power plants. But the EPA attempted to read the law to allow it to regulate the air pollution from the entire electrical grid. Congress itself has repeatedly declined to enact a nationwide system of controls on the pollution that may be contributing to global warming. In 2009 and 2010, Congress even rejected plans very similar to the one at issue in *West Virginia*, despite sizeable Democrat majorities in both houses.

Despite these setbacks in Congress, the Obama administration EPA was determined to force a fundamental transition in the way the nation's electricity was produced. It first envisaged a shift in electricity production from higher-emitting coal plants to lower-emitting natural gas plants. Then it required another shift to renewables, chiefly wind and solar power. EPA's plan required an electricity producer to reduce or cease its own production from coal plants, build or invest in lower-emitting plants, or buy emissions allowances or credits through a cap-and-trade regime. The EPA was mandating a switch to zero-carbon renewable-energy sources that would force coal and gas plants to cease operating altogether. Coal would fall from 38 percent of electricity generation to 27 percent by 2030. Dozens of power plants would be shuttered by 2025, and tens of thousands of jobs would be eliminated. By some estimates, the EPA's plan would raise the price of electricity to consumers by over $200 billion and reduce the gross domestic product "by at least a trillion 2009 dollars by 2040."[10]

It can be argued that the plan was nonetheless good public policy, despite its heavy costs. But the question before the Court was not how best to save the planet from global warming or what costs were acceptable to achieve that goal. The question for the Court was whether the EPA had tried to escape the legal guard rails that limit its actions. And the Court ruled that Congress, not the EPA, should make a policy decision with such massive consequences. It rejected the EPA's core argument that Congress had delegated that power to the agency in the 1970s in an obscure and little-used "gap-filler provision" of the Clean Air Act. Instead, the Court invoked "the major questions doctrine" to require that Congress "speak clearly if it wishes to assign to an agency decisions of vast economic and political significance."[11]

The Court decided against the EPA on the basis *not* of a revived delegation doctrine, but of what it called the "major questions doctrine"—on which the Court relied three times in the 2021–2022 term to set aside regulatory actions. The first was an unwarranted extension of the COVID eviction moratorium by the Centers for Disease Control.[12] The second was a vaccination mandate imposed on much of the workforce by the Occupational Safety and Health Administration.[13] The EPA's generation transition plan was the third, and it got the fullest treatment from the Court.[14]

The major questions doctrine was not newly minted. The Court had in effect applied it over two decades before to rein in the Food and Drug Administration, which had claimed that its statutory authority over "drugs" and "devices" gave it the power to regulate or even ban tobacco products,[15] and again in 2006, to deny that Congress had authorized the attorney general to rescind the licenses of physicians who prescribed controlled drugs for assisted suicides even in states where such prescriptions were legal.[16] A variant of the major questions doctrine appeared also in the 2006 *Rapanos* case, where the Court (in a plurality opinion by Justice Scalia) rejected the Army Corps of Engineers' expansive interpretation of key terms in the Clean Water Act, saying that "we ordinarily expect a 'clear and manifest' statement from Congress to authorize an unprecedented intrusion into traditional state authority." In that case federalism rather than separation of powers provided the constitutional underpinning for the rule.[17]

"Chief Justice Roberts Delivered the Opinion of the Court"

In *West Virginia*, unfortunately, the Chief Justice's majority opinion did a poor job of explaining the basis of the major questions doctrine and when it will apply. Roberts gave little guidance for lower courts, insisting that the doctrine is limited to "exceptional" or "extraordinary" cases—without explaining *why* it should be so limited.[18] Perhaps Roberts meant to say that the doctrine would apply only to *new* administrative mandates, rather than to those that were promulgated years ago. Past overreaching by the executive agencies would thus be "grandfathered" in.

Roberts also did not explain the constitutional underpinnings of the major questions doctrine. He seemed to characterize the doctrine as consisting of an assortment of clues culled from a selection of Court precedents that should inform the judiciary's interpretation of statutes. He added that applying the doctrine called for "a practical understanding of legislative intent." But apart from a single reference to "separation of powers principles," Roberts did nothing to illuminate the doctrine's constitutional foundations or otherwise to provide a coherent rationale for it.[19] The doctrine could possibly flow from any of several sources: enforcement of the Administrative Procedure Act, which sets general procedural rules for agency actions and regulations; rules of construction for vague statutes; or a broader agenda to limit the unknowing delegation of lawmaking power.

Roberts ultimately compressed the major questions doctrine into a single, basic test: Is the defendant agency "asserting [a] highly consequential power beyond what Congress could *reasonably* be understood to have granted?"[20] This formulation invites uncertainty and dispute, however. Lower courts, agencies, and Congress simply may not know what the Supreme Court expects of them. And Roberts's flexible standard may also encourage the justices to indulge their ideological preferences in future cases: conservative justices may be prone to apply it against environmental regulations, liberal justices, not so much. Finally, judges have incentives not to challenge outcomes that both the political branches find satisfactory, and both Congress and the executive branch may be content to allow agencies to take major but controversial policy choices out of their hands. Given the judicial temptation to accept inter-branch arrangements, the major questions doctrine as Roberts articulated it may prove to be a speed bump, not a traffic light, for delegations of congressional power.

Roberts's failure to root the major questions doctrine firmly in constitutional soil indicates that it is a stopgap and nothing more. Roberts was prescribing a palliative for a cancer that is eating away at the constitutional separation of powers. The major questions doctrine may slow down metastasis of the Administrative State. But without any deeper grounding in the Constitution, it cannot stop it.

To illustrate—the major questions doctrine has a corollary called the "clear statement rule." Under that rule, the Court requires Congress to provide a clear statement of its intent before the Court will take Congress to have authorized the agency to make major policy decisions. Roberts explains the clear statement rule by saying that the Court *presumes* that Congress intends to make major policy decisions by itself. Thus, he would presume that the "basic and consequential tradeoffs" that the EPA had sought to make were in fact ones that "Congress *would likely*" have reserved to itself. He concludes that a "decision of such magnitude and consequence [as the nationwide transition away from coal as a source of electricity] rests with Congress itself, *or an agency acting pursuant to a clear delegation from that representative body*" [emphases added].[21]

The problem, of course, is that the clear statement rule does not *bar* Congress from delegating away its powers. The clear statement rule at best flashes a yellow light to Congress, not a red one. Congress can delegate away its powers without hindrance, provided only that it does so in plain terms. Suppose Congress enacted a law saying, "We delegate *all* policy decisions concerning the environment—and we really mean *all*—to the EPA." In Roberts's view, that delegation would stand, even if the major questions doctrine applied. Congress could hardly have spoken more clearly.

"Gorsuch, J., Concurring"

In contrast to Roberts's opinion for the majority, Justice Gorsuch's concurring opinion provides ample intellectual firepower for the campaign against the Administrative State.

Justice Gorsuch is the Court's leading revolutionary on administrative law. His 2019 *Gundy* dissent set out the original meaning of the separation of powers, explained the purpose of vesting federal lawmaking power exclusively in Congress, delineated the traditional limits on legislative authority to delegate to the executive, and described the rise of the Administrative State during the Progressive Era, the New Deal, and the 1970s. Gorsuch also observed in *Gundy* that "enforcing the Constitution's demands [does not] spell doom for . . . the 'administrative state,'" nor drive "any particular policy outcome, let alone dictate any conclusion about the proper size and scope of government." Separation of powers is "a procedural guarantee that requires Congress to assemble a social consensus before choosing our nation's course on policy questions."[22]

Gorsuch lowered his sights in *West Virginia.* There he was primarily concerned with answering three questions: (1) the constitutional basis for the "major questions doctrine" and its corollary "clear statement rule"; (2) the circumstances likely to trigger the application of the doctrine; and (3) the "clear congressional statement" needed to authorize agency action.

Gorsuch argued that the clear statement rule presupposes that "Congress means for its laws to operate in congruence with the Constitution rather than test its bounds."[23] Here the bounds are those set by the Article I Vesting Clause. Following *Wayman v. Southard,*[24] Gorsuch interprets the Vesting Clause to deny Congress the power to divest itself of the responsibility for making important policy decisions. Under the Court's current Commerce Clause jurisprudence, Congress could have enacted the EPA's plan itself or a similar national cap-and-trade scheme. But it could not have delegated the power to make that policy to an executive agency, at least without entering constitutionally problematic territory. The EPA, Gorsuch reasons, would have to show that Congress in fact did grant it the relevant authority to make the policy. And that requires a clear and specific statement by Congress.

What, specifically, triggers the need for the agency to show a clear statement? Drawing on the Court's case law, Gorsuch identified three situations where that need can arise (though he suggests that there may be others): First, when the challenged agency rule or mandate seeks to resolve a matter of great political significance or of national debate (such as in the case of the vaccine mandates). Second, when the agency is seeking to regulate "a significant portion of the American economy" or requires the private sector to spend billions of dollars. Third, when the agency is trenching on the structural constitutional principle of federalism by attempting to regulate in an area traditionally reserved to the States. Gorsuch had no difficulty proving that all three of these signs of a "major question"—along with other "suggestive factors"—were present in the case of the EPA's plan.

Gorsuch also described the features of a clear statement. He helpfully identified four tests. First, courts should look at the structure of the statute and the place in that structure of the provision on which the agency relies. A "gap-filler" provision like the one cited by EPA will likely not do. Second, courts should consider the age and focus of the statute. If the agency is attempting to address a novel problem (climate change) on the basis of a fifty-year-old statute (the Clean Air Act), then again it will likely come up short. Third, the courts should examine the agency's own interpretation of the statute in the past. If its challenged interpretation marks a significant departure from the past, then again it is unlikely that Congress authorized the agency action. Finally, courts should ask whether there is "a mismatch between the agency's challenged action and its congressionally assigned mission and expertise"—as there was when the Centers for Disease Control, a public health agency, incongruously sought to regulate landlord-tenant relations.[25]

Gorsuch's analysis brought the far-reaching implications of the major questions doctrine into clearer focus. While Roberts obscured the potential for conflict between the separation of powers and the broad congressional delegations characteristic of the Administrative State, Gorsuch's concurrence prepares for the battle. Gorsuch's opinion does not limit the major questions doctrine to statutory grants of authority of an older vintage, to vague or unclear laws, or to regulations that deviate from past agency practices or interpretations. In his view *any* statute, including the Clean Air Act, will be constitutionally problematic if it purports to grant significant discretion to an agency, and *any* major agency policy reliant on that discretion will be under a constitutional cloud. The "clear statement" rule is simply a judicial device for defusing the potential constitutional conflict in a limited set of cases. But the deeper conflict between Article I and congressional delegation looms on the horizon.

A Constitution of Necessity

Progressive critics of the *West Virginia* decision were loud and vociferous. Their condemnation of the Court was laden with doomsday predictions—as if the Court, not Congress, were supposed to be making climate change policy. As we were writing this chapter, some progressives were urging President Biden to declare a climate "emergency" to take measures to reduce carbon emissions.[26] On the more recognizably jurisprudential side, the criticisms of the decision recapitulated the "living constitution" themes that progressives had been promoting since Woodrow Wilson wrote them up in in the 1880s.[27]

Like Woodrow Wilson, the Court's progressive critics believe in a "Constitution of Necessity." If there is a pressing political or economic problem that Congress fails to resolve, then, they assume, the necessity for action falls to the president and the executive agencies. And since Congress drags its heels on so many urgent problems—immigration reform and global warming among them—it is imperative for the executive branch to act unilaterally.

On the Sidelines

Congress is often content to pass the buck. It prefers to play the part of a Greek chorus and let the president be Oedipus.

Progressives nowadays are quite unabashed about their belief that "necessity" justifies them in bypassing Congress—even more unabashed than Wilson dared to be. After the Democratic Party lost control of Congress in the 2010 midterm elections, President Obama revealed his support for a Constitution of Necessity that would enable him to act without, or in defiance of, Congress. He pledged in October 2011 to "do everything in my power right now to act on behalf of the American people with or without Congress. We can't wait for Congress to do its job. So where they won't act, I will."[28] In the manner that Wilson had prescribed for a president who was to be the nation's "Leader," Obama was appealing to (what he supposed to be) the will of the people to justify bypassing the awkward and inconvenient Article I lawmaking process. The EPA's proposed regime for the nation's electric power production—eventually the subject of *West Virginia v. EPA*—was originally one of these unilateral acts by Obama, based on his claim that "we can't wait." Obama was channeling Wilson's contention in 1891 that "*Administration cannot wait upon legislation,* but must be given leave, or take it, to proceed without specific warrant in giving effect to the characteristic life of the State."[29]

Supreme Confidence

"My fellow Americans, I am confident we will succeed in this mission because we are on the right side of history." —Barack Obama in 2015[30]

And it is not only presidents but justices of the Supreme Court who channel Wilson's Progressive ideas. Like Wilson, these justices assume that members of Congress are simply not competent to deal with urgent contemporary

No Kind of Government for a Free People

Whether championed by Wilson or Obama, Blackmun or Kagan, the Progressives' Constitution of Necessity is not a government for a free people. Today's feverish controversies over voting rights and election rules make little sense if the only important question up for grabs in federal elections is the choice of a presidential "Leader" and a Congress that merely "oversees" the bureaucracy. The president himself has a shaky hold on the bureaucracy, as every president since Harry Truman has found. The Constitution of Necessity is fit to govern what the French call "the administered," not a polity of *citizens*. Whatever else it is, it is not the Republic that the Founders left us.

problems. Justice Kagan wrote for the dissent in *West Virginia* that "Members of Congress often don't know enough . . . to regulate sensibly on an issue."[31] Justice Harry Blackmun, writing in the 1989 *Mistretta* case, opined that "in our increasingly complex society . . . Congress simply cannot do its job absent an ability to delegate power under broad general directives."[32] A deep aversion to democratic politics, coupled with a naïve faith in purportedly unpolitical "experts," is coded into the DNA of the Progressive ideology.

Recall that Woodrow Wilson maintained that "administration" was best entrusted to neutral, apolitical "experts," while the president was to concern himself with the "politics" of "Leadership." During the first half of the twentieth century, this conception led to the creation of several major "independent" agencies. These were entities formally located within the executive but whose heads (typically, collective boards of five to seven members, rather than single individuals) were to be insulated from "politics." Their independence was to be ensured by placing restrictions on the president's power to remove their heads from office. Typically, for example, Congress barred the president from removing the heads of such agencies except "for cause," such as inefficiency, incapacity, malfeasance in office, or neglect of duty.

Undistracted by the fear that a president might remove him or her for refusing to implement White House policies, the agency head would be able to act on his or her own independent, "expert" judgment. Though not life-tenured, heads of independent agencies would be sheltered from the gusts and squalls of presidential politics. Several of the most important early independent agencies were established in the Wilson and FDR administrations, including the Federal Reserve System (1913), the Federal Trade Commission (1914), the Federal Communications Commission (1934), the Securities and Exchange Commission (1934) and the National Labor Relations Board (1935). Congress thereafter continued to establish new independent agencies such as the Environmental Protection Agency (1970) and the Consumer Financial Protection Bureau (2010).

Precedents Distinguished, Not Overruled

In *Humphrey's Executor* (1935), the Supreme Court upheld the constitutionality of the Federal Trade Commission against a challenge brought by the Roosevelt administration. Roosevelt had discharged Humphrey, an FTC commissioner, despite statutory restrictions on the president's removal power. After Humphrey's death, his executor sued for back pay, charging that Humphrey's dismissal had violated the statute's tenure protections. The Court sided with the executor, relying on a rationale that captured the essence of Wilsonian thinking about the Administrative State: "The commission is to be non-partisan; and it must, from the very nature of its duties, act with entire impartiality. It is charged with the enforcement of no policy except the policy of the law. Its duties are neither political nor executive, but predominantly quasi-judicial and quasi-legislative. . . . Its members are called upon to exercise the trained judgment of a body of experts 'appointed by law and informed by experience.'"[33]

In practical terms, the Court concluded, if Congress could create agencies furnished with the power to make and enforce regulations that had the effect of law, that could frustrate the president in implementing the policies that the voters had elected him to pursue. Decisions made by a "trained judgment of a body of [unelected] experts," some of whom might have been appointed by the president's predecessors in office, could prevail over the policy choices of an incumbent president who had stood before the voters and might well do so again. There might be certain advantages in maintaining continuity from one administration to another in an agency's priorities and policies, but the voters also might have elected a new president precisely to *disrupt* existing policies.

Apart from practical questions, there was a deeper constitutional issue. Could Congress impede the president from removing officials who headed up federal agencies without violating separation of powers? Would not such obstacles interfere with the president's constitutional authority to execute the law? Vigorous debates over the president's removal power had flared up on two major occasions in the country's history: once in the first Congress in 1789, when no fewer than four different views about the removal power emerged, and then again when President Andrew Johnson was impeached (though not removed from office) for suspending Edwin Stanton, his secretary of war, in defiance of the 1867 Tenure of Office Act. These debates echo still.

Although the Constitution speaks to the power to appoint high-ranking executive officials, it is not explicit (except for in the Impeachment Clauses) in addressing their removal. This ambiguity gave rise to the controversy in 1789, when the first Congress began organizing the government. One view was that the silence of the Constitution on this issue meant that high executive officials were simply not removable except through impeachment. A second view was that they could only be removed through the same process by which they had been appointed, which in the case of cabinet officers was by the joint action of the president and Senate. A third view was that since Congress had the power to create executive offices, it also had the power to define the tenure of offices and the modes of removal from them. The fourth view, espoused by James Madison, was that the president had the sole authority to remove high-ranking executive officials at will.

There is much to be said for Madison's view. For one thing, in the English Constitution as explained by Blackstone, the king had the removal power (except as to judges and certain municipal officers), and the conception of the president's executive power laid out in the U.S. Constitution was derived to a great extent from the English model. The power to remove, therefore, could be found to have a textual basis in the Vesting Clause of Article II, which places the "executive power" exclusively in the president. Madison argued that "if any power whatever is in its nature executive, it is the power of appointing, overseeing, and controlling those who execute the laws." And to "control," Madison contended, the president had to be able to "displac[e]."[34] Moreover, the text of Article II also charges the president with the duty to execute the laws faithfully. Fisher Ames, a leading Federalist member of the first Congress, staked the defense of presidential removal power on that clause: "The President is required to see the laws faithfully executed. He cannot do this without he has a control over officers appointed to aid him in the performance of his duty. Take this power out of his hands, and . . . you virtually destroy his responsibility."[35]

Arguments like Madison's and Ames's persuaded the Supreme Court in the 1926 case of *Myers v. United States*. The Court's opinion was written by William Howard Taft, who enjoys the unique distinction of having been president before becoming chief justice.[36]

When the Court came down with *Humphrey's Executor* only nine years later, it did not *overrule Myers*, but it certainly swerved from the course set by that decision. *Humphrey's Executor* green-lighted the creation of additional independent agencies, with the effects that Madison and Ames had foreseen: the president's power under Article II's Vesting Clause was drained off, and his ability to discharge his duty to execute the laws faithfully was impaired.

In the 1988 *Morrison v. Olson* case, the Court affirmed that legislative restrictions on the president's power to remove an "independent" prosecutor from office were permissible when the prosecutor had a limited jurisdiction, a relatively short tenure, and no policy-making or significant administrative authority. Even though the investigation and prosecution of federal crimes lie at the very core of presidential powers and duties, the Court reasoned that an officer operating within the limits defined by Congress was not "so central to the functioning of the Executive Branch" as to require that that officer be "terminable at will by the President."[37] Justice Scalia issued a powerful but solitary dissent in *Morrison*, an opinion that has rightly come to be regarded as a classic, that has increasingly been woven into the law and that enjoys bipartisan approval.[38] Also of note, however, is the fact that the majority opinion in *Morrison* itself had taken down key load-bearing parts of *Humphrey's Executor*—notably its attempt to find a new type of governmental power that was neither legislative nor "purely" executive nor judicial, and to situate the Federal Trade Commission within that previously unknown category.[39]

The Roberts Court has begun to unwind the legal structure erected by *Humphrey's Executor*, restoring to the presidency the power that Madison and Ames argued it possessed. In doing so, it has chipped away at the foundations of the Administrative State. "Politics" has been allowed to reoccupy some of the ground that had been ceded to "administration." Two other cases mark this trend: *Free Enterprise Fund v. Public Company Accounting Oversight Board* (2010) and *Seila Law LLC v. Consumer Financial Protection Bureau* (2020). Both opinions for the Court were written by Chief Justice Roberts and both are signature examples of his judicial style.

The Roberts Court did not overrule *Humphrey's Executor* in either of these decisions, though Justice Thomas urged it to do so. Instead it chose to marginalize *Humphrey* (and *Morrison*) by, in effect, confining them to their special facts. In *Seila Law*, for instance, Roberts said that the Court was being asked to extend those precedents to "a new configuration: an independent agency that wields significant executive power and is run by a single [tenure-protected] individual," but it refused to take that extra step.

Rather, the Court distinguished and limited the scope of *Humphrey's Executor* by saying that that case had dealt with a traditional independent agency headed by a multimember board, not with one under the leadership of a single director.[40] The rationale of *Free Enterprise* was much the same: rather than overturning its precedents, the Court again preferred to narrow them by saying that it was confronted with "a new situation" in which an official was "protected by two layers of for-cause removal."[41] In *Seila Law*, it read *Humphrey's Executor* merely to have "permitted Congress to give for-cause removal protections to a multimember body of experts, balanced along partisan lines, that performed legislative and judicial functions and was said not to exercise any executive power."[42] This was somewhat (but only somewhat) better than saying that the crucial distinction was that *Humphrey's Executor* had been decided on a Tuesday, while *Free Enterprise* had been decided on a Wednesday and *Seila Law* on a Thursday. But its ostensibly conciliatory and disarming approach to precedent served the Court's purposes in two ways. First, it avoided the inevitable controversy that would have ensued if the Court had openly and honestly overruled *Humphrey's Executor* instead of merely disemboweling it. Second, it signaled to Congress that it would not tolerate the creation of new independent agencies that differed by even a jot or tittle from the template it had approved in 1935. Even if a new agency were a mere clone of the FTC, *Morrison v. Olson*'s rejection of *Humphrey*'s conception of "purely executive power" could be brought to bear against it.

The Court pared *Morrison* back as well. Unlike *Humphrey's Executor*, *Morrison* had not involved a multimember board, but only a single officer: the independent counsel. To slip through this difficulty, the Court emphasized that the independent counsel was merely an "inferior officer" in a constitutional sense—an officer who could be appointed by executive or judicial officials without need for Senate confirmation, whose duties were limited, and whose policy-making power and administrative authority were not significant. Bluntly, this was to say that the independent counsel was more like a career civil servant working in a U.S. attorney's office than like a Senate-confirmed U.S. attorney. Whether that was a fair description of the special counsel, it served the Court's purpose, signaling that the Court would view removal restrictions on "principal" or high-ranking executive officers (especially those who head agencies and whose appointments require Senate confirmation) much more skeptically.

If in these two cases the Court has drawn a line in the sand against new independent agencies, where does that leave the older established ones? Would a constitutional challenge to the Federal Reserve, the SEC, or the EPA prevail? On the reasoning of *Free Enterprise* and *Seila Law*, the answer ought to be yes. Those opinions endorsed a Madisonian understanding of the executive power—and hence of the president's removal authority. They reinvigorated *Myers*. And they stripped down the two key precedents in support of the constitutionality of independent agencies to the bare bones. Essentially nothing was left standing of either *Humphrey's Executor* or *Morrison*.

But the Court still left them on the books.

So will the Court extend its recent removal decisions to the older independent agencies? To borrow from the legendary movie mogul Sam Goldwyn, "We can give you a definite maybe." Perhaps a cautious Roberts Court is just testing the waters to see how far it can go before it encounters (what it would consider to be) unacceptable political pushback. Or perhaps it will follow the more intrepid course suggested by Justice Thomas. We shall see.

PART V

In Conclusion

CHAPTER 13

Looking Ahead

Our politically incorrect tour has explored the Supreme Court's past and present. From the earliest days of the American Republic, the justices have had to reconcile the Court's awesome power to overturn the decisions of the president, the Congress, and the states with the democratic basis of the Constitution. Allowing a majority of five justices to block a majority of 330 million Americans raises profound problems for popular self-government. On the other hand, the American people have chosen, through a process of constitutional ratification and amendment, to place beyond the reach of majorities certain individual rights and the structures of the separation of powers and federalism. The Court has had to strike a balance between the Constitution and popular government; it has often erred. The challenge facing the Roberts Court in the years ahead asks it to reconcile its new vision of the Constitution with popular self-government.

A Turning Point

The 2021–2022 term was a turning point in the Roberts Court's jurisprudence. *Dobbs* marked the end of the Warren Court's era of activism. The overruling of *Roe v. Wade* concluded the fifty-year struggle over the Warren Court's non-textual approach to constitutional interpretation and its expansion of an unenumerated "right to privacy." It is no mistake that *Dobbs* relied heavily on Chief Justice Rehnquist's analysis in *Washington v. Glucksberg* (1997), which had denied a right to euthanasia based on the constitutional text, its original understanding, and subsequent historical practice.[1]

If *Dobbs* defined the Roberts Court's treatment of the past, *Bruen* expressed its present. In *Bruen*, the Roberts Court went where no Court before had gone on gun rights. In *Heller* and *McDonald*, the Court had identified a right to possess firearms under the Second Amendment despite the possibility that it might apply only to state militias, not individuals. But it was not until *Bruen* that the Court made clear that it would vigorously protect the individual right to bear arms as part of a broader individual right to self-defense. The Court would no longer treat the Second Amendment as a second-class right but would put the right to bear arms on a par with other core liberties such as freedom of speech. It would require the government to prove it has a compelling reason to limit a constitutional right, rather than require Americans to explain why the government should allow them the freedom to exercise that right. Just as the Court does not allow utilitarian considerations to override freedom of speech, it will not permit policy consequences alone to restrict the right to gun ownership. *Bruen* announced that the Roberts Court intends to be as energetic as its predecessors in the protection of individual rights—once it agrees that that the constitutional text indeed establishes the right.[2]

If *Dobbs* marks the Roberts Court's past, and *Bruen* its present, *West Virginia v. EPA* hints at its future. Both *Dobbs* and *Bruen* addressed the fundamental conflict between majority rule and minority rights that has driven constitutional law since *Brown v. Board of Education*, if not before. This struggle is not new: the great majority of the Court's constitutional law cases involve the scope of individual rights. *West Virginia* announces a new object of the Supreme Court's attention—the structure of government. In the original constitutional structure, individual rights came second; separation of powers and federalism came first. Naturally the Framers thought first of the internal workings of their new national government, before they devised its external limits. They established a Spartan system in which each of three branches would perform specialized functions suited to its design. A large Congress of representatives would deliberate and devise policy in generally applicable rules. An executive headed by a single president would enforce the laws and protect the national security. A hierarchical judiciary would interpret the laws in the course of resolving legal cases and controversies. The Founders expected that states would continue as the primary makers and enforces of law and order, with the federal government intervening on discrete specialized subjects.

But the innovations of the Progressive and New Deal Eras overlaid a different vision upon the Founders' design. The Progressive vision transferred lawmaking power from political legislatures to agencies whose expert officials were insulated from political control and whose decisions were unreviewable by the courts. The Roberts Court has already invalidated the provisions insulating the leaders of these agencies from direct presidential control.[3] These recent Supreme Court decisions allow a chief executive, elected by and responsible to the American people, to advance a coherent agenda across the entire executive branch. In *West Virginia v. EPA*, the justices began to correct the Administrative State's next distortion of the constitutional structure: while the major questions doctrine does not insert courts into reviewing every delegation of lawmaking authority from Congress to the president, it does bar future delegations on questions of major economic or social importance without a clear statement of congressional intent. If Congress wishes the executive branch to re-engineer the economy out of concern over global warming, or if it wants agencies to impose environmental, social, and governance rules upon businesses and even individuals, it must say so in the text of the law. Agencies will no longer have the freedom to invoke broad powers out of vague statutes, and Congress will no longer have the ability to escape political responsibility for these decisions.

A New Direction

The major questions doctrine signals the Roberts Court's agenda of policing the rampant delegation of legislative power to the agencies that has accelerated the growth of the Administrative State. Not only is the Roberts Court revising the New Deal settlement, which allowed the growth of administrative government after the ill-fated confrontation between FDR and the Hughes Court, it is also turning its back on past conservative jurisprudence. The Burger and Rehnquist Courts, led by justices appointed by conservative Republican presidents, developed the doctrines that liberated the agencies to exercise power so freely under the new social and economic laws of the 1960s and 1970s. Chief Justice Rehnquist, for example, wrote the majority opinion in *Morrison v. Olson* (1988), which reaffirmed that Congress could vest agency heads with independence from presidential control if the public interest demanded it.[4] Justice Scalia wrote the majority opinion in *Whitman v. American Trucking Associations, Inc.* (2001), which refused to place substantive limits on the power that Congress could transfer to the EPA.[5] Justice Stevens's opinion in *Chevron, U.S.A., Inc. v. National Resources Defense Council, Inc.* (1984), which required all federal courts to defer to an agency's interpretation of vague statutes that Congress had charged the agency with administering so long as they were reasonable, was for a unanimous Court.[6]

Chevron, which the Rehnquist and Roberts Courts have never overruled but also have not applied consistently, allows agencies to read vague statutes to expand their own powers with few restraints. *Chevron*'s defenders have included Justice Scalia, who argued that when a statutory ambiguity results from congressional intent to leave the resolution of a question to an agency, the only question for the courts was whether the agency's resolution was reasonable.[7] Scalia's successor, Justice Gorsuch, has been highly critical of *Chevron*. As a lower court judge, he argued that *Chevron* "permit[s] executive bureaucracies to swallow huge amounts of core judicial and legislative power and concentrate federal power in a way that seems more than a little difficult to square with the Constitution of the framers' design."[8] Justice Thomas has also criticized *Chevron.* In his concurring opinion in *Michigan v. EPA* (2015), Thomas declared that the case "wrests from Courts the ultimate interpretative authority to 'say what the law is.'"[9] Taming the Administrative State will require the Court's new conservative majority to turn aside past precedent and bring new thinking to bear on old problems.

A similar tension between new approaches and past precedent may arise in several other important areas long neglected by the Court. In addition to the creation of the independent agencies of the Administrative State, the New Deal settlement has also allowed the practically limitless exercise of power from Washington, D.C. After FDR's failed Court-packing plan and the retirement of four justices who had opposed the New Deal, the Court allowed the federal government to draw more and more of daily life into its grasp. Under the Interstate Commerce Clause, Congress placed under federal control most economic activity in the nation. Federal agencies, for example, regulate all factories and offices in the country, set minimum wages and maximum hours, and dictate most working conditions. They set the rules for the buying and selling of most products, the terms for most investments, and the provision of most information on the internet, networks, and communication services. The government's regulatory reach extends beyond purely economic issues to the environment, matters of racial and social justice, and crime. For most of the twentieth century, the Supreme Court allowed Congress, under the Interstate Commerce Clause, to exercise authority to regulate society with few limits.

Congress has also been allowed to extend its control not just through direct command, but through indirect persuasion—by using taxes and spending to create incentives for the states to follow federal policy. Although the government cannot command individuals to buy houses or have larger families, it can provide financial subsidies to encourage these goals. Even when the Court has held that the government cannot force all Americans to purchase a health insurance policy, it has allowed the government to tax the recalcitrant and subsidize the compliant.[10] After the New Deal confrontation between the Court and FDR, the Court allowed Congress to use the power of the purse with little restraint. Today, Congress advances its policies for health care, retirement and old age, education, transportation, and housing through a mixture of grants, taxes, and subsidies, rather than direct regulation.

For decades the courts deferred to the elected branches in identifying the limits of federal power. According to some justices and scholars, if the states were concerned that Congress was exceeding its enumerated authority, they could exercise their influence through the Senate—where states receive an equal representation.[11] In its later years, the Rehnquist Court began to move away from reliance on such political safeguards of federalism and to identify substantive limits on the Commerce Clause, though not in any case involving legislation of significance. It was only when the Roberts Court encountered the Affordable Care Act, popularly known as Obamacare, in *National Federation of Independent Business v. Sebelius* (2012) that the justices struck down a congressional claim to authority on the basis of the Commerce Clause on an issue of true national importance. But even as it prohibited Congress from commanding every adult American to purchase health insurance, it still allowed Congress to impose a tax penalty on everyone who refused.[12]

Overrule This! (A Supreme Court Wish List)

If the Roberts Court is to press forward its campaign to resurrect a true balance between federal and state power, it will have to undo past decisions. Earlier efforts to limit the Commerce Clause solely to commercial activity will place few obstacles in Congress's way. It remains far too easy to claim an economic motive for most human activities. Take the current push to overrule *Dobbs* and restore the rule of *Roe v. Wade* nationwide. Congress could claim that it is not creating abortion rights per se, but only regulating the safety of medical procedures, over which it has power because of the interstate market in health care. Federal resources gathered through the income and corporate taxes might be spent to make an end around that evades the limits on direct regulation. In order to restrict federal power to the boundaries originally laid out by the Framers, the Court will have to carefully identify the subjects and institutions that remain under the control of the states and those that fall within national competence. This will require the Court to overturn past precedents that still give Congress broad discretion to regulate anything that has a minimal economic character.

The Roberts Court's new conservative majority has displayed an interest in restoring all constitutional rights to an equal status. This motive seems to have moved the justices to their conclusion in *Bruen*. The Second Amendment presumptively protects an individual right to keep and bear arms, and government must justify its gun control regulation as consistent with historical tradition, Justice Thomas wrote for the Court, because that is "how we protect other constitutional rights." Again, "The constitutional right to bear arms in public for self-defense is not 'a second-class right, subject to an entirely different body of rules than the other Bill of Rights guarantees,'" he observed. In its conclusion *Bruen* made clear that constitutional rights must exist on an equal plane: "We know of no other constitutional right that an individual may exercise only after demonstrating to government officers some special need. That is not how the First Amendment works when it comes to unpopular speech or the free exercise of religion. It is not how the Sixth Amendment works when it comes to a defendant's right to confront the witnesses against him. And it is not how the Second Amendment works when it comes to public carry for self-defense."[13]

Equal Rights

If the constitutional text recognizes a right, the Court made clear, the government must prove why it has any legitimate need to restrict it. This will be true whether the right involves speech or guns.

The Second Amendment is not the only right for which, it is to be hoped, the Court will reject precedent in favor of treating rights equally. Perhaps the most salient area of interest in 2023 will be race-based affirmative action. In two cases argued in fall 2022, with decisions expected by summer 2023, the Court will examine whether universities that are run by states or that receive federal funding can consider race when admitting students. The Court has long read the Equal Protection Clause to prohibit the use of race except when advancing a compelling government interest and employing the narrowest means possible—a legal standard known as strict scrutiny. Virtually no government policies have survived strict scrutiny in its original sense. Although the notorious *Korematsu* case approved the World War II use of race to justify internment of loyal Japanese American citizens,[14] the Roberts Court recently disavowed *Korematsu* in *Trump v. Hawaii*.[15] The major area that remains where the government can use race is in college and university admissions. In *Regents of the University of California v. Bakke* (1978), *Grutter v. Bollinger* (2003), and *Fisher v. University of Texas* (2016), the Supreme Court allowed school administrators to consider race on the ground that ethnic diversity would promote the ideological diversity necessary for a successful education.[16] This anomaly makes no sense: compare the many areas where the government might use race for public health and safety reasons—in wartime or law enforcement, for example—but cannot. In order to render uniform the operation of constitutional rights with regard to race, the Roberts Court will likely remove the exception from strict scrutiny for affirmative action in college admissions. But it will have to overrule thirty-five years of precedent to do it.

Another area where the Roberts Court has pointed a more skeptical eye at the government is religion. In 2022 the Court struck down several state policies that interfered with the freedom of religion. *Carson v. Makin* held that Maine could not provide tuition for families to use at high schools but then prohibit religious schools from participating in the program.[17] In *Kennedy v. Bremerton School District*, the Court found that a high school could not prohibit a football coach from praying privately at the end of the game, even if students joined him.[18] *Shurtleff v. City of Boston* struck down Boston's refusal to fly a Christian flag in front of city hall when it allowed secular groups to fly their own flags.[20] These cases continued a series of Roberts Court decisions that have required government to treat religious organizations equally with secular groups. Justice Gorsuch explained for a 6–3 majority in *Kennedy* that the state could not "ferret out and suppress religious observances even as it allows comparable secular speech." *Kennedy* explicitly overruled *Lemon v. Kurtzman* (1971), which had forbidden the government from aiding religious groups if a reasonable observer would believe the state had endorsed religion.[21]

"Like some ghoul in a late-night horror movie that repeatedly sits up in its grave and shuffles abroad, after being repeatedly killed and buried, *Lemon* stalks our Establishment Clause jurisprudence once again, frightening the little children and school attorneys of Center Moriches Union Free School District." —Justice Scalia, comparing the long-lingering (but now finally overruled) precedent to a zombie that keeps rising from the dead[19]

The Roberts Court may also shed some of the traditional skepticism of conversative jurisprudence towards unenumerated rights, particularly the rights of parents to supervise the education of their children. The last two years have seen bitter struggles between public school bureaucracies and angry parents over such issues. Originalist jurisprudence by no means prevents the recognition of unenumerated parental rights, and there are sturdy early-twentieth-century cases that would support parents' claims.[22]

While some conservative justices have feared that the Ninth Amendment—"The enumeration in the Constitution, of certain rights, shall not be construed to deny or disparage others retained by the people"—is a Pandora's box whose opening will conjure a whirlwind of imaginary rights, the amendment's text is plain. In *Troxel v. Granville* (2000), even Justice Scalia recognized that the unenumerated right of parents to direct the upbringing of their children was sheltered within the Ninth Amendment, though he denied it was judicially enforceable.[23] The Roberts Court will probably be called on to explore these questions.

One last issue the new Roberts Court majority might scrutinize is property rights. The Constitution contains explicit textual protections for the right to property, such as its declaration: "Nor shall private property be taken for public use, without just compensation." In that short phrase, the Framers required that any governmental infringement on property ownership have a public purpose and be accompanied by a fair and effective payment. Nevertheless, past judicial decisions have eroded the clear meaning of the text, primarily by blessing regulations that, while they do not physically seize property, do radically restrict its uses and reduce its value. In *Penn Central Transportation Company v. New York City* (1978), the Court introduced an amorphous balancing test that generally permits most such "regulatory takings," especially those pursued for environmental protection.[24] Another case, *Kelo v. City of New London* (2005), weakened the requirement that the government's taking of property be for a public use by approving local programs that effectively seize small homes and transfer the land to developers.[25] But in recent years the Roberts Court has begun to question whether the environment can justify severe restrictions on the use and development of property. If equality among constitutional rights becomes its lodestar, the Court may well seek to elevate the protection of property rights with bright lines that match those for speech and firearms.

We do not mean to demean the achievements of the New Deal Court and the Warren Court. On the contrary, we recognize them and salute them. The New Deal Court threw its weight behind the powerful democratizing forces of the period. It created a constitutional jurisprudence that deferred to the majoritarian will—indeed, that rubber-stamped it—across a wide range of contested political issues, especially regarding business regulation. At the same time, it began the process of protecting the free speech and religious rights of unpopular minorities—a process that was carried forward by the Warren Court and that remains vital in the Roberts Court. More hesitantly, the New Deal Court also began to breathe life into the Fourteenth Amendment's protection of racial minorities, which had been moribund before. The Warren Court's greatest achievement was to take the New Deal Court's tentative steps much further, to deliver landmark constitutional opinions on that subject, beginning the long-delayed task of dismantling Jim Crow and integrating African Americans fully into the life of the nation. And what the Warren Court began to do for African Americans, the Burger Court did for women.

Magnificent as these judicial accomplishments were, they came at a price. Even as it was attempting to fashion a jurisprudence that emphasized democracy, the New Deal Court was enabling the rise of the Administrative State and the emergence of a bloated, remote, and unresponsive federal government. In its decisions, the New Deal Court was caught in the paradox that seems intrinsic to the Progressive ideology. On the one hand, it professed faith in the democratic political process. On the other hand, it promoted rule by "experts" insulated from political accountability and hostile to democratic self-government.

The Irony

"In a real sense, Western societies have attained universal suffrage only after popular democracy has disappeared." —James Buchanan[26]

In the seventy years between the rise of the New Deal Court and the momentous 2021–2022 term, the Court was little concerned with upholding the principles of federalism. That was largely because "states' rights" had been so often invoked to cover racial oppression and inequality. Yet the Court ought to appreciate the merits of federalism. Perhaps it will. For one thing, federalism could be the means by which the strife arising from deep political polarization and rending divisions over issues such abortion might be overcome. *Dobbs* certainly holds out that promise. To be sure, a "checkerboard" solution, in which California and Vermont enact one abortion policy and Texas and South Dakota another, will not appeal to everyone. But it might promote national unity. Surely there is much to be said for that.

In addition to reviving separation of powers and federalism, the Roberts Court should also be more protective than its predecessors of individual property rights, and more vigilant against rent-seeking by influential special interests via the legislative process. Political economists have shown that that process can be exploited by disproportionately influential business or professional lobbies. There can be, as the leading political economist Mancur Olson demonstrated, a "tyranny of the minority"—no less to be feared than Madison's tyranny of the majority.[27] These special interests may be able to use their leverage in the legislative process to suppress competition and secure advantages to themselves, without regard to the common good. For example, special licensing requirements for lawyers, doctors, or undertakers may operate as unjustifiable transfers of wealth to those groups, to the detriment of the great majority of citizens and consumers.[28] The Roberts Court should revisit the longstanding jurisprudence of its predecessors on economic rights and liberties.[29]

Predicting the course of the Roberts Court in the decade is difficult. As Yogi Berra famously said, "It's tough to make predictions, especially about the future." But property, race, religion, and federalism are all areas where the justices of the new majority have suggested that reform is in order. On the other hand, as in *Dobbs*, there are all areas where past Supreme Court decisions stand in the way of reaching what the Court believes is the correct interpretation of the Constitution. If the Roberts Court is going to follow its initial intuitions, it must have a clear and coherent doctrine of *stare decisis* that is true to the originalist tenor of its recent cases. Such a doctrine began to emerge in the *Dobbs* decision. But it has some way to go. To conclude our discussion of the Court's possible future, we need to consider how it views its own past. The remainder of this chapter is dedicated to considering how much weight the Court has given and should give to its precedents.

Grappling with *Stare Decisis*

The question of *stare decisis* was at the heart of the *Dobbs* decision. As Justice Kavanaugh put it in concurrence, the issue of precedent was a "more difficult question" than whether or not *Roe* had correctly decided that there was a constitutional right to abortion. Even if *Roe* had been wrongly decided as an original matter, the Court had maintained for almost half a century that the Constitution recognized (some form of) that right.[30] Furthermore, *Roe* had survived a constitutional challenge thirty years earlier. In *Planned Parenthood v. Casey* (1992), a fractured Court had reaffirmed the "core holding" of *Roe.* Granted, four justices in *Casey* would have overruled *Roe*, and only two would squarely have upheld it as it was. But a plurality of three justices voted to reaffirm it, albeit with substantial modifications. Thus *Roe* had been the law from 1973 to 2022—enduringly controversial, clinging to life by narrow majorities, and acknowledged even by its defenders to have been poorly reasoned, but still on the books. So in *Dobbs*, Justice Alito had to deal with the argument, pressed hard by the dissent, that the Court should reaffirm *Roe* and *Casey* because they had been the law for half a century.[31]

Exacerbating the dispute was the fact that the Court had overturned another precedent only shortly before *Dobbs.* In the First Amendment case

Kennedy v. Bremerton School District (2022), the Court discarded the long-standing *Lemon v. Kurtzman* (1971).[32] And the Roberts Court has rejected or at least whittled down other important constitutional precedents as well. *Janus v. AFSCME* (2018) overturned, on the basis of freedom of speech, a 1977 precedent on the right of unions to collect dues from non-members.[33] Critics of *Heller* argue that it overruled *United States v. Miller*, a precedent of some seventy years standing.[34] The campaign finance case *Citizens United v. FEC* (2010) repudiated two earlier decisions that had upheld legislative restrictions on corporate spending for political purposes.[35] Yet the Roberts Court treated other precedents differently. In *Dobbs* itself Justice Alito rejected the argument that a "potential home for the abortion right" might be found in the Fourteenth Amendment's Equal Protection Clause on the grounds that that possibility was "squarely foreclosed by our precedents."[36]

Stare decisis loomed large in *Dobbs* because respect for precedent was the best defense of *Roe*. *Roe*'s reasoning was notoriously weak and unconvincing. When the *Casey* Court had been invited to overturn *Roe*, it did not even attempt to rehabilitate the precedent on substantive, doctrinal grounds. If anything, the *Casey* plurality implicitly admitted that *Roe* was wrong as an original matter and instead affirmed core *parts* of *Roe* on the basis of *stare decisis*.[37] If that was still the main reason to reaffirm *Roe*, thirty years later, then the Court needed to examine it.

So *Dobbs* brought the question of *stare decisis* to the fore. But what is that doctrine? What practical considerations count for and against it? What has the actual practice of the Court been as to its own precedents? And what is the basis of the doctrine of *stare decisis* in the Constitution?

Simply put, *stare decisis*—standing by the thing decided, or adhering to precedent—is a rule made by the courts for the courts. The Supreme Court has characterized it in various ways. A recent, though pre-*Dobbs*, formulation can be found in Justice Gorsuch's majority opinion in *Ramos v.*

Louisiana (2020). Gorsuch summarized the Court's standard view: "The precedents of this Court warrant our deep respect as embodying the considered views of those who have come before. But *stare decisis* has never been treated as an inexorable command. And the doctrine is 'at its weakest when we interpret the Constitution,' because a mistaken judicial interpretation of that supreme law is often 'practically impossible' to correct through other means."[38]

There are three main points here. First, the Court ought to show "deep respect" for its own precedents. But, second, showing respect for precedents does *not* entail having to follow them in every case: *stare decisis* is *not* an inexorable command. Indeed, if a precedent is known to have been erroneous, then it may be best not to heed it. As Gorsuch put it, "*Stare decisis* isn't supposed to be the art of methodically ignoring what everyone knows to be true."[39] Third, there is a distinction between constitutional and statutory *stare decisis*. If the Court misconstrues a statute, and belatedly comes to recognize its error, it can still follow the erroneous precedent and Congress can always correct the error.[40] But the Court should show more alacrity in correcting constitutional errors, because in practical terms the only alternative is the cumbersome process of amending the Constitution under Article V. That can be done, of course. As we have seen, Section One of the Fourteenth Amendment corrected *Dred Scott*'s error about African Americans' citizenship. But by and large, we must look to the Court itself to correct its own constitutional blunders.

Having explained what *stare decisis* is, Justice Gorsuch then identified the considerations that weigh on whether or not to reaffirm an arguably mistaken constitutional precedent: "When it revisits a precedent this Court has traditionally considered 'the quality of the decision's reasoning; its consistency with related decisions; legal developments since the decision; and reliance on the decision.'"[41] These four considerations may, and often do, overlap. A precedent's consistency with past and future case law, for example, can promote "reliance" on the Court's decisions. The "reliance" factor is especially important in many circumstances. When the Supreme Court decides a constitutional question, behavior may have to change, often drastically. For example, if the Court announces a rule for criminal procedure, the behavior of police, prosecutors, juries, judges, and the general public will change to conform to it. Evidence may be admissible or inadmissible that was not so before; prosecutions may be successful or unsuccessful because of the rule; sentences may become longer or shorter; convictions may be vacated; the public may engage in conduct that once was unlawful. Everyone concerned will form expectations in reliance on the Court's rule. And if the Court shifts its ground and reverses the rule, those expectations will be disappointed, and widespread or longstanding patterns of behavior will have to be readjusted. The costs of readjustment may well be severe. Among other costs may be a sense that the law is unstable and unpredictable, and that the Court's decision-making is erratic and unprincipled.

Justice Alito's dissent in *Ramos* (in most of which the chief justice and Justice Kagan joined him) succinctly stated the most common justifications for the doctrine. *Stare decisis*, Alito said, "exists to promote" several "important objectives," including "evenhandedness, predictability, and the protection of legitimate reliance." Alito also called for a more coherent formulation of the doctrine and a more consistent application of it. "We begin with the presumption that we will follow precedent, and therefore when the Court decides to overrule, it has an obligation to provide an explanation for its decision," he wrote. "This is imperative because the Court should have a body of *neutral* principles on the question of overruling precedent. The doctrine should not be transformed into a tool that favors particular outcomes" [emphasis in the original].

This approach conceptualizes *stare decisis* as a "presumption"—and presumptions can be overcome. Alito wrote that "as we have said many times, it is not an 'inexorable command.' . . . There are circumstances when past decisions must be overturned." At most, "When the Court decides to overrule, it has an obligation to provide an explanation for its decision." That seems to make the presumption in favor of precedent very weak. The Court merely has to "provide an explanation" for overruling it.[42] What Alito here called a "presumption" seems very close to what Justice Frankfurter called a "policy." Policy is and should be variable, as circumstances require.

Justice Alito was not the only member of the Court in *Ramos* who expressed discomfort at the state of the Court's *stare decisis* doctrine. Justice Kavanaugh wrote a lengthy concurrence, much of it dedicated to *stare decisis*. Kavanaugh identified no fewer than seven factors that the Court had used in the past when deciding whether to apply *stare decisis*. These included the quality of the precedent's reasoning; its coherence and consistency with other decisions; changes in the law and changes in the facts since the precedent was issued; the precedent's workability; its age; and the reliance interests at stake. Not surprisingly, Kavanaugh found that the Court had applied these factors "without establishing any consistent methodology or roadmap." He called the Court's practice a "muddle [that] poses a problem for the rule of law."

Kavanaugh's proposal was to distill from the Court's past decisions "three broad considerations" that would guide the Court towards a more "neutral and consistent" application of *stare decisis*. (He repeated these three considerations in his concurrence in *Dobbs*.) In essence the considerations were these: (1) Was the precedent not merely wrong, but "grievously or egregiously wrong"?; (2) Has the precedent caused "significant negative jurisprudential or real-world consequences"?; and (3) Would overruling the precedent "unduly upset reliance interests"?[43]

Even when winnowed down from seven factors to three, however, it seems unlikely that *stare decisis* could be applied in a "neutral and consistent" manner. Each of the tests Kavanaugh identified required judgments, in which justices would be likely to differ. When was a precedent not merely "wrong," but "egregiously" so? When should its effects be deemed to have caused "significant negative consequences"? When would overruling it "unduly" upset reliance interests? And what in any case *were* the "reliance interests" to be considered? The problem was essentially the same as with *any* test requiring the application of judgement: every factor involved subjectivity. Even if the justices were answering the same three questions, each of them would answer the questions differently and give different weights to the answers they yielded. Kavanaugh was offering a flexible *standard* for evaluating the salience of *stare decisis,* not a mechanical *rule* that would generate certainty and predictability. His proposal might marginally *reduce* disagreement on the Court over the application of *stare decisis*, but it was chimerical to think that it would *eliminate* outcome-driven uses of the doctrine. It would remain a makeweight, invoked primarily to bolster dissenting opinions. The differences among the justices in *Dobbs* only underscored the difficulty—or impossibility—of achieving a consensus on the matter, even if there were agreement about what set of factors was relevant.

But the problem goes deeper than that. Justices who wish to accord significant weight to *stare decisis* usually do so out of concern for the rule of law. Chief Justice Roberts put this point well in his *Citizens United* concurrence: the "greatest purpose" of the doctrine of *stare decisis* "is to serve a constitutional ideal—the rule of law."[44] But what if one believes (as we do) that a decision like *Roe* was fundamentally a *lawless* one, made up by the justices out of whole cloth, without foundation in constitutional text or structure, legal history or judicial precedent, but merely a matter of judicial *fiat*? If *Dobbs* had affirmed *Roe*, as *Casey* had, purely on the basis of *stare decisis*, would the Court have been upholding the rule of law, or negating it? We think it would have been giving a veneer of legality to what was originally, and remained, a lawless act—an exercise of raw power, not of reason and judgment. The "rule of law" tells in favor of precedent. Precedent can serve as a check on judicial arbitrariness and caprice. But more important, the rule of law speaks in favor of *law*. And by any fair reckoning, *Roe* was not "law," but only the semblance of it.

Principle versus Practice

Both in *Ramos* and later in *Dobbs*, Justice Kavanaugh demonstrated that, in practice, the Court was not especially respectful of its own precedents. The practice of overturning important constitutional precedents did not begin with the Roberts Court, nor was it a peculiarity of "activist" conservative justices. In fact, as Kavanaugh noted, *every* justice sitting on the *Ramos* Court had voted in recent years to overrule constitutional precedents. Furthermore, he observed, "some of the Court's most notable and consequential decisions have entailed overruling precedent." *Brown v. Board of Education* (1954), which Kavanaugh called "the single most important and greatest decision in this Court's history," had "repudiated the separate but equal doctrine of *Plessy v. Ferguson* [1896]," and it was but one of many examples.[45]

In overturning its precedents, the Court has been willing to defeat very deeply entrenched reliance interests. Take *Brown*. *Brown* did not merely upend *Plessy*, a precedent that had been on the books longer than *Roe v. Wade* before meeting its demise. Nor did *Brown* merely uproot more recent precedents that had relied on *Plessy*, such as *Gong Lum v. Rice* (1927), a twenty-seven-year-old precedent at the time.[46] (*Casey* was a twenty-nine-year-old precedent at the time of *Dobbs*.) *Brown* began the dismantling of the entire social structure of the segregated South, spelling the end of an entire way of life that depended on judicial enforcement of white supremacy. Should *Brown* have protected the reliance interests at stake there? The question answers itself.

More Honored in the Breach

The doctrine of *stare decisis* seems to have been more honored in the breach than in the observance. Whether from an originalist perspective, a progressivist perspective, or neither, the Supreme Court has regularly revisited and purged its precedents. And the efforts by some justices to promote a more disciplined and coherent doctrine of *stare decisis*, however well-intentioned, seem overwhelmingly likely to fail. If we go by the Court's precedents—as opposed to going by what the Court says about precedent—then there is ample precedent for overturning precedents.

Stare Decisis versus the Constitution

We may well question the constitutional basis for affirming precedents, or even for regarding them as *presumptively* correct, when they were in fact wrongly decided. What constitutional text or feature entitles the Court to give precedent a sufficient weight that it, rather than the Constitution, can determine the outcome of later constitutional cases? Why should the Court apply *stare decisis* even at the cost of perpetuating constitutional error? And the problem is even more acute when the precedent is widely understood to have been clearly mistaken, and when members of the Court have insisted or acknowledged that the precedent was in error. What could justify deliberately perpetuating egregious constitutional mistakes?

The argument that the Court has a *duty* to overturn mistaken precedents, or at least egregiously mistaken ones, rests on the Supremacy Clause, Article VI, Clause 2 of the Constitution. The clause states, "This Constitution, and the Laws of the United States which shall be made in Pursuance thereof; and all Treaties . . . which shall be made, under the Authority of the United States, shall be the supreme Law of the Land."

It appears to follow that, when adjudicating a challenge to a statute or regulation, the Supreme Court must test its consistency with "this Constitution." And consistency with "this Constitution" is not the same as "consistency with this Court's constitutional precedents." Indeed, the two tests *cannot* be identical, once it is admitted (as it must be) that the Court can err. On this understanding, the Court has a duty not to follow a constitutional precedent that is contrary to the Constitution itself.

Looking for *Stare Decisis* in the Constitution

Efforts to find a constitutional foothold for *stare decisis* in the face of objections like this ordinarily involve appealing to Article III, Section 1, of the Constitution, which vests the "judicial Power of the United States" in the Supreme Court and such lower federal courts as Congress may establish. Justice Kavanaugh, for one, has made that appeal. In his Senate confirmation hearings, Kavanaugh testified that "the system of precedent comes from Article III itself."[47] More recently, in *Ramos*, Kavanaugh argued that "the Framers of our Constitution understood that the doctrine of *stare decisis* is part of the 'judicial Power' and rooted in Article III of the Constitution."[48]

Yet Kavanaugh's argument that the Framers nestled *stare decisis* within "the judicial Power" is surprisingly weak. In support of it, he said, "Writing in Federalist 78, Alexander Hamilton emphasized the importance of *stare decisis:* To 'avoid an arbitrary discretion in the courts, it is indispensable' that federal judges 'should be bound down by strict rules and precedents, which serve to define and point out their duty in every particular case that comes before them.'"[49]

Assuming that Hamilton had constitutional precedents (rather than common law or statutory cases) in mind when he wrote this, and assuming also that he was speaking about horizontal *stare decisis* (affirming the Supreme Court's own precedents) as opposed to vertical *stare decisis* (following the precedents of a higher court), his remarks would make *stare decisis* an "inexorable command" (in Gorsuch's phrase) that the Court was duty-bound to obey "in every particular case that comes before them." No one on the Supreme Court, including Justice Kavanaugh, believes that. Moreover, if Hamilton was making the point that *stare decisis* is a core

Perverse Incentive

Taking constitutional *stare decisis* to be an inflexible command would entail perverse consequences. It would encourage justices to lay down extreme and indefensible precedents that codified their personal policy preferences, knowing that later Courts could not expunge their errors.

component of the "judicial Power," he put the idea in an odd place: in the part of *The Federalist* No. 78 where the remark appears, he is discussing why judges should have life tenure, not what the elements of the "judicial Power" are. He is arguing that they should have life tenure because their duties require deep learning in the case law, and that that study should be encouraged by the promise that life tenure will reward it. Finally (as discussed later in this chapter), the jurisprudence of the Founding period, both in England and in this country, assumed that the courts could and, when appropriate, should, overrule precedents. It is implausible to think that Hamilton denied that.

Gamble v. United States: Justice Thomas Weighs In

The question of whether and when the Court has a duty to overturn constitutional precedents that it knows to be erroneous remains open. That question was explored in Justice Thomas's fascinating concurrence in *Gamble v. United States* (2019), to which we now turn.

The underlying issue in *Gamble*—whether the Fifth Amendment's Double Jeopardy Clause permits or forbids successive federal and state criminal prosecutions for the same offense—is not especially relevant here. Instead, it is crucial that the Court had repeatedly permitted such successive prosecutions to go forward, on the basis of what is known as the "dual sovereignty doctrine." *Gamble* posed the question of how much weight the Court should give to those established precedents. Thomas came up with a provocative answer.

Thomas began with an account of "the judicial Power." Tracking Chief Justice John Marshall's foundational decision in *Marbury v. Madison*, which established the power of judicial review of the constitutionality of federal law, Thomas characterized "the judicial Power" as the power to say what the law is. This entailed that the courts had no power to "alter" the law; instead, they had a duty to "expound" it.

In a period (like the Founding) when the bulk of the work of the courts concerned the unwritten common law, the role of precedent was vital. The task of the traditional common law judge was to *discover* the "law" which was given by nature or custom. This "discovery" was an act of reason and judgment; common law judges did not see themselves as "inventing" or "making" law, which would have been an activity of the will, not the intellect. Precedent provided the principal and most authoritative *evidence* of what the law was. But even in that kind of legal system, precedent, if "flatly absurd or unjust," should not be followed. It was recognized that in their effort to discern what the law was, judges might be mistaken. Despite being the best evidence of what the law was, precedent was a fallible guide.

But the American judiciary had to work with written law, not uncodified and unwritten common law, to discover foundational legal principles and rules. In particular, they had to interpret the Constitution's text. That Constitution was supreme over any other law, including judicial opinions. In the event of a conflict between the Constitution and a judicial interpretation of it, the Court was bound to follow the former. Thus, the role of a precedent in the American constitutional system was fundamentally different from its role in the English common law. Precedent might be evidence of the meaning of the Constitution's text, but it was not necessarily conclusive evidence. "Because the Constitution is supreme over other sources of law, it requires us to privilege its text over our own precedents when the two are in conflict."[50]

Chief Justice Marshall's reasoning in *Marbury* supports Justice Thomas's view. Marshall's defense of judicial review is premised on the assumption that the Court must declare "what the law is," not what the Court *has said* the law is. If the Court could apply its own mistaken precedents to invalidate the actions of the other federal branches or the states, judicial review would be stripped of its justification. The constitutionality of challenged statutes would be measured, not against the Constitution, but against mistaken accounts of the Constitution.

Thomas bolstered his argument by pointing to the constitutional requirement (Article VI, Clause 3) that federal judges take an oath to "support this Constitution." He pointedly remarked that "the Constitution does not mandate that judicial officers swear to uphold judicial precedents."

Justice Thomas also identified two kinds of judicial precedents. The first category includes cases that are "demonstrably erroneous," or not "permissible interpretation[s] of the text." When presented with such a precedent, "the Court should correct the error, regardless of whether other factors support overruling the precedent. . . . A demonstrably incorrect judicial decision . . . is tantamount to *making* law, and adhering to it both disregards the supremacy of the Constitution and perpetuates a usurpation of the legislative power." In such a case, the Court simply has no business considering what weight to accord reliance interests, or whether the precedent conforms with other decisions, or if it has proven to be "workable." There is a duty to overrule a "demonstrably erroneous" precedent.

The other category includes those that are not "demonstrably erroneous" and are "permissible interpretations" of the text. Textual indeterminacy could arise from "the inability of human language to be fully unequivocal in every context." Therefore, "Reasonable people may arrive at different conclusions about the original meaning of a legal text after employing all relevant tools of interpretation." In that situation, the "judicial policy of *stare decisis*" may come in, so as to allow "courts to constitutionally adhere to that interpretation, even if a later court might have ruled another way as a matter of first impression." *Stare decisis* would permit, not require, adherence to a precedent. In other words, the Court can decide whether to overrule it or not.[51]

Thomas's theory of *stare decisis* is clearly superior to the multi-factor "tests" proposed by the other justices; it is a more clear and consistent doctrine, rooted in a deeper and more searching account of "the judicial Power" than Justice Kavanaugh's. Had the *Dobbs* majority followed Thomas's lead, it could have made quick work of *Roe*: the precedent was "demonstrably erroneous," and *stare decisis* could not uphold it.

But critics have noted that it too permits discretion. When the Court is evaluating a plausible or "permissible" precedent, Thomas's theory would allow the Court to reject the precedent if it wishes. Perhaps a better rule is that, when a precedent is "permissible," the Court should uphold it. On that principle the only question before the Court would be whether the precedent was "demonstrably erroneous" or not.

Casey versus *Dobbs*

The *Dobbs* Court adopted neither Justice Thomas's account of *stare decisis* nor Justice Kavanaugh's proposal. Instead, it went with the framework that it had typically used in its discussions of *stare decisis*, the method that the *Casey* plurality had used in 1992 to uphold *Roe*. Granted, the Court's reluctance to innovate was prudent: If there were a case where the Court should have used its existing benchmarks for *stare decisis*, it would be one that would overturn precedents as important as *Roe* and *Casey*. The *Dobbs* Court wished to be seen as treating *Roe* and *Casey* just as it had treated other challenged constitutional precedents—there was to be no thumb on the scale.

Accordingly, *Dobbs* posited a five-factor test in deciding whether *Roe* and *Casey* were to be upheld on *stare decisis* grounds. The factors were (1) the "nature" of the precedents' error; (2) the quality of their reasonings; (3) the "workability" of the precedents, or "whether [the precedents] can be understood and applied in a consistent and predictable manner"; (4) the disruptive effects the precedents had on other areas of law; and (5) the "reliance interests" that would be affected by overruling them.[52]

This framework was similar to the one applied by the *Casey* plurality. But the *Dobbs* Court argued that *Casey* had customized the doctrine of *stare decisis* specifically to serve the purpose of affirming *Roe*—in other words, *Casey*'s account of *stare decisis* was actually "a novel version" of the doctrine. *Casey*'s rendition of *stare decisis* "placed great weight on an intangible form of reliance with little if any basis in prior case law." As a precedent about precedents, *Casey* was itself a significant deviation from precedent: it relied on a newly minted *ad hoc* sense of "reliance."[53]

Let us, therefore, focus on *Dobbs*'s treatment of the "reliance" factor in its account of *stare decisis*.

Reliance Interests

The concept of reliance is rooted in contract and property. In *Payne v. Tennessee* (1991), the Court stated that "considerations in favor of *stare decisis* are at their acme in cases involving property and contract rights, where reliance interests are involved."[54] Reliance enables precise and coherent future planning. If we can take a legal rule to be settled, we can reasonably base our future conduct on it.

Consider a simple example involving private contracts. A contract binds private parties to certain conduct: A agrees to build a table for B in exchange for B's promise to pay a certain sum of money to A. Suppose that A prepares to make the table and incurs certain out-of-pocket expenses in making those preparations. B then announces that the deal is off and that she will not pay A the agreed amount. A is legally entitled to recover his out-of-pocket costs from B. A has reasonably relied on B's promise to his detriment.

Detrimental reliance is not confined to economic losses that ensue from breaching a promise. Consider a scenario in which a criminal defendant, to avoid the risks of a trial, takes a plea bargain, after which a precedent-overturning Supreme Court decision makes the evidence against him inadmissible in court. The defendant here would lose liberty, not property.

The concept of detrimental reliance appears in various forms in the case law. A common thread is that the "reliance" that the law protects must leave one worse off than he or she would have been but for an earlier mistake. Merely being surprised or disappointed does not amount to detrimental reliance in the legal sense. The reliance must also be "reasonable." For instance, if an investor bought beach-front property knowing that the risk of significant regulatory change "inhered" in his title, he could not complain if such changes later caused the value of his property to decline.

The *Dobbs* Court found—in full agreement with *Casey*—that "conventional, concrete reliance interests" would not be unfairly defeated if *Roe* were overruled. "Traditional" reliance interests arise and deserve protection where advanced planning is a necessity. But, as *Casey* noted, abortion is generally "unplanned activity," and "reproductive planning could take virtually immediate account of any sudden restoration of state authority to ban abortions." In other words, both the *Dobbs* majority and the *Casey* plurality assumed that most abortions occurred as a result of unplanned and unwanted pregnancies. If the states were allowed to reassert the power to ban abortion, then the response would be less unprotected sex and fewer unexpected pregnancies.

If *Casey* conceded that the more traditional kind of reliance was not at stake, then what type of reliance interests did the plurality protect? According to *Dobbs,* this is the point at which *Casey* diverged from the Court's normal view of *stare decisis. Casey* had invented "a more intangible form of reliance": "It wrote that 'people [had] organized intimate relationships and made choices that define their views of themselves and their places in society . . . in reliance on the availability of abortion in the event that contraception should fail' and that '[t]he ability of women to participate equally in the economic and social life of the Nation has been facilitated by their ability to control their reproductive lives'" (brackets in the original).

Dobbs's best counter to this was simply that those were not the kind of reliance interests that the pre-*Casey* Court had protected. If *Casey* had merely distilled the Court's prior jurisprudence on reliance and found that reversing *Roe* would have damaged "reliance" in that sense, then its application of *stare decisis* in defense of *Roe* would have been more convincing. But *Casey* had more or less openly created a new kind of reliance interest that seemed to be custom-made for upholding *Roe*. *Casey* seemed to be trying to have it both ways: appealing to established precedent in order to preserve *Roe* and rewriting the precedent it was invoking in that defense.[55]

The *Dobbs* Court's insistence that the "reliance interests" in question be "concrete" is correct. The dissenting justices had been applying a supercharged version of reliance. In his dissent in *Franchise Tax Board of California v. Hyatt*, for example, Justice Breyer had offered a very generalized account of reliance: "The people of this Nation rely upon stability in the law. Legal stability allows lawyers to give clients sound advice and allows ordinary citizens to plan their lives. Each time the Court overrules a case, the Court produces increased uncertainty."[56]

By this standard, the Court should hardly ever overrule a precedent; the social cost is simply too high. But this neither correctly describes the Court's actual conduct nor provides a compelling normative standard. "Legal stability" would hardly have justified the Court in upholding *Plessy*, or a multitude of other bad precedents. Justice Breyer simply gave too much weight to stability and not enough to redressing errors and wrongs.

There were other reasons for the majority in *Dobbs* to insist that the reliance interests at stake would have to be "concrete" to justify upholding an erroneously decided precedent. If they were not "concrete," what metric could the Court use to determine and evaluate the effects of reversing a challenged precedent? Could the Court say, with reasonable confidence, that keeping *Roe* was necessary to maintain "the ability of women to participate equally in the economic and social life of the Nation"? The experts who submitted amicus briefs were sharply divided over whether *Roe* was necessary in 1973 to advance women's rights, whether preserving *Roe* was necessary to that end in 2022, and what was the best concept of equality for women.

If the Court decides to retain *Dobbs*'s five-factor test, it will have to develop another account of "reliance," especially of the kinds of reliance that are "concrete." While it may often be true that consistency is more important than correctness when the latter would destabilize property and contract rights, that is not always the case. Consider *Shelley v. Kraemer* (1948), which ruled that the judicial enforcement of a racially restrictive covenant barring white homeowners from selling their houses to African Americans was a state action that denied equal protection and hence was unconstitutional.[57] *Shelley* necessarily caused the values of some properties that had been subject to restrictive covenants to decline.

A Concrete Reliance Interest the Court Didn't Consider

The Court's analysis of reliance, despite its considerable merits, is not beyond cavil. For example, at least some of those who had acted in reliance on *Roe* and *Casey* might be exposed to the risk of criminal prosecution as a result of those cases being overruled. Some state laws criminalizing abortion had remained on the books after 1973, though *Roe* had rendered them unenforceable. Would they spring back into life if *Roe* were overruled? And if so, could they be retroactively applied to women who had procured abortions or to abortionists who had provided them, even though both parties relied on *Roe*? This is not a likely outcome. Nonetheless, it seems to be the right kind of reliance interest to consider.

Before *Shelley*, white homeowners who desired such covenants might reasonably have thought that they were protected by a 1926 precedent, *Corrigan v. Buckley*, which had rejected a constitutional challenge to racially restrictive covenants in the District of Columbia.[58] *Shelley* distinguished *Corrigan* rather than overruling it,[59] but it still had a tangible, negative impact on the economic interests of the parties to restrictive covenants who might reasonably have relied on *Corrigan* when purchasing their houses. And yet that reliance interest should have counted for nothing when the Court came to decide *Shelley*. In that case, correctness was more important than consistency.

Casey was simply not a credible precedent for at least three other reasons. First, despite purporting to preserve *Roe*'s "core," the reasoning in *Casey* differed significantly from the reasoning in *Roe*. For one thing *Casey* replaced the "right to privacy" foundation that *Roe* had offered for the abortion right with the "Liberty" Clause of the Fourteenth Amendment. *Casey* discarded *Roe*'s trimester system in favor of its own system pegged to fetal "viability."[60] And *Casey* overturned two major *Roe*-related abortion precedents.[61] *Casey* was hardly a respectable model for respecting precedent. Why did it deserve respect itself?

Second, *Casey*'s substantive jurisprudence of "liberty," which underpinned its affirmation of *Roe*, did not cohere with its professed deference to procedural tradition and judicial circumspection in its discussion of *stare decisis*. The *Casey* Court appealed to tradition in support of a radical innovation and to judicial circumspection in support of unprecedented judicial audacity.

Third, *Casey*'s account of *stare decisis* would soon prove to be at odds with the Court's development of that doctrine. In *Lawrence v. Texas*, Justice Kennedy led the Court in overturning *Bowers v. Hardwick*, a precedent from only seventeen years before. Kennedy paid the merest lip service to *stare decisis* in *Lawrence*. *Lawrence* confirmed that *Casey*'s invocation of *stare decisis* was opportunistic and unprincipled—a mere stratagem for making the affirmation of *Roe* seem more plausible.[62]

Institutional Positioning

Casey was a self-congratulatory decision. The controlling plurality of Justices O'Connor, Kennedy, and Souter were appointed by pro-life Republican presidents. A Republican administration was calling on the Court to overturn *Roe*. If the *Casey* Court had done so, there would have been charges that the Court had been "politicized." Concerned with the Court's prestige, these justices wished to seem to be "above" politics. That led to the plurality's strangest claim: its avowal that it was upholding *Roe* in order not to have seemed to have succumbed to "political pressure."

That avowal was entirely unconvincing. For in affirming *Roe*, the Court yielded to another kind of "political pressure." The Court would have been accused of playing politics regardless of its decision. So the accusations should have been a wash, and the Court should not have felt any pressure about the inevitable charge. The Court's avowed intent to seem unpolitical was itself a transparent political ploy. The controlling plurality's reasoning seemed to be more strategic than principled, more concerned with institutional positioning than with legal doctrine. Rather than simply saying "what the law is" and letting the chips fall, the plurality tried to gain some positional advantage for the Court. The Court's determination to shore up its own "legitimacy" ended up delegitimizing it.

Then, having cast itself in the role of a neutral and unpolitical actor, the Court appealed to the American people to lay down their arms in the abortion war. It called on "the contending sides of a national controversy to end their national division."[63] The justices in the *Casey* plurality appeared to think that their ruling formed a balanced and reasonable compromise that the voters might well have reached themselves, but they seemed to be blind to the fact that they had declared a "winner." Why should the losing side surrender? Because it, the Court, had declared that the matter was closed?

The *Casey* Court was as foolish to think it could end the controversy over abortion as the *Dred Scott* Court was to think it had ended the controversy over slavery in the territories. Justice Alito's *Dobbs* opinion is pitch-perfect on this: "We cannot allow our decisions to be affected by any extraneous influences such as concern about the public's reaction to our work. . . . That is true both when we initially decide a constitutional issue *and* when we consider whether to overrule a prior opinion. . . . 'The Judicial Branch derives its legitimacy, not from following public opinion, but from deciding by its best lights whether enactments of the popular branches of Government comport with the Constitution.'"[64] The best way to serve the Court as an institution is not to strive to serve the Court as an institution. It is simply to try to get the law right.

What Would the Founders Do?

Some *Dobbs* critics have argued that it gives an account of *stare decisis* that is false to the Founders' understanding of precedent. In the Founding period, they maintain, precedent was considered to be far more binding than *Dobbs* supposed. Even if *stare decisis* was not an unbreakable rule, it had a far greater weight than the *Dobbs* Court assumed. In their view *Dobbs* rejects the method that the Founders' jurisprudence would have used to assess earlier decisions.

Anglo-American judges at the time of the Founding did attribute considerable authority to precedents. But they also believed that courts were bound to overrule, narrow, or otherwise repudiate erroneous precedents. They accepted that reliance interests could play some roles in sustaining mistaken precedents, but chiefly in cases involving land or commerce. In other areas of the law, the most important task of a judge was to get the law right.

The jurisprudence of the Founding period encapsulated a vision of law in which the common law, statutory law, and the Law of Nations (what we now call international law) were seen as subordinate parts of a greater scheme, the Law of Nature. The task of judges was not to "make" law but to find it. Precedents were "evidence" of the law, but they did not constitute it. As respectable as precedents were, they could also be misleading. As Charles Reid put it in a major study of Founding era jurisprudence, "If judicial decisions were evidence of law, they were necessarily subject to the rules of evidence: they might be subject to further evaluation, scrutiny, consideration, and deliberation to ascertain their fidelity to fundamental legal principles and also to the higher law."[65]

"The Laws of Nature and of Nature's God"

The "naturalist" jurisprudence of the Founding period had ontological, moral, and epistemological foundations: it presupposed that there was a "higher" Law of Nature (which itself was often thought to be anchored in the will of God); that in the event of a conflict between the Law of Nature and man-made law, the former should prevail; and that the Law of Nature could be discerned by human reason and reflection, especially by judges deeply versed in the common law. In this vision the judge-made common law was an attempt to discover a higher law and to bring human law into alignment with it.

Custom was important to common law judges because human communities tend to organize themselves in ways that are natural and so to conform to the Law of Nature, as applied to the circumstances in which those communities find themselves. Thus, although "natural justice and reason are the same in all countries and in all ages,"[66] common law judges were expected to adjust the universal principles of natural law to fit particular circumstances. Montesquieu had remarked in *The Spirit of Laws* that "law in general is human reason, inasmuch as it governs all the inhabitants of the earth," but also that laws "should be adapted in such a manner to the people for whom they are made, as to render it very unlikely for those of one nation to be proper for another."[67]

The Classical and Christian Origins of American Politics: Political Theory, Natural Law, and the American Founding by Kody W. Cooper and Justine Buckley Dyre. Cambridge: Cambridge University Press, 2022.

Because the common law, despite being derived from the Law of Nature, also had to respect local situations and customs, post-revolutionary American judges regarded English common law precedents as relevant and material evidence of the law, but not as binding. The principles behind the common law were immutable; their particular applications were not. Chief Justice John Marshall stated in an 1808 case that English precedents "can only be considered as the opinions of men distinguished for their talents and learning, expounding a rule, by which this country, as well as theirs, professes to be governed."[68] In an 1806 case, St. George Tucker, a Virginia Supreme Court judge and the author of an important early commentary on the Constitution, cited a recent English precedent—not as binding, but as "an apposite case decided by able Judges upon the same law which as to this point prevails in this country."[69] His colleague Judge Spencer Roane characterized English precedents "merely as affording evidence of the opinions of eminent Judges as to the doctrines in question."[70]

During the latter half of the nineteenth century, the Founders' naturalist understanding of law gave way to a "positivist" conception of law, which saw law as expressing the command of a human sovereign will, not as a reflection of the Law of Nature.[71] In Justice Oliver Wendell Holmes Jr.'s epigram, "the common law is not a brooding omnipresence in the sky, but the articulate voice of some sovereign or quasi-sovereign that can be identified."[72] The most influential justice since John Marshall, Holmes derided the notion of natural law not only in his opinions but in his other legal writings. Among these was a 1918 article, "Natural Law," in which Holmes wrote that "the jurists who believe in natural law seem to me to be in that naïve state of mind that accepts what has been familiar and accepted . . . by all men everywhere." In the end, law serves "the interest of society, that is, of the predominant power in the community."[73]

The Supreme Court eventually came around to Holmes's positivistic way of thinking in a foundational 1938 case, *Erie Railroad v. Tompkins*,[74] which overruled the Court's antebellum decision *Swift v. Tyson* (1842).[75] *Erie* was authored by Justice Louis Brandeis, an eminent Progressive judge whom Woodrow Wilson had appointed to the Court. The *Erie* Court explicitly acknowledged Holmes's impact: "The fallacy underlying the rule declared in *Swift v. Tyson* is made clear by Mr. Justice Holmes. The doctrine rests upon the assumption that there is 'a transcendental body of law outside of any particular State but obligatory within it unless and until changed by statute,' that federal courts have the power to use their judgment as to what the rules of common law are; and that in the federal courts 'the parties are entitled to an independent judgment on matters of general law.'"[77]

This tectonic shift from a jurisprudence of natural law to a jurisprudence of positivism carried with it a different conception of precedent. Precedent was no longer to be seen as "evidence" of a higher law. The world of Founding-era jurisprudence receded into the dim past; its evidentiary conception of *stare decisis*

Might Makes Right

Holmes denied that there were "natural" rights or duties rooted in the very structure of things; for him, legal duties arose from the fact that "if I do live with others they tell me that I must do and abstain from doing various things or they will put the screws on me." Eventually, I may come "not only [to] accept the rules but . . . [also] to accept them with sympathy and emotional affirmation and begin to talk about duties and rights." But in truth "a right is only the hypostasis of a prophecy—the imagination of a substance supporting the fact that the public force will be brought to bear upon those who do things said to contravene it."[76]

A Book You're Not Supposed to Read

Law without Values: The Life, Work, and Legacy of Justice Holmes by Albert W. Alschuler. Chicago: University of Chicago Press, 2002

Stare Decisis: It's "More than a Feeling"[78]

"We can get from those who preceded a sense of the continuity of a society. We can draw from their learning a feel for the durability of a doctrine and a sense of the origins of principles. But we have experience that they never knew. Our vision may be shorter or longer. But it is ours. It is better that we make our own history than be governed by the dead. We too must be dynamic components of history if our institutions are to be vital, directive forces in the life of our age."

—Justice William O. Douglas, who served on the New Deal Court, articulates the Progressive-positivist view of precedent in a 1949 lecture on "Stare Decisis" to the New York City Bar Association[79]

became unfamiliar to courts and scholars. As a now-dominant Holmesian positivism was conjoined with Wilsonian Progressivism in the first half of the twentieth century, the courts came to be seen as instruments for adjusting the law dynamically to fit the perceived needs of the present. This change necessarily devalued precedent.

It was only in comparison with this fluid, evolutionary approach to precedent that the Founders' understanding of it came to appear rigid, inflexible, and static. But the judges and lawyers of the Founding period had not taken precedent to be static, let alone binding. It only looked that way when the Founders were viewed through positivist and progressive lenses.

In sum, there is a mass of material from the Founding period revealing that precedent was not considered sacrosanct; that at best it was fallible evidence of what the law was; and that the Founders believed that precedent merited respect while also holding that later courts should generally not hesitate to correct it when it was erroneous. Those who have charged the *Dobbs* Court with betraying the Founders' conception of *stare decisis* are mistaken.

The Constitution is a masterpiece. It is a great vehicle for self-governance—perhaps the greatest ever created. It was founded on centuries of political experience and embodies deep insights about human nature and the dangers of power. It has stood the test of time.

But masterpieces may suffer from the shocks of time. Classic works of architecture may fall into disrepair or be disfigured by careless additions. They may stand in need of careful, patient restoration so that the beauty, sweep, and symmetry of their original designs can show forth again.

The same goes for our Constitution. It needs a careful restoration. The pillars on which it was originally constructed—limited and defined powers, federalism, individual rights and liberties, separation of powers—are as true and necessary as ever. But they have been obscured, overgrown, altered, and permitted to decay.

The work of restoration has fallen to the current Supreme Court. Let us hope it is equal to the task.

Acknowledgments

Acknowledgments

The authors thank a group of dedicated research assistants who went above and beyond to see this manuscript through the writing and editing process: Justin Folk, Ka Ho Patrick Mok, Maguire Radosevic, and Daniel Schneider.

Robert J. Delahunty would like to thank his former colleagues Teresa S. Collett and Charles J. Reid Jr. for their advice and encouragement and the Claremont Institute Center for the American Way of Life in Washington, D.C., for its support.

John Yoo would like to thank colleagues at the Law School at the University of California at Berkeley, the American Enterprise Institute, and the Hoover Institution at Stanford University for many conversations about the Supreme Court. He is also grateful for the generous support of the Thomas Smith Foundation and the Darling Foundation. Yoo expresses his deep gratitude to the late Judge Laurence H. Silberman of the U.S. Court of Appeals for the D.C. Circuit, who spent three decades struggling to correct his Yale law clerk's high opinion of a "quasi-court Court."

Notes

Chapter 1: Least Dangerous?

1. Alexander Hamilton, *The Federalist*, no. 78, in Alexander Hamilton, John Jay, and James Madison, *The Federalist*, ed. George W. Carey and James McClellan, 1818 Gideon ed. (Indianapolis: Liberty Fund, 1990), 402.
2. *Dobbs v. Jackson Women's Health Organization*, 142 S. Ct. 2228 (2022), reversing *Roe v. Wade*, 410 U.S. 113 (1973).
3. Nancy Pelosi and Chuck Schumer, "Schumer, Pelosi Joint Statement on Reported Draft Supreme Court Decision to Overturn Roe v. Wade," press release, May 2, 2022, https://www.democrats.senate.gov/about-senate-dems/dpcc/press-releases/schumer-pelosi-joint-statement-on-reported-draft-supreme-court-decision-to-overturn-roe-v-wade.
4. *New York State Rifle & Pistol Association v. Bruen*, 142 S. Ct. 2111 (2022).
5. *West Virginia v. EPA*, 142 S. Ct. 2587 (2022).
6. *Kennedy v. Bremerton School District*, 142 S. Ct. 2407 (2022).
7. *Alabama Association of Realtors v. Department of Health and Human Services*, 141 S. Ct. 2320 (2021); *National Federation of Independent Business v. Occupational Safety and Health Administration*, 142 S. Ct. 661 (2022).
8. *Department of Homeland Security v. Regents of the University of California*, 140 S. Ct. 1891 (2020).
9. *Trump v. Hawaii*, 138 S. Ct. 2392 (2018).
10. *Trinity Lutheran Church of Columbia, Inc. v. Comer*, 137 S. Ct. 2012 (2017).
11. *McCutcheon v. FEC*, 572 U.S. 185 (2014); *Citizens United v. FEC*, 558 U.S. 310 (2010).
12. *Pennsylvania Democratic Party v. Boockvar*, 662 Pa. 39 (2020); Cert. Denied, *Republican Party of Pennsylvania. v. Degraffenreid*, 141 S. Ct. 732 (2021) (mem.).
13. *Rucho v. Common Cause*, 139 S. Ct. 2484 (2019).
14. Ibid.

15. *Students for Fair Admissions v. University of North Carolina*, Docket No. 21-707; *Students for Fair Admissions v. President and Fellows of Harvard College*, Docket No. 20-1199.
16. *Sackett v. EPA*, Docket No. 21-454.
17. Alexis de Tocqueville, *Democracy in America: Historical-Critical Edition of* De la démocratie en Amérique, ed. Eduardo Nolla, trans. James T. Schleifer, French-English ed. (Indianapolis: Liberty Fund, 2010), 2:441.
18. *Marbury v. Madison*, 5 U.S. (1 Cranch) 137 (1803).
19. *Dred Scott v. Sandford*, 60 U.S. 393 (1857).
20. Abraham Lincoln, "First Inaugural Address—Final Text: March 4, 1861," in *The Collected Works of Abraham Lincoln*, ed. Roy P. Basler (New Brunswick: Rutgers University Press, 1953), 4:268.
21. Ibid.
22. *McCulloch v. Maryland*, 17 U.S. (4 Wheat.) 316 (1819).
23. *Obergefell v. Hodges*, 576 U.S. 644 (2015).
24. Janet Hook and Christi Parsons, "Obama Says Empathy Key to Court Pick," *Los Angeles Times*, May 2, 2009, https://www.latimes.com/archives/la-xpm-2009-may-02-na-court-souter2-story.html.
25. Robert Alt and Deborah Malley, "Key Questions for Sonia Sotomayor," The Heritage Foundation, July 10, 2009, https://www.heritage.org/report/key-questions-sonia-sotomayor/#_ftn1.
26. "Chief Justice Roberts Statement—Nomination Process," United States Courts, 2005, https://www.uscourts.gov/educational-resources/educational-activities/chief-justice-roberts-statement-nomination-process.
27. John Yoo and James C. Phillips, "A Clash of Judicial Visions," *National Review*, October 19, 2018, https://www.nationalreview.com/2018/10/supreme-courtjudicialphilosophy-constitutional-system/.
28. "Chief Justice Roberts Statement."
29. Hamilton, *Federalist*, no. 78, 402.
30. H. Jefferson Powell, *Constitutional Conscience: The Moral Dimension of Judicial Decision* (Chicago: University of Chicago Press, 2008), 16.
31. Hamilton, *Federalist*, no. 78, 405.

Chapter 2: *Marshall, Marbury*, and *McCulloch*

1. *Marbury v. Madison*, 5 U.S. (1 Cranch) 137, 176 (1803).
2. James Rosen, *Scalia: Rise to Greatness, 1936–1986* (Washington, D.C.: Regnery Publishing, 2023), 382.
3. *Marbury*, 5 U.S. (1 Cranch) 137, 177.

4. Ibid., 180.
5. Ibid., 177.
6. *McCulloch v. Maryland*, 17 U.S. (4 Wheat.) 316, 421 (1819).
7. *McCulloch*, 17 U.S. 316.
8. Ibid., 415.
9. Letter from James Madison to Judge Roane, September 2, 1819, in *The Records of the Federal Convention of 1787*, ed. Max Farrand (New Haven: Yale University Press; London: Henry Frowde and Oxford University Press, 1911), 3:435.
10. *Gibbons v. Ogden*, 22 U.S. (9 Wheat.) 1, 194 (1824).
11. *United States v. Morrison*, 529 U.S. 598, 627 (2000) (Thomas, J., concurring).

Chapter 3: From the Civil War to the New Deal

1. *Scott v. Sandford*, 60 U.S. (19 How.) 393, 404 (1857).
2. Ibid., 404–5.
3. Ibid., 410.
4. *Ex parte Milligan*, 71 U.S. (4 Wall.) 2 (1866).
5. Keith E. Whittington, *Political Foundations of Judicial Supremacy: The Presidency, the Supreme Court, and Constitutional Leadership in U.S. History* (Princeton: Princeton University Press, 2007), 254.
6. Abraham Lincoln, "First Inaugural Address—Final Text: March 4, 1861," in *The Collected Works of Abraham Lincoln*, ed. Roy P. Basler (New Brunswick: Rutgers University Press, 1953), 4:268.
7. *Prize Cases*, 67 U.S. (2 Black) 635 (1862).
8. *Slaughter-House Cases*, 83 U.S. (16 Wall.) 36 (1873).
9. *Plessy v. Ferguson*, 163 U.S. 537, 548 (1896).
10. *Hammer v. Dagenhart*, 247 U.S. 251, 272 (1918).
11. David E. Bernstein, *Rehabilitating Lochner: Defending Individual Rights against Progressive Reform* (Chicago: University of Chicago Press, 2011).
12. *Lochner v. New York*, 198 U.S. 45, 53 (1905).
13. *Lochner v. New York*, 198 U.S. 45, 75 (1905) (Holmes, J., dissenting).
14. John Yoo, *Crisis and Command: The History of Executive Power from George Washington to George W. Bush* (New York: Kaplan Publishing, 2009), 259–60.
15. Ibid., 260.
16. Franklin D. Roosevelt, "Acceptance Speech for the Renomination for the Presidency, Philadelphia, Pa.," June 27, 1936, The American Presidency Project, https://www.presidency.ucsb.edu/documents/acceptance-speech-for-the-renomination-for-the-presidency-philadelphia-pa.
17. *Panama Refining Co. v. Ryan*, 293 U.S. 388 (1935).

18. *A. L. A. Schechter Poultry Corp. v. United States*, 295 U.S. 495, 528 (1935).
19. Franklin D. Roosevelt, "Press Conference #209," Executive Offices of the White House, May 31, 1935, http://www.fdrlibrary.marist.edu/_resources/images/pc/pc0022.pdf.
20. Ibid.
21. *United States v. Butler*, 297 U.S. 1, 74 (1936).
22. *Carter v. Carter Coal Co.*, 298 U.S. 238, 309–10 (1936).
23. *Jones v. SEC*, 298 U.S. 1, 27, 28 (1936).
24. *Morehead v. New York ex rel. Tipaldo*, 298 U.S. 587 (1936).
25. Franklin D. Roosevelt, "Message to Congress on the Reorganization of the Judicial Branch of the Government," The American Presidency Project, February 5, 1937, https://www.presidency.ucsb.edu/documents/message-congress-the-reorganization-the-judicial-branch-the-government.
26. *NLRB v. Jones & Laughlin Steel Corp.*, 301 U.S. 1, 41 (1937).

Chapter 4: Equality before the Law

1. *Slaughter-House Cases*, 83 U.S. (16 Wall.) 36, 78 (1873).
2. See *Duncan v. Louisiana*, 391 U.S. 145, 163, 170–71 (1968) (Black, J., concurring). Justice Thomas has argued that incorporation should proceed under the Fourteenth Amendment's Privileges or Immunities Clause instead. See, e.g., *Timbs v. Indiana*, 139 S. Ct. 682, 691 (2019) (Thomas, J., concurring in judgment).
3. See *Gitlow v. New York*, 268 U.S. 652 (1925) (incorporating freedom of speech); *De Jonge v. Oregon*, 299 U.S. 353 (1937) (incorporating freedom of assembly); *Near v. Minnesota*, 283 U.S. 697 (1931) (incorporating freedom of the press); *Cantwell v. Connecticut*, 310 U.S. 296 (1940) (incorporating free exercise of religion); *Everson v. Board of Education*, 330 U.S. 1 (1947) (incorporating the prohibition against government establishment of religion).
4. *Engel v. Vitale*, 370 U.S. 421 (1962).
5. *Mapp v. Ohio*, 367 U.S. 643 (1961); *Gideon v. Wainwright*, 372 U.S. 335 (1963); *Miranda v. Arizona*, 384 U.S. 436 (1966).
6. *Wong Sun v. United States*, 371 U.S. 471, 488 (1963).
7. Holly Thomas, "What Are 'Miranda Rights'—and How Does This Latest Supreme Court Decision Affect Them?," Katie Couric Media, June 24, 2022, https://katiecouric.com/news/what-are-miranda-rights-and-how-does-this-latest-supreme-court-decision-affect-them/.
8. *Brown v. Board of Education* (*Brown I*), 347 U.S. 483, 495 (1954).
9. *Brown v. Board of Education* (*Brown II*), 349 U.S. 294, 301 (1955).

10. Reva B. Siegel, "Equality Talk: Antisubordination and Anticlassification Values in Constitutional Struggles over Brown," *Harvard Law Review* 117, no. 5 (2004): 1487.
11. Michael J. Klarman, *From Jim Crow to Civil Rights: The Supreme Court and the Struggle for Racial Equality* (New York: Oxford University Press, 2006).
12. *Reynolds v. Sims*, 377 U.S. 533, 558 (1964).
13. *Griswold v. Connecticut*, 381 U.S. 479, 485–86 (1965).
14. Ibid., 484.
15. *Roe v. Wade*, 410 U.S. 113, 152–53, 159, 163 (1973).
16. *Doe v. Bolton*, 410 U.S. 179 (White, J., dissenting).
17. John Hart Ely, "The Wages of Crying Wolf: A Comment on *Roe v. Wade*," *Yale Law Journal* 82, no. 5 (April 1973): 947.
18. Ruth Bader Ginsburg, "Speaking in a Judicial Voice," *New York University Law Review* 67, no. 6 (December 1992): 1208.
19. *Planned Parenthood v. Casey*, 505 U.S. 833, 867 (1992).
20. *Poe v. Ullman*, 367 U.S. 497, 546 (1961) (Harlan, J. dissenting).
21. *Lawrence v. Texas*, 539 U.S. 558, 567 (2003).
22. *Obergefell v. Hodges*, 576 U.S. 644, 675 (2015).
23. *Lawrence v. Texas*, 539 U.S. 558, 590 (2003) (Scalia, J., dissenting).
24. "Attitudes on Same-Sex Marriage: Public Opinion on Same-Sex Marriage," Pew Research Center, May 4, 2019, https://www.pewresearch.org/religion/fact-sheet/changing-attitudes-on-gay-marriage.
25. Abner J. Mikva, "A Rejoinder to 'The Judge's Role in Educating the Public about the Law," *Catholic University Law Review* 31, no. 2 (Winter 1982): 211, quoting Finley Peter Dunne, *Mr. Dooley At His Best*, ed. Elmer Ellis (New York: Scribner's Sons, 1938), 77, with modifications to the original spelling.

Chapter 5: Abortion and the Current Supreme Court

1. Drew Desilver, "Up until the Postwar Era, U.S. Supreme Court Confirmations Usually Were Routine Business," Pew Research Center, February 7, 2022, https://www.pewresearch.org/fact-tank/2022/02/07/up-until-the-postwar-era-u-s-supreme-court-confirmations-usually-were-routine-business.
2. Kathryn Jean Lopez, "When the 'Dogma Lives Loudly' within One—What Judge Amy Barrett Can Teach Us," *National Review*, November 6, 2017, https://www.nationalreview.com/2017/11/dogma-lives-loudly-within-judge-amy-barrett-thank-goodness.
3. *National Federation of Independent Business v. Sebelius*, 567 U.S. 519 (2012); Joan Biskupic, "The Inside Story of How John Roberts Negotiated to Save Obamacare,"

CNN, March 25, 2019, https://www.cnn.com/2019/03/21/politics/john-roberts-obamacare-the-chief/index.html.

4. *Gonzales v. Carhart*, 550 U.S. 124 (2007) and *Gonzales v. Planned Parenthood*, 550 U.S. 124 (2007); *Whole Woman's Health v. Hellerstedt*, 136 S. Ct. 2292 (2016); *June Medical Services v. Russo*, 140 S. Ct. 2103 (2020).
5. Biskupic, "Inside Story."
6. "Kagan Confirmation Hearing, Day 2, Part 1," C-SPAN, June 29, 2010, https://www.c-span.org/video/?294264-2/kagan-confirmation-hearing-day-2-part-1.
7. "Ketanji Brown Jackson and Antonin Scalia" (editorial), *Wall Street Journal*, March 24, 2022, https://www.wsj.com/articles/ketanji-brown-jackson-and-antonin-scalia-supreme-court-senate-confimation-hearings-originalism-11648159368.
8. "Questions for the Record for Ketanji Brown Jackson, Nominee to Be Associate Justice of the United States Supreme Court," (written responses to questions from Sen. Ted Cruz for the record), U.S. Senate Committee on the Judiciary, 117th Congress, 2022, page 79, https://www.judiciary.senate.gov/imo/media/doc/Judge%20Ketanji%20Brown%20Jackson%20Written%20Responses%20to%20Questions%20for%20the%20Record.pdf.

Chapter 6: The Leak

1. *Planned Parenthood v. Casey*, 505 U.S. 833, 851 (1992).
2. John Hart Ely, "The Wages of Crying Wolf: A Comment on *Roe v. Wade*," *Yale Law Journal* 82, no. 5 (April 1973): 947.
3. Ruth Bader Ginsburg, "Speaking in a Judicial Voice," *New York University Law Review* 67, no. 6 (December 1992): 1199–1209.
4. *Obergefell v. Hodges*, 135 S. Ct. 2584 (2015).
5. Alexander Hamilton, *The Federalist*, no. 78, in Alexander Hamilton, John Jay, and James Madison, *The Federalist*, ed. George W. Carey and James McClellan, 1818 Gideon ed. (Indianapolis: Liberty Fund, 1990), 405.
6. Abraham Lincoln, "First Inaugural Address—Final Text: March 4, 1861," in *The Collected Works of Abraham Lincoln*, ed. Roy P. Basler (New Brunswick: Rutgers University Press, 1953), 4:268.
7. Hamilton, *Federalist*, no. 78, 402.
8. Ibid., 405.

Chapter 7: Overruling *Roe*: The *Dobbs* Decision

1. *Dobbs v. Jackson Women's Health Organization*, 142 S. Ct. 2228 (2022) (reversing *Roe v. Wade*, 410 U.S. 113 (1973)).
2. Ibid.

3. Ibid.
4. *District of Columbia v. Heller*, 554 U.S. 570 (2008).
5. See, for example, *Meyer v. Nebraska*, 262 U.S. 390 (1923); *Pierce v. Society of Sisters*, 268 U.S. 510 (1925); and *Troxel v. Granville*, 530 U.S. 57 (2000).
6. *Washington v. Glucksberg*, 521 U.S. 702, 703 (1997).
7. See, e.g., *Gregg v. Georgia*, 428 U.S. 153 (1976); *United States v. Quinones*, 313 F.3d 49 (2d. Cir. 2002).
8. *Dobbs*, 142 S. Ct. 2228.
9. Ibid., 2235.
10. Colleen Walsh, "Softer Tone Post-Leak? Maybe, Says Tribe, but Ruling Will Remain an 'Iron Fist,'" *Harvard Gazette*, May 3, 2022, https://news.harvard.edu/gazette/story/2022/05/laurence-tribe-on-scotus-leak.
11. *Dobbs*, 142 S. Ct. at 2258.
12. Ibid., 2243.
13. *Slaughter-House Cases*, 83 U.S. (16 Wall.) 36 (1873).
14. See, e.g., *Saenz v. Roe*, 526 U.S. 489 (1999) (Thomas, J., dissenting); *Troxel v. Granville*, 530 U.S. 57, 80 (2000) (Thomas, J., concurring); *McDonald v. City of Chicago*, 561 U.S. 742, 805 (2010) (Thomas, J., concurring in part and concurring in the judgment); *Timbs v. Indiana*, 139 S. Ct. 682 (2019), (Thomas, J., concurring in the judgment).
15. George F. Will, "Gorsuch's Chance to Correct Scalia on the Constitution," *Washington Post*, February 1, 2017, https://www.washingtonpost.com/opinions/gorsuchs-chance-to-correct-scalia-on-the-constitution/2017/02/01/765d2980-e8b6-11e6-bf6f-301b6b443624_story.html.
16. *Dobbs v. Jackson Women's Health Organization*, 142 S. Ct. 2228, 2301 (2022) (Thomas J., concurring).
17. Ibid., 2301–2.
18. *Roe*, 410 U.S. 113.
19. Abraham Lincoln, "Fifth Debate with Stephen A. Douglas at Galesburg, Illinois, October 7, 1858," in *The Collected Works of Abraham Lincoln*, ed. Roy P. Basler (New Brunswick: Rutgers University Press, 1953), 3:225–26.
20. Gary Bauer, "Obama and the Politics of Empathy," *POLITICO*, April 7, 2010, https://www.politico.com/story/2010/04/obama-and-the-politics-of-empathy-035499.
21. Olga R. Rodriguez, "Archbishop: Pelosi Will Be Denied Communion over Abortion," Associated Press, May 20, 2022, https://apnews.com/article/abortion-congress-nancy-pelosi-san-francisco-religion-cd68155b976a60fc4f6b948acb217858.
22. Catherine Lucey, "Upholding Roe v. Wade Is Supported by Most Americans, WSJ Poll Finds," *Wall Street Journal*, June 2, 2022, https://www.wsj.com/articles/upholding-roe-v-wade-is-supported-by-most-americans-wsj-poll-finds-11654162200.

23. Victoria Balara, "Fox News Poll: Support for Abortion Depends on Circumstance and Timing," Fox News, July 17, 2022, https://www.foxnews.com/official-polls/fox-news-poll-support-abortion-depends-circumstance-timing; Mary Rooke, "Most Americans Want an Abortion Ban after 15 Weeks: POLL," Daily Caller, July 5, 2022, https://dailycaller.com/2022/07/05/harvard-caps-harris-poll-americans-abortion-ban-15-weeks-democrats-republicans.
24. See Jeff Diamant and Besheer Mohamed, "What the Data Says about Abortion in the U.S.," Pew Research Center, updated January 11, 2023, https://www.pewresearch.org/fact-tank/2022/06/24/what-the-data-says-about-abortion-in-the-u-s-2.
25. Lauren Egan, "Biden Administration Says Hospitals Must Provide Abortions in Emergencies," NBC News, July 11, 2022, https://www.nbcnews.com/politics/politics-news/biden-administration-says-hospitals-must-provide-abortions-emergencies-rcna37715.
26. *City of Boerne v. Flores*, 521 U.S. 507 (1997); *Employment Division v. Smith*, 494 U.S. 872 (1990).
27. *City of Boerne*, 521 U.S. at 508.
28. *Gonzales v. Carhart*, 550 U.S. 124 (2007).
29. Ibid.
30. *United States v. Lopez*, 514 U.S. 549 (1995).
31. *United States v. Morrison*, 529 U.S. 598 (2000).

Chapter 8: *Heller*: The Court Takes Up the Second Amendment

1. Thomas Black, "Americans Have More Guns than Anywhere Else in the World and They Keep Buying More," Bloomberg, May 25, 2022, https://www.bloomberg.com/news/articles/2022-05-25/how-many-guns-in-the-us-buying-spree-bolsters-lead-as-most-armed-country?leadSource=uverify%20wall.
2. Gary Klek, Tomislav Kovandzic, and Jon Bellows, "Does Gun Control Reduce Violent Crime?," *Criminal Justice Review* 41, no. 4 (December 2016): 488–513, https://journals.sagepub.com/doi/abs/10.1177/0734016816670457?journalCode=cjra. In spite of gun control regulations, a vast majority of public shootings continue to occur in "gun free" zones. John Lott, "Updated: Mass Public Shootings Keep Occurring in Gun-Free Zones: 94% of Attacks since 1950," Crime Prevention Research Center, June 15, 2018, https://crimeresearch.org/2018/06/more-misleading-information-from-bloombergs-everytown-for-gun-safety-on-guns-analysis-of-recent-mass-shootings/.
   In 2015 it was found that 80–88 percent of mass shooting incidents, defined as shootings with four or more fatalities, were associated with other criminal activity or

domestic violence. William J. Krouse and Daniel J. Richardson, *Mass Murder with Firearms: Incidents and Victims, 1999–2013*, (Washington, D.C.: Congressional Research Service, 2015).

A 2015 analysis of 358 mass shootings resulted in the determination that one-third were a result of drive-by or gang-related shootings, another third were the result of arguments (often between "people who were drunk or high"), and a tenth were the result of domestic violence. The tenth of mass shootings that were attributable to domestic violence caused 31 percent of total fatalities from mass shootings. Ninety percent of zip codes with mass shootings had "higher-than-average poverty rates." Lois Beckett, "Most Victims of US Mass Shootings Are Black, Data Analysis Finds," *The Guardian*, May 23, 2016, https://www.theguardian.com/us-news/2016/may/23/mass-shootings-tracker-analysis-us-gun-control-reddit.

3. Illinois and New York, alongside California, are recognized as some of the strictest states with regards to their gun control laws, yet they are the states where some of the most severe mass shooting incidents of the previous year occurred. In May 14, 2022, the Buffalo shooting in New York resulted in thirteen casualties. Artemis Moshtaghian et al., "10 People Killed in a Racially Motivated Mass Shooting at a Buffalo Supermarket, Police Say," CNN, May 14, 2022, https://www.cnn.com/2022/05/14/us/buffalo-ny-supermarket-multiple-shooting/index.html. On July 4, 2022, the Highland Park shooting in Illinois resulted in seven fatalities and more than forty wounded. Meryl Kornfield, "Highland Park Shooting Suspect Indicted on More than 100 Felony Counts," *Washington Post*, July 27, 2022, https://www.washingtonpost.com/nation/2022/07/27/highland-park-indictment/.
4. James Madison, *The Federalist*, no. 46, in Alexander Hamilton, John Jay, and James Madison, *The Federalist*, ed. George W. Carey and James McClellan, 1818 Gideon ed. (Indianapolis: Liberty Fund, 1990), 247.
5. Joseph Story, *Commentaries on the Constitution* (Boston: Hilliard, Gray, and Company; Cambridge: Brown, Shattuck, and Co., 1833), 3:746.
6. *District of Columbia v. Heller*, 554 U.S. 570 (2008); *McDonald v. City of Chicago*, 561 U.S. 742 (2010); and *New York State Rifle & Pistol Association v. Bruen*, 142 S. Ct. 2111 (2022).
7. For an overview and defense of originalism, see Ilan Wurman, *A Debt against the Living: An Introduction to Originalism* (New York: Cambridge University Press, 2017).
8. On the roots of "living constitutionalism" in the thought of the Progressive movement, see Bradley C. S. Watson, *Living Constitution, Dying Faith: Progressivism and the New Science of Jurisprudence* (Wilmington, Delaware: ISI Books, 2009).
9. *Saenz v. Roe*, 526 U.S. 489 (1999), (Thomas, J., dissenting).
10. *Timbs v. Indiana*, 139 S. Ct. 682 (2019), (Gorsuch, J., concurring).

11. For an account of Justice Thomas's jurisprudence, see Myron Magnet, *Clarence Thomas and the Lost Constitution* (New York: Encounter Books, 2019).
12. *United States v. Miller*, 307 U.S. 174 (1939).
13. *Barron v. Baltimore*, 32 U.S. 243 (1833).
14. *Heller*, 554 U.S. at 576.
15. Remarks of Representative James Madison on February 2, 1791, 2 Annals of Congress, 1946, 1945.
16. *Heller*, 554 U.S. at 578; Platt Potter, ed., *A General Treatise on Statutes* (Sydney, Australia: Wentworth Press, 2019), 268–69.
17. *Heller*, 554 U.S. at 643.
18. Walter Hartwell Bennett, ed., *Letters from the Federal Farmer to the Republican* (Tuscaloosa: University of Alabama, 1978), 21–22. On the identity of "The Federal Farmer," see Gordon S. Wood, "The Authorship of the *Letters from the Federal Farmer*," *William and Mary Quarterly* 31, no. 2 (April 1974): 299–301.
19. Quoted in Jonathan Gienapp, *The Second Constitution: Fixing the American Constitution in the Founding Era* (Cambridge: Belknap Press, 2018), 89.
20. *Heller*, 554 U.S. at 579–80.
21. Ibid, 583–85.
22. Ibid., 592–93.
23. *Alden v. Maine*, 527 U.S. 706, 715 (1999).
24. William Blackstone, "Commentary 41," in *Commentaries on the Laws of England: A Facsimile of the First Edition of 1765–1769* (Chicago: University of Chicago Press, 1979), 1:139–40.
25. *Heller*, 554 U.S. at 598–99.
26. Ibid., 600.
27. Ibid.
28. Richard A. Posner, "In Defense of Looseness," *New Republic*, August 28, 2008, https://newrepublic.com/article/62124/defense-looseness.
29. Saul Cornell, *A Well-Regulated Militia: The Founding Fathers and the Origins of Gun Control in America* (New York: Oxford University Press, 2008), 63.
30. John Paul Stevens, *Six Amendments: How and Why We Should Change the Constitution* (Boston: Little, Brown and Company, 2014), x.
31. *District of Columbia v. Heller*, 554 U.S. 570, 636–37 (2008) (Stevens, J., dissenting).
32. Ibid., 640–43.
33. Ibid., 646–48
34. Ibid., 657.
35. "Ratification of the Constitution by the State of New Hampshire, June 21, 1788," Yale Law School: The Avalon Project, 2008, https://avalon.law.yale.edu/18th_century/ratnh.asp.

36. *Heller*, 554 U.S. at 658–60 (Stevens, J., dissenting).
37. Ibid., 660.
38. *Ramos v. Louisiana*, 140 S. Ct. 1390 (2020).
39. William Blackstone, "Of Homicide," in *Commentaries on the Laws of England: A Facsimile of the First Edition of 1765–1769* (Chicago: University of Chicago Press, 1979), 4:176–88.
40. *District of Columbia v. Heller,* 554 U.S. 570, 682 (2008) (Breyer, J., dissenting).
41. Ibid., 689–90.
42. *National Socialist Party of America v. Village of Skokie,* 432 U.S. 43 (1977).
43. *Nixon v. Shrink Missouri Government PAC*, 528 U.S. 377, 402 (Breyer, J., concurring) (2000).
44. *Snyder v. Phelps*, 562 U.S. 443 (2011).

Chapter 9: *McDonald*: Incorporating the Second Amendment

1. *McDonald v. City of Chicago*, 561 U.S. 742 (2010).
2. For a review of the state of the debate, see Michael P. Zuckert, "Coping with the 14th Amendment," *Claremont Review of Books* 22, no. 1 (Winter 2021–2022), https://claremontreviewofbooks.com/coping-with-the-14th-amendment/.
3. *Pierce v. Society of Sisters*, 268 U.S. 510 (1925)
4. *Slaughter-House Cases*, 83 U.S. (16 Wall.) 36 (1873).
5. For example, in *Bradwell v. Illinois*, 83 U.S. 130 (1872), the Court denied that the Privileges or Immunities Clause protected the right of a woman to obtain a license to practice law. The Court wrote (at 139): "We agree . . . that there are privileges and immunities belonging to citizens of the United States, in that relation and character, and that it is these and these alone which a state is forbidden to abridge. But the right to admission to practice in the courts of a state is not one of them." See also *United States v. Cruikshank*, 92 U.S. 542 (1875); *O'Neil v. Vermont*, 144 U.S. 323 (1892); *Maxwell v. Dow*, 176 U.S. 581 (1900); *Twining v. New Jersey*, 211 U.S. 78 (1908).
6. *McDonald v. City of Chicago*, 561 U.S. 742 (2010) (Stevens, J., dissenting).
7. *Adamson v. California*, 332 U.S. 46 (1947).
8. For a stimulating and persuasive example of revisionist scholarship, see Randy H. Barnett and Evan D. Bernick, *The Original Meaning of the Fourteenth Amendment: Its Letter and Spirit* (Cambridge: Belknap Press, 2021).
9. Solo opinions by the justices are not always the products of quirkiness or eccentricity. Justice Scalia was the sole dissenter in the 1988 *Morrison* case, which upheld the constitutionality of a special counsel charged with investigating and prosecuting alleged wrongdoing within the executive branch. In part because the ability of the attorney general (and of the president) to remove the special counsel

from office was constrained, Scalia regarded the appointment as a violation of separation of powers, and hence unconstitutional. Scalia's opinion is now widely regarded as correct, indeed a classic. *Morrison v. Olson*, 487 U.S. 654 (1988).

10. *McDonald v. City of Chicago*, 561 U.S. 742, 805–6 (2010) (Thomas, J., concurring).
11. Ibid., 813.
12. Ibid., 828.
13. Ibid.
14. Cong. Globe, 39th Cong., 1st Sess., 2765 (1866).
15. Ibid., 2766.
16. Ibid., 2675.
17. *McDonald*, 561 U.S. at 813 (Thomas, J., concurring).
18. Ibid., 812.
19. Ibid., 811–12.

Chapter 10: *Bruen*: Do You Need a "Special Need" to Carry a Gun?

1. *New York State Rifle & Pistol Association, Inc. v. Bruen*, 142 S. Ct. 2111 (2022).
2. Ibid.
3. *New York State Rifle & Pistol Association, Inc. v. Bruen*, 142 S. Ct. 2111 (2022) (Breyer, J., dissenting).
4. *New York State Rifle & Pistol Association, Inc. v. Bruen*, 142 S. Ct. 2111 (2022) (Alito, J., concurring).
5. *New York State Rifle & Pistol Association, Inc. v. Bruen*, 142 S. Ct. 2111 (2022) (Kavanaugh, J., concurring).
6. *New York State Rifle & Pistol Association, Inc. v. Bruen*, 142 S. Ct. 2111 (2022) (Barrett, J., concurring).
7. *Bruen*, 142 S. Ct. 2111 (Alito, J., concurring).
8. Transcript of Oral Argument at 67, *New York State Rifle & Pistol Association, Inc. v. Bruen*, 142 S. Ct. 2111 (2022).
9. Jeff Spross, "How Obama Addressed Trumpism Way Back in 2008," *The Week*, March 8, 2016, https://theweek.com/articles/610945/how-obama-diagnosed-trumpism-way-back-2008.
10. *Bruen*, 142 S. Ct. 2111 (2022).
11. Ibid.
12. Ibid.
13. Ibid.
14. *Bruen*, 142 S. Ct. 2111 (Alito, J., concurring).
15. *Bruen*, 142 S. Ct. 2111 (Kavanaugh, J., concurring).

16. Letitia James, "Understanding Recent Changes to New York's Gun Laws," Letitia James: NY Attorney General, 2022, https://ag.ny.gov/new-york-gun-laws; "Senate Bill S51001, 2021–2022 Legislative Session: Relates to Licensing and Other Provisions Relating to Firearms," The New York State Senate, July 1, 2022, https://www.nysenate.gov/legislation/bills/2021/S51001; "Governor Hochul Signs Landmark Legislation to Strengthen Gun Laws and Bolster Restrictions on Concealed Carry Weapons in Response to Reckless Supreme Court Decision," New York State, July 1, 2022, https://www.governor.ny.gov/news/governor-hochul-signs-landmark-legislation-strengthen-gun-laws-and-bolster-restrictions.
17. Bipartisan Safer Communities Act, Pub. L. No. 117-159, 136 Stat. 1313 (2022). On the "loophole," see Rachel Treisman, "The Senate Gun Bill Would Close the 'Boyfriend Loophole.' Here's What That Means," NPR, June 23, 2022, https://www.npr.org/2022/06/23/1106967037/boyfriend-loophole-senate-bipartisan-gun-safety-bill-domestic-abuse.
18. *Caniglia v. Strom*, 141 S. Ct. 1596 (2021).
19. *Plessy v. Ferguson*, 163 U.S. 537 (1896).
20. *Bruen*, 142 S. Ct. 2111.
21. See John F. Stinneford, "The Origins of the Meaning of 'Unusual': The Eighth Amendment as a Bar to Cruel Innovation," *Northwestern University Law Review* 102, no. 4 (2008): 1739–1825.
22. *Griswold v. Connecticut*, 381 U.S. 479 (1965).

Chapter 11: The "Living Constitution" and the Fourth Branch

1. Often enough, outside experts are highly critical of the claims by "experts" working for the administrative agencies, arguing that the latter disregard scientific data and are driven by a political agenda. See, for example, Marty Makary, "Why America Doesn't Trust the CDC," *Newsweek*, June 10, 2022, https://www.newsweek.com/why-america-doesnt-trust-cdc-opinion-1713145. Such skepticism is shared by much of the public.

   In April of 2022, the American Enterprise Institute published a study called "Attitudes about the Federal Government: Major Trends." The study reported the results of decades of polling by various organizations about public attitudes towards the federal government. For example, the study tabulated responses recorded by the Gallup organization between September 2002 and September 2021 to the question, "Do you think the federal government today has too much power, has about the right amount of power or has too little power?" In 2002, 39 percent answered, "Too much power," 52 percent answered, "About the right amount of power," and 7 percent answered, "Too little power." In 2021, the answers were 54, 36, and 9 percent respectively. According to Pew polling, responses to the question "How much of the time do you think you can trust the government in Washington to do what is right—just about always, most of the time, or only some of the time?"—shifted from 2 percent "Just about always," 36 percent "Most of the time," 60 percent "Only some of the time," and 2 percent "Never" in 1997 (when polling began) to 2, 22, 61, and 14 percent, respectively, in 2021. In other words, by 2021 three quarters of the American public trusted the government only some of the time or not at all. Karlyn Bowman and Samantha Goldstein, "Attitudes about the Federal Government: Major Trends," American Enterprise Institute, April 15, 2022, https://www.aei.org/research-products/report/attitudes-about-the-federal-government-major-trends/.

In 2019 the Niskanen Center published an interview with two scholars who had recently written books on public attitudes towards the bureaucracy. Both scholars agreed that government was facing a "reputation crisis, not unlike those in business scandals." Amy Lerman of the University of California, Berkeley, one of the scholars interviewed, said, "We're really in a reputation crisis, which goes beyond what we think of as the usual low-trust in government, and is really this downward spiral, a cycle of public opinion that is self-reinforcing. . . . We have now decades of research on declining trust in government and perceptions of government that are increasingly negative." "Why Americans Dislike Government, Even When It Works," Niskanen Center, September 3, 2019, https://www.niskanencenter.org/why-american-dislike-government-even-when-it-works/.

2. Cass R. Sunstein and Adrian Vermeule, *Law & Leviathan: Redeeming the Administrative State* (Cambridge: Belknap Press, 2020), 3.
3. *Rapanos v. United States*, 547 U.S. 715, 721 (2006).
4. *West Virginia v. EPA*, 142 S. Ct. 2587 (2022).
5. See, for example, *Seila Law LLC v. Consumer Financial Protection Bureau*, 140 S. Ct. 2183 (2020); *Collins v. Yellen*, 141 S. Ct. 1761 (2021); and *Free Enterprise Fund v. Public Accounting Oversight Board*, 561 U.S. 477 (2010).
6. Albert J. Beveridge, *"Pass Prosperity Around"* (New York: Stoddard-Sutherland Press, 1912), 15.
7. William Howard Taft and Elihu Root, *Speech of William Howard Taft Accepting the Republican Nomination for President of the United States: Together with the Speech of Notification by Senator Elihu Root* (Washington, D.C.: U.S. Government Printing Office, 1912), 3–4.
8. Woodrow Wilson, "The Study of Administration," *Political Science Quarterly* 2, no. 2 (June 1887): 204.
9. Ibid.

10. Woodrow Wilson, "The Art of Governing," November 15, 1885, in *The Papers of Woodrow Wilson*, vol. 5, *1885–1888*, ed. Arthur S. Link (Princeton: Princeton University Press, 1968), 52.
11. Woodrow Wilson, *Constitutional Government in the United States* (New York: Columbia University Press, 1908), 192.
12. Wilson, "Study of Administration," 199–200, 204, 210.
13. Woodrow Wilson, *Congressional Government: A Study in American Politics*, 15th ed. (Boston: Houghton, Mifflin and Company; Cambridge: The Riverside Press, 1901), 284.
14. Woodrow Wilson, *The New Freedom: A Call for the Emancipation of the Generous Energies of a People* (New York and Garden City, New York: Doubleday, Page & Company, 1913), 47.
15. Wilson, "Study of Administration," 201.
16. Ibid., 213.
17. Ibid., 213–14.
18. Woodrow Wilson, "Notes on Administration," in *The Papers of Woodrow Wilson*, vol. 7, *1890–1892*, ed. Arthur S. Link (Princeton: Princeton University Press, 1969), 121.
19. *Perez v. Mortgage Bankers Association*, 575 U.S. 92, 130 n. 6 (2015).
20. Woodrow Wilson, "Shorthand Diary," in *The Papers of Woodrow Wilson*, vol. 1, *1856–1880*, ed. Arthur S. Link (Princeton: Princeton University Press, 1966), 143.
21. Woodrow Wilson, "Marginal Notes on John Richard Green," in *The Papers of Woodrow Wilson*, vol. 1, *1856–1880*, ed. Arthur S. Link (Princeton: Princeton University Press, 1966), 388.
22. Wilson, "Study of Administration," 209.
23. Woodrow Wilson, *The State: Elements of Historical and Practical Politics*, ed. Edward Elliott (Boston, New York, and Chicago: D. C. Heath & Co., Publishers, 1918), 305.
24. Woodrow Wilson, "Random Notes for 'The Philosophy of Politics,'" in *The Papers of Woodrow Wilson*, vol. 9, *1894–1896*, ed. Arthur S. Link (Princeton: Princeton University Press, 1970), 132.
25. Wilson, *Constitutional Government*, 54.
26. Ibid., 67–68.
27. Ibid., 66.
28. Ibid., 66–67.
29. *Wayman v. Southard*, 23 U.S. 1 (1825).
30. *Gundy v. United States*, 139 S. Ct. 2116, 2123 (2019).
31. *INS v. Chadha*, 462 U.S. 919, 951 (1983).
32. *Mistretta v. United States*, 488 U.S. 361, 415 (1989) (Scalia, J., dissenting).

33. James Madison, *The Federalist*, no. 48, in Alexander Hamilton, John Jay, and James Madison, *The Federalist*, ed. George W. Carey and James McClellan, 1818 Gideon ed. (Indianapolis: Liberty Fund, 1990), 256.
34. John Locke, *Second Treatise of Government* (1690), § 141.
35. *Gundy v. United States*, 139 S. Ct. 2116 (2019) (Gorsuch, J., dissenting).
36. *Whitman v. American Trucking Associations, Inc.*, 531 U.S. 457, 472 (2001).
37. *Whitman*, 531 U.S. 457 (2001). See *Panama Refining Co. v. Ryan*, 293 U.S. 388 (1935) and *A. L. A. Schechter Poultry Corp. v. United States*, 295 U.S. 495 (1935).
38. *Whitman*, 531 U.S. at 474.
39. *Skinner v. Railway Labor Executives' Association*, 489 U.S. 602 (1989).
40. *Touby v. United States*, 500 U.S. 160 (1991).
41. *Lichter v. United States*, 334 U.S. 742 (1948).
42. *American Power & Light Co. v. SEC*, 329 U.S. 90 (1946).
43. *New York Central Securities Corp. v. United States*, 287 U.S. 12 (1932).
44. James Madison, *The Federalist*, no. 51, in Alexander Hamilton, John Jay, and James Madison, *The Federalist*, ed. George W. Carey and James McClellan, 1818 Gideon ed. (Indianapolis: Liberty Fund, 1990), 268.
45. See, for example, John O. McGinnis, "Constitutional Review by the Executive in Foreign Affairs and War Powers: A Consequence of Rational Choice in the Separation of Powers," *Law & Contemporary Problems* 56, no. 4 (Fall 1993): 293–325.
46. Code of Federal Regulations, 29 CFR 1910.2(f).
47. Occupational Safety and Health Act of 1970, Pub. L. No. 91-596, 94 Stat. 1590 (1970), section 6.
48. Peter J. Wallison, *Judicial Fortitude: The Last Chance to Rein in the Administrative State* (New York: Encounter Books, 2018), 48, quoting Christopher DeMuth Sr., "Can the Administrative State Be Tamed?," *Journal of Legal Analysis* 8, no. 1 (Spring 2016): 132.
49. Ibid.
50. *Industrial Union Department v. American Petroleum Institute*, 448 U.S. 607 (1980).
51. Gary Lawson's classic 1994 article "The Rise and Rise of the Administrative State" presses this objection. Gary S. Lawson, "The Rise and Rise of the Administrative State," *Harvard Law Review* 107, no. 6 (April 1994): 1231–54.

Chapter 12: Is It Too Late?

1. Charles Murray, *By the People: Rebuilding Liberty without Permission* (Crown Forum, 2015), 27.
2. Ibid.

3. Keith E. Whittington, *Repugnant Laws: Judicial Review of Acts of Congress from the Founding to the Present* (Lawrence, Kansas: University Press of Kansas, 2019), 238.
4. *United States v. Windsor*, 570 U.S. 744 (2013); *Obergefell v. Hodges*, 135 S. Ct. 2584 (2015).
5. *National Federation of Independent Business v. Sebelius*, 567 U.S. 519 (2012).
6. Yuval Levin, *The Fractured Republic: Renewing America's Social Contract in the Age of Individualism* (New York: Basic Books, 2017).
7. John Yoo, "Conclusion," in *The Administrative State before the Supreme Court: Perspectives on the Nondelegation Doctrine*, ed. Peter J. Wallison and John Yoo (Washington, D.C.: AEI Press, 2022), 385.
8. *Seila Law LLC v. Consumer Financial Protection Bureau*, 140 S. Ct. 2183 (2020); *Free Enterprise Fund v. Public Company Accounting Oversight Board*, 561 U.S. 477 (2010)
9. *West Virginia v. EPA*, 142 S. Ct. 2587 (2022).
10. Ibid.
11. Ibid., 2605.
12. *Alabama Association of Realtors v. Department of Health and Human Services*, 141 S. Ct. 2320 (2021).
13. *National Federation of Independent Business v. Occupational Safety and Health Administration*, 142 S. Ct. 661 (2022).
14. *West Virginia*, 142 S. Ct. 2587.
15. *Food and Drug Administration v. Brown & Williamson Tobacco Corporation*, 529 U.S. 120 (2000).
16. *Gonzales v. Oregon*, 546 U.S. 243 (2006).
17. *Rapanos v. United States*, 547 U.S. 715 (2006).
18. *West Virginia*, 142 S. Ct. 2587.
19. Ibid.
20. Ibid., 2609.
21. Ibid., 2616.
22. *Gundy v. United States*, 139 S. Ct. 2116, 2145 (2019) (Gorsuch, J., dissenting).
23. *West Virginia v. EPA*, 142 S. Ct. 2587 (2022) (Gorsuch, J., concurring).
24. *Wayman v. Southard*, 23 U.S. 1 (1825).
25. *West Virginia*, 142 S. Ct. 2587 (Gorsuch, J., concurring).
26. See Brigid Kennedy, "Should Biden Declare a National Climate Emergency?," *The Week*, July 21, 2022, https://theweek.com/environmental-news/1015285/should-biden-declare-climate-emergency.
27. *West Virginia v. EPA*, 142 S. Ct. 2587 (Kagan, J., dissenting).
28. Barack Obama, "Remarks at the University of Colorado-Denver in Denver, Colorado," GovInfo, October 26, 2011, https://www.govinfo.gov/content/pkg/DCPD-201100797/pdf/DCPD-201100797.pdf.

29. Woodrow Wilson, "Notes on Administration," in *The Papers of Woodrow Wilson*, vol. 7, *1890–1892*, ed. Arthur S. Link (Princeton: Princeton University Press, 1969), 121.
30. Barack Obama, "Address to the Nation by the President," The White House, December 6, 2015, https://obamawhitehouse.archives.gov/the-press-office/2015/12/06/address-nation-president.
31. *West Virginia*, 142 S. Ct. at 2642 (2022) (Kagan, J, dissenting).
32. *Mistretta v. United States*, 488 U.S. 361, 372 (1989).
33. *Humphrey's Executor v. United States*, 295 U.S. 602, 624 (1935).
34. 17 Cong. Rec. 2398 (1886).
35. Fisher Ames, "President's Power of Removal," in *The Debates in the Several State Conventions on the Adoption of the Federal Constitution*, ed. Jonathan Elliot, 2nd ed. (New York: Burt Franklin, 1854), 4:395.
36. *Myers v. United States*, 272 U.S. 52 (1926).
37. *Morrison v. Olson*, 487 U.S. 654, 691–92 (1988).
38. *Morrison v. Olson*, 487 U.S. 654 (1988) (Scalia, J., dissenting). See Adrian Vermeule, "Morrison v. Olson is Bad Law," Lawfare, June 9, 2017, https://www.lawfareblog.com/morrison-v-olson-bad-law.
39. *Morrison*, 487 U.S. 654.
40. *Seila Law LLC v. Consumer Financial Protection Bureau*, 140 S. Ct. 2183 (2020).
41. *Free Enterprise Fund v. Public Company Accounting Oversight Board*, 561 U.S. 477, 483, 505 (2010).
42. *Seila Law*, 140 S. Ct. at 2199.

Chapter 13: Looking Ahead

1. *Washington v. Glucksberg*, 521 U.S. 702 (1997).
2. *New York State Rifle & Pistol Association, Inc. v. Bruen*, 142 S. Ct. 2111 (2022).
3. See, e.g., *Seila Law LLC v. Consumer Financial Protection Bureau*, 140 S. Ct. 2183 (2020).
4. *Morrison v. Olson*, 487 U.S. 654 (1988).
5. *Whitman v. American Trucking Associations, Inc.*, 531 U.S. 457 (2001).
6. *Chevron U.S.A., Inc. v. National Resources Defense Council, Inc.*, 467 U.S. 837 (1984).
7. See Antonin Scalia, "Judicial Deference to Administrative Interpretations of Law," *Duke Law Journal* 1989, no. 3 (June 1989): 511–21. Scalia's view of *Chevron* grew markedly more critical over time. See *Perez v. Mortgage Bankers Association*, 575 U.S. 92 (2015) (Scalia, J., concurring in the judgment).
8. *Gutierrez-Brizuela v. Lynch*, 834 F.3d 1142, 1149 (10th Cir. 2016) (Gorsuch, Circuit Judge, concurring).
9. *Michigan v. EPA*, 576 U.S. 743, 761 (2015) (Thomas, J., concurring).

10. *National Federation of Independent Business v. Sebelius*, 567 U.S. 519 (2012).
11. See, e.g., *Garcia v. San Antonio Metropolitan Transit Authority*, 469 U.S. 528 (1985); Herbert Wechsler, "The Political Safeguards of Federalism: The Rôle of the States in the Composition and Selection of the National Government," *Columbia Law Review* 54, no. 4 (April 1954): 543–60.
12. *Sebelius*, 567 U.S. 519.
13. *Bruen*, 142 S. Ct. 2111.
14. *Korematsu v. United States*, 323 U.S. 214 (1944).
15. *Trump v. Hawaii*, 138 S. Ct. 2392 (2018).
16. *Regents of the University of California v. Bakke*, 438 U.S. 265 (1978); *Grutter v. Bollinger*, 539 U.S. 306 (2003); *Fisher v. University of Texas*, 579 U.S. 365 (2016).
17. *Carson v. Makin*, 142 S. Ct. 1987 (2022).
18. *Kennedy v. Bremerton School District*, 142 S. Ct. 2407 (2022).
19. *Lamb's Chapel v. Center Moriches Union Free School District*, 508 U.S. 384 (1993) (Scalia, J., concurring in the judgment).
20. *Shurtleff v. City of Boston*, 142 S. Ct. 1583 (2022).
21. *Kennedy*, 142 S. Ct. at 2433; *Lemon v. Kurtzman*, 403 U.S. 602 (1971).
22. *Meyer v. Nebraska*, 262 U.S. 390 (1923); *Pierce v. Society of Sisters*, 268 U.S. 510 (1925).
23. *Troxel v. Granville*, 530 U.S. 57 (2000).
24. *Penn Central Transportation Company v. New York City*, 438 U.S. 104 (1978).
25. *Kelo v. City of New London*, 545 U.S. 469 (2005).
26. James Buchanan, *The Collected Works of James M. Buchanan*, vol. 13, *Politics as Public Choice* (Carmel, Indiana: Liberty Fund, 2000), 62.
27. Mancur Olson, *The Logic of Collective Action: Public Goods and the Theory of Groups* (Cambridge: Harvard University Press, 1965).
28. For an illustration of "rent-seeking" behavior, see *St. Joseph Abbey v. Paul Wes Castille*, No. 11-30756 (5th Cir. 2013), in which the Court of Appeals held that rules issued by the Louisiana Board of Funeral Directors granting funeral homes an exclusive right to sell caskets were unconstitutional.
29. This would require the Court to revisit such precedents as *Williamson v. Lee Optical Co.*, 348 U.S. 483 (1955).
30. *Dobbs v. Jackson Women's Health Organization*, 142 S. Ct. 2228, 2304 (2022) (Kavanaugh, J., concurring).
31. *Dobbs*, 142 S. Ct. 2228, 2317 (2022) (Breyer, Sotomayor, and Kagan, JJ., dissenting).
32. *Kennedy*, 142 S. Ct. at 2427 (reasoning that the "Court long ago abandoned *Lemon*).
33. *Janus v. AFSCME*, 138 S. Ct. 2448 (2018).
34. *United States v. Miller*, 307 U.S. 174 (1939).

35. *Citizens United v. FEC*, 558 U.S. 310 (2010), overturning *Austin v. Michigan Chamber of Commerce*, 494 U.S. 652 (1990) and overturning *McConnell v. FEC*, 540 U.S. 93 (2003) in part.
36. *Dobbs*, 142 S. Ct. at 2304 (2022).
37. *Planned Parenthood v. Casey*, 505 U.S. 833 (1992).
38. *Ramos v. Louisiana*, 140 S. Ct. 1390, 1405 (2020).
39. *Ramos*, 140 S. Ct. at 1405.
40. "The burden borne by a party advocating the abandonment of an established precedent is greater where the Court is asked to overrule a point of statutory construction, which, unlike constitutional interpretation, may be altered by Congress." *Patterson v. McLean Credit Union,* 491 U.S. 164 (1989).
41. *Ramos*, 140 S. Ct. at 1405.
42. *Ramos v. Louisiana*, 140 S. Ct. 1390, 1429, 1432 (2020) (Alito, J., dissenting).
43. *Ramos v. Louisiana*, 140 S. Ct. 1390, 1414–15 (2020) (Kavanaugh, J., concurring in part); *Dobbs v. Jackson Women's Health Organization*, 142 S. Ct. 2228, 2307 (2022) (Kavanaugh, J., concurring).
44. *Citizens United v. FEC*, 558 U.S. 310, 378 (2010) (Roberts, C.J., concurring).
45. *Ramos*, 140 S. Ct. at 1411–12 (Kavanaugh, J., concurring in part).
46. *Gong Lum v. Rice*, 275 U.S. 78 (1927).
47. Committee on the Judiciary, *Confirmation Hearing on the Nomination of Hon. Brett M. Kavanaugh to Be an Associate Justice of the Supreme Court of the United States* (Washington, D.C.: U.S. Government Publishing Office 2020), 173, https://www.govinfo.gov/content/pkg/CHRG-115shrg32765/pdf/CHRG-115shrg32765.pdf.
48. *Ramos*, 140 S. Ct. at 1411 (Kavanaugh, J., concurring in part).
49. Ibid.
50. *Gamble v. United States*, 139 S. Ct. 1960, 1985 (2019) (Thomas, J., concurring).
51. Ibid., 1986.
52. *Dobbs*, 142 S. Ct. at 2265, 2272, 2276.
53. *Dobbs*, 142 S. Ct. 2228.
54. *Payne v. Tennessee*, 501 U.S. 808, 828 (1991).
55. *Dobbs*, 142 S. Ct. at 2241–42.
56. *Franchise Tax Board of California. v. Hyatt*, 139 S. Ct. 1485, 1506 (2019) (Breyer, J., dissenting).
57. *Shelley v. Kraemer*, 334 U.S. 1, 20 (1948).
58. *Corrigan v. Buckley*, 271 U.S. 323, 332 (1926).
59. *Shelley*, 334 U.S. at 13–14.
60. *Casey*, 505 U.S. at 846, 873.
61. Ibid, 858.

62. *Lawrence v. Texas*, 539 U.S. 558, 577 (2003), overruling *Bowers v. Hardwick*, 478 U.S. 186 (1986).
63. *Casey*, 505 U.S. at 867.
64. *Dobbs*, 142 S. Ct. at 2278.
65. Charles J. Reid Jr., "Judicial Precedent in the Late Eighteenth and Early Nineteenth Centuries: A Commentary on Chancellor Kent's Commentaries," *Ave Maria Law Review* 5, no. 1 (Winter 2007): 51.
66. John M. Goodenow, *Historical Sketches of the Principles and Maxims of American Jurisprudence* (Steubenville, Ohio: James Wilson, 1819), 36.
67. Charles de Secondat Montesquieu, *The Spirit of Laws*, trans. Thomas Nugent, 2nd ed. (London: J. Nourse and P. Vaillant, 1752): 8–9.
68. *Murdock v. Hunter*, 17 F. Cas. 1013, 1015 (C.C.D. Va. 1808).
69. *Baring v. Reeder*, 11 Va. 154, 158 (1806).
70. Ibid., 162
71. On the transition, see Stuart Banner, *The Decline of Natural Law: How American Lawyers Once Used Natural Law and Why They Stopped* (New York: Oxford University Press, 2021).
72. *Southern Pacific Co. v. Jensen*, 244 U.S. 205, 222 (1917).
73. Oliver Wendell Holmes, "Natural Law," *Harvard Law Review* 32, no. 1 (1918): 41–42, https://archive.org/details/jstor-1327676/mode/2up.
74. *Erie Railroad v. Tompkins*, 304 U.S. 64 (1938).
75. *Swift v. Tyson*, 41 U.S. 1 (1842).
76. Holmes, "Natural Law," 42.
77. *Erie Railroad*, 304 U.S. at 79.
78. With apologies to Boston. Tom Scholz, "More than a Feeling," on *Boston* (Epic Records, 1976).
79. William O. Douglas, "Stare Decisis," *Columbia Law Review* 49, no. 6 (June 1949): 739.

Index

D

E

F

M

N

T

About the Authors

Peter Holden Photography © AEI

JOHN YOO is Emanuel S. Heller Professor of Law at the University of California at Berkeley and a fellow of the American Enterprise Institute and the Hoover Institution. He has served as Deputy Assistant Attorney General and General Counsel for the U.S. Senate Judiciary Committee. He holds an A.B. from Harvard University and a J.D. from Yale Law School, and he was a law clerk for Justice Clarence Thomas.

© Becky Hansen

ROBERT J. DELAHUNTY is a fellow at the Claremont Institute Center for the American Way of Life in Washington, D.C. He held the LeJeune Chair of Law at the University of St. Thomas Law School in Minneapolis until his retirement and has published widely in constitutional law. Delahunty served in the U.S. Department of Justice for seventeen years and was Deputy General Counsel in the White House Office of Homeland Security.